IAA Interdisciplinary Series
Studies in Archaeology, History, Literature and Art
Volume I

UNIVERSITY OF
BIRMINGHAM

Children, Childhood and Society

Edited by

Sally Crawford
Gillian Shepherd

BAR International Series 1696
2007

This title published by

Archaeopress
Publishers of British Archaeological Reports
Gordon House
276 Banbury Road
Oxford OX2 7ED
England
bar@archaeopress.com
www.archaeopress.com

BAR S1696
IAA Interdisciplinary Series: Studies in Archaeology, History, Literature and Art
Series Editor Gillian Shepherd
Volume I

Children, Childhood and Society

ISBN 978 1 4073 0138 9

Cover illustration: Greek Geometric krater (c. 750-735 BC), attributed to the Hirschfeld Workshop.
The Metropolitan Museum of Art, Rogers Fund, 1914 (14.130.14) (detail)
Image © The Metropolitan Museum of Art

Printed in England by Chalvington Digital

All BAR titles are available from:

Hadrian Books Ltd
122 Banbury Road
Oxford
OX2 7BP
England
bar@hadrianbooks.co.uk

The current BAR catalogue with details of all titles in print, prices and means of payment is available
free from Hadrian Books or may be downloaded from www.archaeopress.com

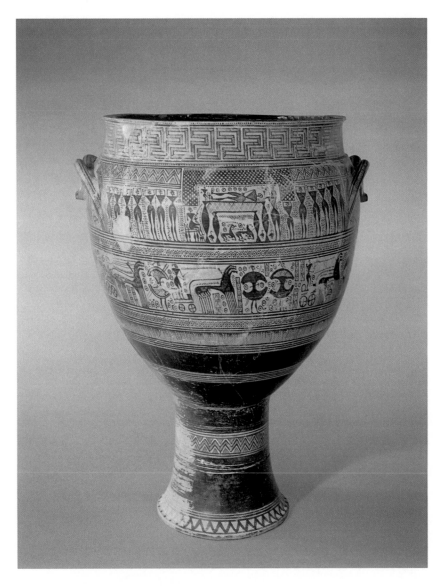

Greek Geometric krater (c. 750-735 BC), attributed to the Hirschfeld Workshop.
The Metropolitan Museum of Art, Rogers Fund, 1914 (14.130.14)
Image © The Metropolitan Museum of Art

IAA Interdisciplinary Series
Studies in Archaeology, History, Literature and Art

Series Editor: Gillian Shepherd

Institute of Archaeology and Antiquity
University of Birmingham

The IAA Series is an interdisciplinary volume reflecting the wide geographical, chronological and disciplinary range of the Institute of Archaeology and Antiquity at the University of Birmingham. The volumes are based on a thematic research seminar series held at the IAA. Contributions from scholars outside the IAA are welcome. For further information on current and future themes, the research seminars and future volumes in the IAA Interdisciplinary Series, please contact the IAA Series Editor, Gillian Shepherd (g.b.shepherd@bham.ac.uk) or visit www.iaa.bham.ac.uk.

Contents

CHAPTER 1

CHILDREN, CHILDHOOD AND SOCIETY: AN INTRODUCTION

Sally Crawford and Gillian Shepherd

In 2003, the Institute of Archaeology and Antiquity (IAA) at the University of Birmingham was founded when the Departments of Archaeology and Ancient History, Classics, and the Centre for Byzantine, Ottoman and Modern Greek Studies were merged. What became immediately apparent as the former departments joined forces were the enormous opportunities for interdisciplinary research that the new Institute offered: its members work within the fields of archaeology, history, literature and art, covering a geographical area ranging from Iceland to Western Asia and a chronological span from prehistory to the modern day. The idea of a thematic research seminar series with a corresponding journal was conceived by the editors of this volume in order to exploit fully both opportunities for research, debate and exchange of ideas across disciplines within the IAA, and also to encourage and facilitate interdisciplinary research within the wider academic community.

'Childhood' was an obvious theme to initiate the new series. The Institute has a strong record of publication in the field, and members of the Institute have made a significant contribution to childhood studies (e.g. Crawford 1991, 1993, 1999; Macrides 2000; Harlow and Laurence 2002; Dowden 1989; Shepherd 2006). The Institute is also host to the Society for the Study of Childhood in the Past (www.sscip.bham.ac.uk), which was established to pursue and foster interdisciplinary approaches to the study of childhood.

It seemed appropriate that this inaugural volume of the IAA Interdisciplinary Series, *Children, Childhood and Society,* should focus on the work of those who were members of the Institute of Archaeology and Antiquity in 2004-5, when the IAA Research Seminar Series was launched, although we are delighted to welcome also Ville Vuolanto (University of Tampere, Finland) who collaborates here with Mary Harlow and Ray Laurence.[1] The second and third volumes in this Series, (*Dress and Identity* and *Warfare, Violence and Conflict;* both in preparation) include contributions from a wider academic field, in addition to those from members of the IAA. Planned future themes in the IAA Research Seminar Series are *Landscapes of Death* and *Cultural Memory.*

The image on the front cover of this volume in many ways sums up a number of the themes explored within it. It is a detail taken from the painted decoration on an enormous krater, or wine-mixing bowl, made in Attica in Greece in the Late Geometric period (c. 750-700 BC) and now in the Metropolitan Museum of Art in New York (Moore 2004: 8-13). At just over a metre high, the krater was not designed for normal domestic use, but instead would have stood above a grave as a marker. One of the scenes on it shows a dead man lying on a bier flanked by mourners; immediately to the left of the bier our figures are depicted (Moore 2004: pls 8-13). A seated figure (possibly a woman, since locks of hair are shown) supports a smaller figure on its lap and raises what appears to be a branch (perhaps to ward off flies) towards the bier; the smaller figure appears to touch the chest and elbow of the larger. The standard interpretation is of an adult and child.

The scene appears to place children (another small figure holding the hand of a larger one is depicted on the bier) well within the sphere of adult life, in this case the elaborate funerary arrangements to which some elite groups aspired in Geometric Greece. Inevitably, approaches to children and childhood in the past are often based in the funerary context and burial evidence is prominent in this volume (Crawford, Garwood and Shepherd): death often provides the most visible evidence of children in past societies in the material record and even in textual evidence (McKeown) while other phases and transitions are harder to recover. Yet, as the Geometric krater implies and the papers in this volume argue, the role of children in the past was far from tangential to the concerns of the adult social world, particularly its public face: children might appear in the role of successors (as possibly on the krater) to emphasise descent and dynastic links or as estate holders (Livingstone, Garwood, Shepherd).

The Geometric painting appears to recognise the presence of children in public life, but does it recognise the particular state of childhood? The distinction is important, and is at the heart of Philippe Ariès' famous assertion that there was no *sentiment* (usually translated as 'idea') of childhood in the past:

> …the idea of childhood did not exist; this is not to suggest that children were neglected, forsaken or despised. The idea of childhood is not to be confused with affection for children; it corresponds to an awareness of the particular nature of childhood, that particular nature which distinguishes the child from the adult, even the young adult. In medieval society, this awareness was lacking. This is why, as soon as the child could live without the constant solicitude of

---
[1] Sally Crawford is now a Departmental Lecturer in Medieval Archaeology at the Institute of Archaeology, Oxford.

his mother… he belonged to adult society. The infant who was too fragile as yet to take part in the life of adults simply 'did not exist' (Ariès 1962: 125).

Aries' general thesis – that a 'concept' of childhood is a relatively modern invention – has by now been thoroughly refuted, but the problematisation of childhood has not been resolved, and the existence of children in the past, though an undeniable fact, remains surprisingly difficult to demonstrate in archaeological and textual records (but cf. Wardle & Wardle and Callow). Studies of childhood continue to offer conflicting ideas about how to separate 'child' from 'adult' in the past, and how to differentiate between what are universal truths about the nature of childhood (and there is no agreement on that one), and what 'truths' are actually part of the cultural baggage modern historians and archaeologists are imposing on childhood (cf. the discussion in Harlow, Laurence & Vuolanto, McKeown, Crawford and Callow).

While Aries' thesis that there was no 'idea' of childhood in the past may have been exploded, his original proposal – that childhood was an idea, a concept – was not properly examined and articulated until the work of James & Prout (1990), who, drawing on advances in childhood sociology, were the first to clarify that childhood is a social construct: 'childhood, as distinct from biological immaturity, is neither a natural nor a universal feature of human groups but appears as a specific structural and cultural component of many societies' (1990: 8-9). As a construct, then, James & Prout argued that there can be no single, clearly-defined condition called 'childhood': childhood 'can never be entirely divorced from other variables such as class, gender or ethnicity. Comparative and cross-cultural analysis reveals a variety of childhoods, rather than a single or universal phenomenon'(1990: 8-9).

Given that childhood is a sociological phenomenon, Christopher Jenks has taken the relationship between the reconstruction of childhood and the variable of adulthood further, arguing that childhood can always and only be understood in reference to adult society, because to categorise childhood – to define the cultural and social place of a child in anthropological terms – is to seek to explain the child by the 'norm' of the adult (Jenks 1996: 3). However, if childhood can only be given shape and form through comparison with adulthood, then the important corollary is that 'it becomes impossible to generate a well-defined sense of the adult, and indeed adult society, without first positing the child' (Jenks 1996: 3). According to this model, childhood is a mirror to society, an assertion that David Archard, a childhood sociologist, has taken as 'self-evident' (1993:161). This is an approach which many of the papers in this volume take into consideration.

The dominance of adult agency in the image of childhood presented in textual and material sources is a recurring theme in the papers offered in this volume. Children are often the objects of adult agency; children can be, in effect, objects (Crawford, Garwood). The decision to include children in an adult context – an adult burial ground, for example – reflects a deliberate decision by adults to include or exclude juveniles; to treat them as adults; or to demarcate them as non-adults (Garwood, Shepherd). When an adult (male) writes about, or describes, or includes, children in a text – whether that text is a poem, a lawcode, a history, or a medical compendium – that inclusion of children as a separate, non-adult group, reflects a tacit adult categorisation of childhood, and an adult decision, for adult reasons, to include or exclude a concept of childhood from the text (Callow, Livingstone, McKeown).

Recent scholarship, however, has stressed that, while it can be extremely difficult to disentangle the actual experience of childhood from its – usually limited – presentation via adults, it is also the case that children were not completely passive beings but actors with the ability, at least, to leave some record other than that constructed by adults. In a determined effort to shift the balance in childhood studies away from seeing children only as they exist as 'not adult' and to offer children agency in their material culture, Joanna Sofaer Derevenski's *Childhood and Material Culture* was intended to 'highlight children as a category and make them visible' (2002: 12). Sofaer Derevenski draws attention to the useful theories of Place (1997), who distinguishes between 'child data' – information derived from the study of the body of the child; and 'data child' – artefacts associated with that child. The possibility that we might be able to recognise children and their agency in life more directly is explored in this volume with calls for the action of children to be given more priority in the analysis and interpretation of the archaeological and textual records (Wardle & Wardle; Livingstone). As Mary Harlow, Ray Laurence and Ville Vuolanto argue here for the study of Roman childhood, there are still many unexplored topics relating to childhood and there is a need for greater theoretical and methodological debate regarding the issues of the representation of childhood. They further stress the need for an interdisciplinary approach to the study of childhood in the past.

The problems of how children might be represented and identified in material culture and the textual record are also highlighted in this volume, including the issue of the transition from child to adulthood in past societies. While the Geometric figures on the New York krater may appear to our eyes as a straightforward representation of an adult and child, there is also evidence that the size of a figure in Geometric art does not necessarily indicate its age (Ahlberg1971: 97-102) and instead other factors – such as social hierarchy or artistic convenience – may dictate the scale of one figure in relation to another. The image may, in fact, be ambiguous or open to other interpretations and a Geometric viewer may have reached different conclusions. Similarly, perceptions of children and childhood are not always straightforward and may be over-ridden by other social concerns or more dominating social personae: as argued in this volume, this might include the depiction of small children performing entirely implausible feats in order to articulate the adult social order (Callow) or the suppression of a primary identity of 'child' in favour of 'possession' (McKeown, Crawford) or, at death, 'adult' (Garwood, Shepherd).

Earlier researchers have tended to present childhood as a developing journey from a savage past to a perfect present; what Harlow, Laurence & Vuolanto describe in this volume as 'a version of social Darwinism that believes in progress towards our current modern age of Western humanity', where past attitudes towards children are understood in terms of their 'difference' to ours (deMause 1974, Shorter 1975). In this volume, we have deliberately avoided a chronological structure, because the history of children is not a linear narrative. Instead, we have chosen to juxtapose different periods to show that other factors beyond chronology determine the way in which different societies treat their children. This juxtaposition has led to often surprising similarities and points of comparison between chronologically and geographically disparate societies.

The study of childhood in the Roman period has a long pedigree and, in their chapter, Mary Harlow, Ray Laurence and Ville Vuolanto place evolving views of Roman childhood in the wider context of the history of childhood, showing trends and developments in this field. Their paper offers an overview of the historiography of childhood with particular reference to the Roman period and offers a valuable framework for the papers which follow. They also offer a plea for broadening the theoretical and methodological approaches to childhood, a challenge taken up in all the later papers in this volume.

In contrast to the long and complex historiography of Roman childhood, childhood in some other cultures and other periods has received relatively limited treatment, despite the wealth of evidence which might be usefully employed to investigate children in those societies. This is particularly true for the ancient Near East, as Alasdair Livingstone's paper makes clear: even major works on daily life fail to discuss children in detail. This is not because evidence for children and childhood in the ancient Near East is in anyway lacking, as Livingstone shows. Rather, it has received treatment only in particular contexts – the study of scribal texts, for example – or has simply been overlooked in the emphasis on other topics of research in ancient Near Eastern studies. The Near Eastern evidence appears particularly promising for the study of children in their own right, because, unlike most ancient societies, there is greater direct evidence for the role of children and even their agency in a variety of social and historical contexts. These include school writing exercises actually produced by children and scribes writing about their own childhood experiences – no doubt with a degree of poetic licence, but writing about them nevertheless.

Diana and Ken Wardle's paper, by contrast, focuses on a single archaeological deposit, but this one enigmatic cache raises important issues, centred on the problem of identifying toys or playthings in the archaeological record. Many playthings are likely to have been made of perishable materials such as bone or wood, since non-perishables such as metal are likely to have been too valuable or simply unsuitable – although here the breakable ceramic dolls and carts of the ancient Greeks may provide an exception (cf. Shepherd). More significant for modern scholars, however, is the issue of how we define a 'plaything' in the archaeological record at all: at what point can we confidently identify an object that was used by a child as opposed to an everyday or ritual object used by adults? In Diana and Ken Wardle's paper, the importance of context and object association in identifying playthings is made clear: as they argue, the particular nature of the assemblage at Assiros rules out other interpretations. Their assertion that there is no good reason for privileging interpretations based on adult actions over those of children in the creation of this cache offers a serious challenge to all archaeologists.

One of the problems in identifying childhood through literary sources is that those who were doing the writing often only mention children in a tangential way, with no intention of providing the reader with any coherent or representative narrative of childhood. In his paper on Icelandic childhood, Chris Callow demonstrates how an idea or ideal of childhood may be teased out of texts. Callow's children emerge in the literature primarily when they are transitional or transgressive. The analysis of stated ages (especially for boys) indicates the chronological phase at which children were expected to begin to take part in the adult social world. Saga writers used children, and children's behaviour, to illustrate and counterpoint adult mores. This paper illustrates how the liminality of children within the adult world allowed them to become a vehicle for conveying a moral, social and political commentary on adult behaviour, particularly with regard to status divisions within medieval Icelandic society. An under-explored topic within the study of children in past societies is the question of gender and childhood (cf. Harlow, Laurence & Vuolanto). Callow's paper also emphasises that gender may have had an impact on how childhood is constructed, and his exploration of the documentary sources raises the question of whether women were ever seen to have had a meaningful transition to adulthood in the same way as men.

Niall McKeown's paper raises the issue that the experience (or existence) of childhood may be contingent on variables other than the age of the child, such as gender and status, when he discusses the point at which Romans were prepared to separate attitudes to slaves and attitudes to childhood. What was the point at which a Roman was prepared to be revolted when ideas about childhood clashed with ideas about slaves as objects and possessions? The answers make uncomfortable reading and offer a cautionary and salutary reminder that childhood has a history – it is not a static construct, and not all modern responses to children are universal to all societies. Sally Crawford's paper also tests modern emotional responses to the past, arguing against conventional interpretations of child/adult pairings in early Anglo-Saxon double or multiple burials as a reflection of emotional or familial bonds between the child and adult in life. Like McKeown's child slaves, Crawford discusses the possibility that some children had a use in the burial ritual, valued not as children but as precious commodities.

Paul Garwood's paper tackles a problem common to a number of archaeological periods and places: why are child burials so rare, and why were the few children found in archaeological deposits placed there? Garwood's exploration of British Bronze Age burials demonstrates that, to make sense of the evidence, children's bodies have to be viewed as a means of expressing adult values, beliefs, ideals and feelings: the child is, as in Callow's Icelandic sagas, Livingstone's ancient Near Eastern texts, and Shepherd and Crawford's cemeteries, a vehicle for the public display and reinforcement of adult values.

Gillian Shepherd's concluding paper draws together many of the themes and problems already explored earlier in the volume. She argues that the burial of children in Archaic Western Greece was an essential tool in defining adult identities at a number of levels: methods of child burial contributed to the development of cultural identities in the ancient Greek world and the representation of children in the funerary record could also be used to highlight social divisions and to articulate lines of descent and inheritance. Limited formal burial of children indicates that such disposal was not a matter of course, but selective: as Crawford and Garwood found, children were in a sense artefacts or accessories to be employed according to the demands of the adult social context. The depiction of children in the funerary record is also highly variable: evidence for a child-specific material culture can be identified in the form of particular objects which might be classified as playthings; at the same time, many children are represented in death in a manner which suppresses distinctions between their social personae and that of adults, indicating that different social roles could take precedence over any concept of children or childhood.

We are very grateful for the assistance of many people in preparing this volume. Special thanks must go to David Davison and Rajka Makjanić at Archaeopress for their support for this Series; to Harry Buglass and Graham Norrie at the Institute of Archaeology and Antiquity for illustrative work; to the Metropolitan Museum of Art in New York for permission to reproduce the cover image; and last, but by no means least, to all those who contributed to the IAA Research Seminar on Children, Childhood, and Society, especially Mike Lally

(University of Southhampton) and Judith Affleck (Head of Classics, Harrow School).

Bibliography

Ahlberg, G. (1971): *Prothesis and Ekphora in Greek Geometric Art*. Göteborg.

Archard, D. (1993): *Children: Rights and Childhood*. London.

Aries, P. (1962): *Centuries of Childhood: a social history of family life*. London. (trans.) R. Baldick, from *L'Enfant et la vie famille sous l'ancien regime* 1960, Paris.

Crawford, S. (1991): 'When do Anglo-Saxon Children Count?' *Journal of Theoretical Archaeology* 2: 17-24.

Crawford, S. (1993): 'Children, death and the afterlife', *Anglo-Saxon Studies in Archaeology and History* 6: 83-92.

Crawford, S. (1999): *Childhood in Anglo-Saxon England*. Stroud.

DeMause, L. (1974): 'The evolution of childhood', in L. deMause (ed.), *The History of Childhood*, 1-73. New York.

Dowden, K. (1989): *Death and the Maiden: Girls' Initiation Rites in Greek Mythology*. London and New York.

Harlow, M. and Laurence, R. (2002): *Growing Up and Growing Old in Ancient Rome: a Life Course Approach*. London and New York.

James, A. and Prout, A. (eds) (1990): *Constructing and reconstructing childhood*. Basingstoke.

Jenks, C. (1996): *Childhood*. London.

Macrides, R. (2000): 'Substitute parents and their children', in M. Corbier, (ed.), *Adoption et fosterage*, 307-319. Paris.

Moore, M.B. (2004): *Corpus Vasorum Antiquorum. United States of America Fasicule 37 The Metropolitan Museum of Art. Greek Geometric and Protoattic Pottery*. New York.

Place, B. (1997): 'The constructing of bodies of critically ill children; an ethnography of intensive care' in A. Prout, (ed.) *The Body, Childhood and Society*. London.

Shepherd, G. (2006): 'Dead but not buried? Child disposal in the Greek West' in E. Herring, I. Lemos, F. Lo Schiavo, L. Vagnetti, R. Whitehouse and J. Wilkins (eds), *Across Frontiers. Etruscans, Greeks, Phoenicians and Cypriots. Studies in honour of David Ridgway and Francesca Romana Serra Ridgway*, 311-25. London.

Shorter, E. (1975): *The making of the Modern Family*. New York.

Sofaer Derevenski, J. (ed.) (2000): *Childhood and Material Culture*. Basingstoke.

CHAPTER 2

PAST, PRESENT AND FUTURE IN THE STUDY OF ROMAN CHILDHOOD

Mary Harlow, Ray Laurence and Ville Vuolanto

Historians do not work in a sealed vacuum and it is often the case that their 'new ideas' are frequently borrowed from other related disciplines. The study of childhood in the Roman world is framed with reference to trends and developments in medieval and modern history, as well as major syntheses that have set out to present an historical overview of the development (or modernisation) of the social institution which we simply know as childhood, and its associated individuals, children. In this paper, we wish to present an overview of the achievement of the first waves of research on Roman childhood. Following from the account that we give of the academic inspirations for the study of the Roman child, we discuss the central debates in the field. At the end of the paper, we offer a perspective on the challenges for future work. In all, we would wish to suggest that the history of Roman childhood is still in its infancy, and has yet to develop from the concerns that were at the heart of the first studies of the Roman family and gender: these tended to be the recording of the institution and its structure, as opposed to the development of an agency-led characterisation of childhood in its cultural context in the Roman Empire.

The paper has a strong emphasis on the views of social historians. This is partly due to our own academic backgrounds. However, the most important and far-reaching debate on childhood and children in Roman studies have been connected to discussions on the power of fathers and the place of emotional attachment in Roman families. In fact, the social history of childhood and the family are at the very centre of Roman history today (as can be seen in the recent editions of the *Cambridge Ancient History*, see e.g. Treggiari 1996).

The present position owes much to the work of Beryl Rawson and Suzanne Dixon based in Australia. Even if the recent retirement of both from academic posts marks, in a way, a semi-colon rather than a full stop, it serves as a convenient moment for an assessment of the development of the history of childhood within Roman culture and the discipline of Roman history.[1] These scholars have been instrumental in shaping the study of Roman children and childhood throughout their careers and particularly in the 1980s and 1990s. They broke new ground with a series of international conferences drawing together a worldwide network of like-minded scholars pursuing similar methodologies for the recovery of social history. There was a focus on Roman law, inscriptions, and literary texts. The important historiographical point is that the early methodologies were derived from their training as classicists and were, by their own testimony, strongly based on empiricism; but, equally, they cast around for parallels from other disciplines studying the social history of the past, and consciously engaged with the modern discussion regarding attitudes to the child in modern societies.

Our contribution to this interdisciplinary volume on children and childhood is written, in part, with a view to inform those writing outside the confines of Roman history of the intellectual developments that may have passed unnoticed due to the fragmentation of the study of the past. Hence, while some Roman social historians might regard this as stating the obvious, for those new to the study of childhood, this is a necessity.

The Legacy of Philippe Ariès

Central to any discussion on the history of childhood is Philippe Ariès, whose seminal work in the 1960s opened up the subject for serious academic study (Ariès 1962). Prior to Ariès, publications on childhood and children primarily focussed on the subject of pedagogy, in terms of a child's upbringing and education. Ariès, however, moved the emphasis towards a greater understanding of the child's life in the context of its family and education, within the context of emotional ties with other members of its family and community. Scholars within the fields of sociology and history, as well as others, quickly adopted his ideas of the historical development or an ideology of progress in the study of childhood. These ideas and preconceptions fitted into a model of modernisation that fundamentally altered the family from a point located close to what we tend to call the period of 'the Enlightenment'.

The crossover of Ariès' ideas can be found in two key publications from the early 1970s: Lloyd deMause's *The History of Childhood* (1974) and Edward Shorter's *The Making of the Modern Family* (1975). These two authors advocated a version of social Darwinism that believes in progress towards our current modern age of Western humanity in the treatment of children. In their view earlier societies were judged as generally brutal to children, and dissimilar to contemporary families in the modern West. DeMause singled out Rome as a paradigm of brutality and a model of what to avoid with its general

---

[1] Rawson made this clear at a conference held at the Finnish Institute in Rome on the subject of *Ancient and Medieval Childhood Reconsidered* in January 2005; for a view of this work at the time see Parkin 1994. Their retirement was marked by a conference organised by the latter to celebrate the former's contribution to the history of childhood, and also by a volume by Rawson herself (Dixon 2001; Rawson 2003).

acceptance of infanticide, corporal punishment and abuse of children.

The end of the 1970s saw a heavy weight of early modern history infiltrate and shape the views of historians of Roman childhood. Lawrence Stone's book, *The Family, Sex and Marriage in England 1500-1800* (1977), identified an evolving family structure over three phases, starting with the fairly remote parent-child relations of the 'open lineage family' (mid-15th/mid-16th centuries), in which the distance between parents and children was exemplified by the use of wet nurses among the upper classes, and by boarding schools by the middle and aspiring upper classes. The next phase (mid-16th/mid-17th centuries) was identified by the use of corporal punishment and the desire to train, control and subject children to the authority of their elders, particularly the father. Most of the elements set out by Stone were familiar to historians working on ancient Rome and, as a consequence, his work was set to appear in bibliographies and footnotes for the next two decades. Underlying Stone's observations was an identification of dramatic change in terms of parent-child relations in the period 1600-1800. By 1800, Stone claimed, a 'domesticated nuclear family' could be identified which privileged affective bonds between parents and children over those with wider kin groups or neighbours. This was, however, only evident among certain classes, and it did not extend across the whole of society. Stone questioned any notion of a single linear evolutionary development in attitudes to children and childhood, but, like deMause and Ariès, he thought major changes could be tracked historically, though he did not always see the change as positive for children.

The approaches of Ariès and Stone and their implications have been discussed and, for the most part, rejected by scholars working in earlier periods. Medievalists, whom the Ariès discussion touched most closely, were quicker to react to these claims than ancient historians. Pierre Riché's refutation of Ariès came out as early as 1962, Barbara Hanawalt published her essay in 1977, and Klaus Arnold in 1980 – to name just a few (Burton 1989 considers ways of moving forward from Ariès). For Roman studies, it was some two decades before reconsiderations were published: Michael Manson's paper on the emergence of the small child in Rome in 1983, and P. Neraudau's monograph in French in 1984. All of these works aimed at attacking the idea that ancient and medieval cultures failed to see childhood as a distinctive phase of the life course, and that parents were unable or unwilling to be emotionally attached to their little children.

Among modern historians, however, there prevailed an almost orthodox position that childhood was a modern development. In 1983, Linda Pollock challenged the orthodoxy in her *Forgotten Children*, which presented the case for continuity in parent-child relations across the period 1500 to 1900. In contrast to Stone's view that high child mortality in some periods may have led to parents investing little emotional capital in children, Pollock used diaries and other individually generated statements, to show that parents did care deeply about their offspring in all periods. She argued from the consistency of evidence of parental grief that the idea that parents were indifferent to their offspring, particularly newborn infants, could not be sustained. All societies could be brutal to children, but this, felt Pollock, was the exception. Thus, the debate was re-focused towards the discussion of the history of sentiment.

This was reflected also in the work of the Roman historians, as in the mid 1980s the Roman family studies entered the discussion on emotional attachment and the study of the household – the *familia* and the *domus* – became central. The notions of the relationship of the child to the wider family and household took over the main focus from education, and childhood became an important approach for the study of the Roman family.[2] At the same time, children became the focus of study in the more specialised studies on the Roman family. Among the legal historians, especially in Italian and German scholarship, children had already been the focus of specific research to understand how the Roman (republican) legislation and values changed in the course the Roman Empire.[3] However, in the new wave of studies, many of these themes, such as *patria potestas*, child abandonment, and guardianship were given attention as the key elements for the social histories of family and childhood, and were linked with studies on family economy, child labour, adoption, illegitimacy, and nursing.[4]

At the same time, a new influence from modern history entered the melting pot of influences that constitutes the history of Roman childhood — demography. This influence has its origin in the interaction between the students of Moses Finley and Keith Hopkins with the Cambridge group studying populations across history led by Peter Laslett and Alan MacFarlane (see Laslett & Wall 1972; Macfarlane 1986). Again the link was made with the early modern period, rather than the medieval. Key questions revolved around how big households were, at what age did people marry and how many children did they have and with what spacing? The flourishing of demography and family studies of the later 1990s had a profound effect also on introducing the serious study of fertility and infant mortality into Roman history.[5]

[2] See Rawson 1966, 1986a, 1991; Dixon 1988, 1992; Wiedemann 1989; Garnsey 1991; Evans 1991; Bradley 1991; Corbier 1991a and 1991b; Saller 1994 (including partly rewritten papers 1984-1991).

[3] Voci 1980 and 1985; Fossati-Vanzetti 1983; Memmer 1991; Fayer 1994; Crifo 1964; Markus 1989.

[4] See Rawson 1986b, 1991; Nielsen 1987; Bellemore & Rawson 1990; Bradley 1991; Saller 1994; Bradley 1994; Petermandl 1997; Arends Olsen 1999; Kehoe 1997; Arjava 1998; Corbier 2000, 1999a and 2001; Lindsay 2001; Harlow & Laurence 2002; Vuolanto 2003.

[5] See Saller & Shaw 1984; Shaw 1987; Saller 1987; Parkin 1992; Harris 1994; Harris 1999; Scheidel 2001. The influence continues to this day; see George 2005.

The other new ingredient was the introduction of women's studies and histories of sexuality. These not only resulted in a new emphasis on children and childhood in connection with the studies on women as mothers and as actors in the domestic sphere (Dixon 1988), but also introduced some new topics. After the pioneering works by Aline Rousselle (1983), Danielle Gourevitch (1984) and Valerie French (1986), the questions of health and medicine were discussed with reference to the Roman family and childhood studies, especially in Francophone countries (including the work of Michel Foucault 1990). Questions on childbirth and maternal care have aroused much attention, alongside questions about abortion, malformation, and children's accidents and illnesses.[6]

The study of the iconography of childhood has not been fully developed although the work of Janet Huskinson has set the tone. It has, however, played a role especially in tracking the emotional side of Roman childhood, and in studying of cultural identities.[7] The study of the material culture has been scarce, perhaps due to a perception that there is a lack of source materials (see, however, Coulon 1994 and now 2004). There has been some research on toys and, for example, amulets and feeding bottles, of which there are numerous archaeological finds. On the other hand, amongst archaeologists, the skeletal remains and associated material culture have aroused considerable interest and have been studied as reflecting practices as diverse as infanticide, health conditions and burial rituals.[8] However, there has not to date been any systematic study that has taken advantage of all the new developments in osteoarchaeology (Gowland 2001, 2004; Redfern 2002, 2007), and there is a feeling from reading some reports that the social history utilised by osteoarchaeologists can be rather dated (see Bisel & Bisel 2002). One key realisation for the study of the material culture of childhood is how those items or artefacts identified as children's toys were a product of an adult's creation of the child and childhood, rather than a representation of a child's own culture. Also, children appropriate the material culture of adults for their own purposes; for example a broom can be carried by a one year old – but no brushing will take place. The very possibility of defining a material culture tied to the child alone is as difficult as identifying a material culture of women.

In spite of the moves towards wider questions and approaches, many of the studies mentioned above have continued to be preoccupied with deconstructing the theses of Ariès or the repetition of Ariès's emphases

echoed and further developed by deMause, Shorter and Stone. It has been only in the last years that this discussion has given way to new studies with a greater stress on the nature of the cultural context. Increasingly sophisticated readings of literary, visual and material evidence have been coupled with a deeper engagement with sociological and anthropological approaches. These have resulted in a critical view of the misconceptions of earlier studies, and a more self-conscious attitude towards methodology. Simultaneously, the material basis for the study of childhood has been enlarged to include many new types of sources, mainly of material culture and iconography.[9] Most significantly the Australian project on the Roman Family, instigated by Beryl Rawson, has consciously sought to incorporate visual and archaeological sources into its remit via invitation to its conferences. The recent interest in the history of childhood among Early Christian studies has also brought the biblical and hagiographical sources and the Church Fathers more to the fore.[10] The evolution of ideas can also be located and charted via seminal works on childhood that have been incorporated, synthesised and rejected or acculturated (consciously or unconsciously) into the academic study of Roman childhood.

Discussing the Roman childhood: paternal power and emotional indifference

The modern works discussed above represent an influential sample of the development of the history of Roman childhood. Their inspiration and paradigms, in many cases, came from the study of the early modern period in Europe. This was seen in a way as a time that had some structures in common with Rome – early modern London reproduced the rates of demographic growth of first century BC Rome. However, what is apparent is that the developments that crossed over were derived from the Roman historian's need for a literature and methodology in which to place their own findings into a context. This was caused in part by the newness of the themes under serious academic discussion, rather than mere illustration of 'daily life in ancient Rome', and a need to create a legitimacy for the new discipline of social history that was battling for a place within the highly conservative discipline of Classics which has tended to be text-based or gives primacy to political history. The effect was that to be any good at social history, you needed to identify key thinkers from early modern history without necessarily having the ability to discriminate between the excellent, bad or mad – let alone to engage with the emphasis of the debate of the changing family and an ideology of modernisation, change or continuity and stability. These themes were to enmesh with the focus of the Roman family in the series of conferences and publications that developed from the

---

[6] Köves-Zulauf 1990; Hanson 1994; Dasen 1997, 1999, 2004; Shaw 2001; Gourevitch 1998; Congourdeau 2000; Kapparis 2002; Laes 2004; Bradley 2005.
[7] Currie 1996; Huskinson 1996; Rawson 1997; Zanker 2000; George 2001; Rawson 2003.
[8] Gourevitch 1991; *Jouer dans l'Antiquité* Anon 1991; Fittà 1997; Dasen 2003; on archaeology: Meskell 1994; Becker 1995; Scott 1999; 2000; Soren & Soren 1999; Norman 2003.

[9] See e.g. Shaw 2001; Harlow & Laurence 2002; Rawson 2003 and several of the papers in Rawson & Weaver 1997; Corbier 2000; Dasen 2004 ; George 2005.
[10] See e.g. Clark 1994; Strange 1996; O'Roark 1999; Nathan 2000 and several of the papers in Moxnes 1997 and Bunge 2000.

mid-1980s through to the present. The Roman context was seen as having some distinctive characteristics, yet can also be seen to have been related to the concerns of historians working on the family in early modern Europe. In short, historians of Roman children and childhood have engaged with these debates – but their work has not necessarily fed back into a period of modern history with rather better documentation.

A discussion on the power of fathers or *patria potestas* is probably the most paradigmatic example of this kind of debate in the study of Roman childhood, as the theme has been subject to considerable re-interpretation and re-theorisation. The standard view of Roman society and the place of the Roman family within it has been characterised and interpreted by those who used the law as a main tool for analysing Roman life: Rome was a patriarchal society with power vested in the eldest male in a family. A legitimate child was in the power (*potestas*) of his father (or grandfather, if still alive) for the life of the elder male, unless legally emancipated. This power was exemplified in the Republic by the father's power of life and death over everyone in his *familia*. While this was rarely invoked it did create an image of a highly authoritarian relationship. The power of the father had particular direct implications for the adult life of offspring: they could not inherit or own property in their own right while they were in *potestas*. David Daube characterised this social institution and postulated an extreme version of paternal power:

> Suppose the head of a family was ninety, his two sons seventy-five and seventy; their sons between sixty and fifty-five, the sons of these in their forties and thirties and the great-great-grandsons in their twenties, none of them, except the ninety-year-old Head owned a penny. If the seventy-five year old senator or the forty-year old general or the twenty-year old student wanted to buy a bar of chocolate, he had to ask the *senex* for the money. This is really quite extraordinary (Daube 1969: 75-6).

Such legal theorising and other extreme examples led deMause to point to Rome as having the dystopian paradigm of familial relations. He refers to the period from antiquity to the 4th century AD as the Infanticidal Mode:

> The image of Medea hovers over childhood in antiquity, for myth here only reflects reality. Some facts are more important than others, and when parents routinely resolved their anxieties about taking care of children by killing them, it affected surviving children profoundly. For those who were allowed to grow up, the projective reaction was paramount, and the concreteness of reversal was evident in the widespread sodomizing of the child (de Mause 1974: 51).

The evidence that deMause uses to support such a conclusion is based partly on the idea that *potestas* allowed a father to treat his child exactly as the whim took him (on this deMause took the most pessimistic view); on evidence for infanticide and abandonment of children in the ancient world; and on ideas of child-rearing which included the practice of swaddling and the use of wet-nurses.

DeMause's interpretation of Roman family relationships, coupled with the view presented in legal texts, was influential up to the late 1980s among some scholars. Paul Veyne, for instance, in the first volume of *A History of Private Life* (1987, orig. 1985) could still invoke the image of the family and household tightly controlled by a powerful, autocratic father who demonstrated little difference between the treatment of his children and that of his slaves. This may reflect the overbearing influence of Ariès on French scholarship (see also Rousselle 1983 and Thomas 1986), but it is also the consequence of reading with a presumption of a negative view of childhood.

The major challenge to the position came from the Cambridge family historians and demographers. Richard Saller's work undermined the legal force of *patria potestas*. While it remained a fact that a son or daughter would be in the power of a father until the father's death, Saller asked the obvious question: 'what proportion of Romans at a given age had a living father and were likely to have been *in potestate*?' Saller's results produced a demographic picture which undercut the idea of lasting and overbearing paternal power. Using Coale-Demeny model life tables and the lower range of age at marriage (12-15 for girls; 18-25 for boys), Saller estimated half of children aged 20 being fatherless, and more than three-quarters by the age of 30. The implication is that most males would be outside of paternal power, be legally independent and in control of any property and income by the time they came to marry (Saller 1984, 1987, 1994: 121). Saller's statistics demonstrated that the phenomenon of the adult child may not have been as widespread as thought, but that was not the end of the story. He also demonstrated through an examination of reported father-son relations from antiquity that the legal power of fathers was not utilised in the manner Daube had suggested and deMause had taken on board. Father-son relations were associated with a quality expressed via the term *pietas* (Saller 1994: 102-54). Having removed the legal theory, we find a very different version of a father's *potestas* – present but seldom utilised.

Arguments over the ubiquity of infanticide and abandonment, and the use of the certain traditions of child care (especially wet nursing and swaddling) as evidence for the absence of affection between parents and children in the ancient world have also been reassessed. The discussion of infanticide in Roman society has been rather meagre after the early 1980s refutations of its large scale, and the discussion has been largely taken over by archaeologists.[11] Abandonment, however, has been subject to more attention in recent years. The accepted opinion is that it was a common means for managing family size.[12] Much of the impetus for discussion of the topic in Roman history came from the publication of syntheses of the practice over longer temporal periods, especially John Boswell's *The Kindness of Strangers* published in 1988. There are, naturally, disagreements: did the rich abandon their healthy new-born; how far was the practice limited to the girls; what was the frequency of exposure – highest estimates are 20-40% of the born infants, the lowest some one tenth of that.[13] Most scholars now recognise that answers to these questions may never be forthcoming. Moreover, it has been often stressed that abandonment might in fact reflect parental concern for the survival of other offspring, and a hope for a better future for the abandoned in the face of limited resources.[14] As the abandonment of one child did not necessarily imply that there was indifference towards it, even less does it carry adverse implications for the treatment of those who were allowed to survive and be brought up in the family.

It is possible to find a similar balance of interpretation for the nursing practices. Whereas Stone saw the practice of wet-nursing for the early modern period as evidence for a 'bleak and uncaring' society (Stone 1977: 65), Keith Bradley viewed the idea of removing a neonate from its mother to a wet nurse in a more sympathetic way for the Romans – as an emotional 'cushion' to protect the feelings of parents in a time of high infant mortality (1986: 220). As Peter Garnsey has stressed, there is a need for establishing a sense of the social norms that underpinned these and other practices of childcare:

> A better understanding of childhood in antiquity is important not only in itself, but also as a contribution to a better founded "history of childhood" – better founded in the sense that it would not privilege the quest for "conscious human emotions" at the expense of the analysis of the norms and practices and the practices and the socio/economic conditions of the society in question (Garnsey 1991: 51).

Thus, to understand Roman ideas about childhood, it is essential to examine the nature of the family in which a child grew up. The upper class Roman household was one that held not only the conjugal group but also extensive slaves, retainers, and perhaps, at some stage, a widowed mother or other elderly relatives.[15] The question that needs to be asked is: did the existence of extra-family members, or of slave carers affect the conjugal group of father-mother and children? There is always a modern agenda at work when such matters are discussed. Today, we cannot approve of slavery – hence are far from objective to begin with. When we add in the modern debate over who should care for the very young child, for example, articles written condemning modern parental practices that facilitate mothers and fathers both working and children from six months attending nurseries or child minders, we can appreciate the extent of the problem. The issues of modern parenting practice can still influence our judgement over the Roman parent-child relations. As our own modern institutional practices of parenting change and alter (e.g. the movement from bottle-feeding to breast feeding infants in western European countries), we may implicitly change our perceptions of slave carers. However, we do not wish to react too strongly to the pessimistic positions. Parental indifference, neglect and cruelty did exist in the past, indeed still exist, but not as general or distinctive features of Roman or any other society; just as today, although the 'smacking' of children is illegal in Britain, there is plenty of evidence that it occurs both here and in other countries. We can construct an alternative view of parental affection by citing individual cases of grief stricken parents. In spite of the problematic nature of some of the sources they do suggest that at least in some circles parents cared about their children deeply from birth (see e.g. Rawson 2003).

Rome had the concept of the child as a biological, social and ideological identity. However, even the meaning of 'child' has to be seen in the Roman context, because it is surrounded by a very Roman and unique set of the adult-child relationships – the potential to be adult in years, but not legally able to operate fully as an adult in society due to the power of a living father. The challenge is to recognise that while we can write about the idea and ideology of childhood, we can only hypothesise about the experience about being a child - Roman historians face the same problems as historians of medieval and early modern societies in that children do not write their own history. As with other 'muted groups' (women, slaves, the poor) children leave little of their own voices in the past; almost all we know of them is seen through the prism of the adult world, and in the Roman case, the world of the elite adult male. Despite this we remain optimistic about reconstructing the lives of children in the past.

Challenges for the future

This overview has sought to show that the history of Roman childhood has been outward looking, taking on

---

[11] Engels 1980; Eyben 1980-1; Harris 1982; Oldenziel 1987; Mays 1993; Lee 1994; Scott 2000, 2001.

[12] See e.g. Dixon 1988; Boswell 1988; Wiedemann 1989; Harris 1994; Corbier 2001; Rawson 2003.

[13] Boswell 1988 for the highest estimate, Harris 1994 speculates 8%, Scheidel 1997 for much less.

[14] Dixon 1992; Garnsey 1991; Corbier 2001. For a bibliographical essay, see Dasen et al. 2001: 11-12.

[15] In the mid-1980s, the important question derived from the research interests of Laslett and the Cambridge group was the structure of the Roman family. The question of whether or not Roman families lived in extended or nuclear groups is no longer an issue (Dixon 1992; Saller 1994; cf Martin 1996). However, Bradley has argued that the term nuclear is too value-laden in modern sociological connotations to be useful and we agree with this position (1991: 6). The nature of Roman family relations, inter-relations and affective ties can all too easily be disguised by a simplistic reading of the term 'nuclear'.

board developments beyond its own discipline. In many ways, we see reaction to the synthesisers such as Ariès, Stone or Boswell, and a feeling of a need for correction of their representation of antiquity. What is interesting is that the synthesisers from beyond the discipline have in many ways shaped the debate. In fact, it possible to suggest a rough four-fold division for the research tradition on ancient childhood based on the relation towards Ariès. First of all, there are the studies not involved in the Ariès discussion, concentrating mostly on pedagogy; second, studies directly opposing the thesis of the lack of childhood in the ancient world introduced by Ariès and propagated by other scholars who were tracking the long term changes in family history; third, studies on ancient childhood expanding to other questions in connection with fields like women's studies and demography – even if still occasionally searching for 'la sentiment de l'enfance'. The fourth and most recent phase has meant the opening up of the field to new topics with a greater reflection on theoretical positions, and with an aim to include the material culture of childhood.

However, it remains unclear and difficult to measure how far the study of Roman childhood has crossed over into other disciplines. Our feeling is that there has been a limited impact even on such closely related fields as archaeology. The archaeology of Roman children and childhood is a developing field, interestingly rather less developed theoretically than the history of Roman childhood. However, there is a mass of relevant data to be derived from the remains of the dead that is of paramount interest for the history of childhood (see Laurence 2005). Skeletal evidence, for instance, provides direct access into the life and health of the child, and can provide a means to contextualise our literary and visual representations of children. Such representations reveal attitudes that are as much about the adult worldview as about attitudes to children.

Often the childhood perceived by archaeologists and those who work in material culture differs from the views of those interested in child labour or representations of children in myths. Similarly, a social historian with an interest in the family needs to develop and continue common interest with scholars studying questions of pregnancy, childbirth, health, nurture and disability, to name just a few. The study of the history of childhood in antiquity has to a certain extent reached a level where specialists are now beginning to fail to make communication between disciplines. For example, the uninitiated reader of Walter Scheidel's *Debating Demography* (2001) may come away with the idea that this is fascinating subject which would seem to have deconstructed itself to a point where demographic angles are essential, yet it is impossible to determine their actual nature. The establishment of a bibliography of more than 30 pages suggests at first sight that everything has been done. However, this is an area which is still wide open for further research.

The areas that have not been covered by historians of childhood are almost as diagnostic of the nature of the historiography as what has actually been published. Topics that remain virtually unexplored include the relationships between children and grandparents, brothers and sisters, as well as the experiences of violence and sexual abuse (the last-mentioned if excluding deMause and his school). There has been a greater interest in the early stages of childhood rather than its later stages. This is particularly true in relation to the child between roughly the ages of 8 and 14, or, we might say, the stage of life in which puberty was experienced. Thus, child labour and apprenticeship have also been rather neglected themes (see however Bradley 1991, Vuolanto 2003). Even the history of education has only recently come into contact with the studies exploring representations, mentalities or the social history of Roman childhood (Cribiore 1996, Vössing 1997, Morgan 1998). There are relatively few studies on socialisation and formation of the identity of children (though Rawson 2003 addresses both). Surprisingly, gender is not yet a big issue in the history of Roman childhood (but see Foucault 1990 for a frame of reference) – literary and visual sources are very one-sided; we should be exploiting all we have to uncover the socialisation of girls and how they become women. At what point was there a gender distinction within childhood? Swaddling might suggest from the start, but that will not be the sole issue. For a girl, the end of childhood was at a different age period to that of her brother, and age stages were very different for girls than for boys (see Harlow and Laurence 2002).

Moreover, while the discussion on the possible changes through time in the perception, representation, and value of children and childhood in the Roman world has taken place, partly due to the work of Ariès (see the critical remarks on this discussion in Bradley 1993 and Dixon 1997), regional representations and variations have only recently been touched on (see George 2005). When we turn to the variation in the experience of childhood between the upper and lower classes, we can see little real interest has been expressed in developing this area of productive research. The presence of papyri from Roman Egypt opens the question of variable childhoods across the Empire, although the lack of comparable evidence from anywhere else will be a hindrance to any attempt to place the evidence into the context of even Rome and Italy, let alone Britain or Mauretania.

The discussion of the Roman family needs to move into greater interaction with other disciplines, and away from the debates that have as their reference point the work of Ariès, which should include those who have developed his thesis as well as those in Roman historiography who have reacted against his viewpoint. As Beryl Rawson pointed out at the summing up of the conference in Rome, January 2005: for studies of childhood, the key to the future lies in interdisciplinarity, and in taking seriously the methodological problems caused both by our own cultural assumptions and the cultural and regional variation already present in the Roman world (see Rawson 2005).

The development of a greater interaction with scholars working on the medieval, rather than the early modern, period is now starting to develop. This might allow us, as Roman historians, to view the history of childhood in a wider context and begin to interact more effectively with historians of other periods. It would also create a sense of why the history of childhood in a particular part of the Roman period was unique or different. Thus, for example, the University of Tampere (Finland) deliberately includes both the ancient and the medieval at their conferences on age related themes. More importantly, only in relating the different periods of history do we really understand the history of the idea of childhood and its reception and reinvention in new social situations or later periods of history. Many of the social institutions, including age systems, of antiquity, were re-invented in the medieval and modern world. At the same time, in drawing on the research of historians studying these periods, we may be cherry-picking their work for similarities between childhoods that were discussed via the language of antiquity regardless whether it was AD 10 or AD 1500. The meaning of that language and the actual experience of childhood might have been quite different.

In moving to meet these new challenges, the work done in disciplines dealing with the modern world will also be of help: so far in Roman history 'childhood as a literary discourse', 'childhood as a social construct', 'childhood and life course', 'childhood and social capital' or 'children and familial strategies' have aroused comparatively little attention. In this, the scholarship of childhood is not alone: historians of antiquity have seldom been known for their methodological self-reflection or innovative use of theoretical standpoints. The very issue of how childhood was represented in literary texts and material sources needs to be deconstructed and problematised. Given the link between Roman historians and their colleagues studying classical literature or archaeology, it seems strange that there has been so little attention paid in this area. The time may have come for the full application of literary and cultural theory to the very evidence on which the history of Roman childhood is based.[16]

Bibliography

Anon (1991): *Jouer dans l'antiquité, Catalogue d'exposition*. Réunion des Musées Nationaux, Marseille.

Arends Olsen, L. (1999): *La femme et l'enfant dans les unions illégitimes à Rome. L'évolution du droit jusqu'au début de l'Empire*. Bern.

Aries, P. (1962): *Centuries of Childhood*. London. [orig. Ariès, P. 1960 *L'enfant et la vie familiale sous l'ancien regime*].

Arjava, A. (1998): 'Paternal Power in Late Antiquity', *Journal of Roman Studies* 88: 147-165.

Arnold, K. 1980. *Kind und Gesellschaft in Mittelalter und Renaissance*. Paderborn.

Becker, M.J. (1995): 'Infanticide, child sacrifice and infant mortality rates: direct archaeological evidence as interpreted by human skeletal analysis', *Old World Archaeology Newsletter* XVIII (2): 24-31.

Bellemore, J. and Rawson, B. (1990): 'Alumni. The Italian evidence', *Zeitschrift für Papyrologie und Epigraphik* 83: 1-19.

Bisel, S.C. and Bisel, J.F. (2002): 'Health and Nutrition at Herculaneum: an examination of human skeletal remains', in W.F. Jashemski and F.C. Meyer (eds), *The Natural History of Pompeii*, 451-75. Cambridge.

Boswell, J. (1988): *The Kindness of Strangers: the Abandonment of Children in Western Europe from Late Antiquity to the Renaissance*. London.

Bradley, K.R. (1986): 'Wet-Nursing at Rome: a Study in Social Relations', in B. Rawson (ed.), *The Family in Ancient Rome: New Perspectives*, 201-229. London.

Bradley, K. (1991): *Discovering the Roman family*. Oxford.

Bradley, K.R. (1993): 'Writing the History of the Roman Family', *Classical Philology* 88 (3): 237-250.

Bradley, K.R. (1994): 'The nurse and the child at Rome. Duty, affect and socialisation', *Thamyris* 1(2): 137-156.

Bradley, K. (2005): 'The Roman Child in Sickness and in Health', in M. George (ed.), *The Roman Family in the Empire*, 67-92. Oxford.

Bunge, M. (ed.) (2000): *The Child in Christian Thought*. Michigan.

Burton, A. (1989): 'Looking forward from Aries? Pictorial and material evidence for the history of childhood and family life', *Continuity and Change* 4: 203-29.

Clark, G. (1994): 'The Fathers and the Children', in D. Wood (ed.), *The Church and Childhood*, 1–28. Studies in Church History 31. Cambridge.

Congourdeau, M.-H. (2000): 'L'embryon dans les premiers siècles chrétiens', in J. Martin et al. (eds), *L'enfant à naître. Tertullien, Grégoire, Augustin, Maxime, Cassiodore, Pseudo-Augustin* (Coll. Les Pères dans la foi 78), 11-35. Paris.

Corbier, M. (1991a): 'Constructing Kinship in Rome: Marriage and Divorce, Filiation and Adoption' , in D. Kertzer, and R. Saller (eds), *The Family in Italy from Antiquity to the Present*, 127-44. New Haven.

Corbier, M. (1991b): 'Divorce and Adoption as Roman Familial Strategies (le divorce et l'adoption en plus)', in B. Rawson (ed.), *Marriage, Divorce and Children in Ancient Rome*, 47-78. Oxford.

Corbier, M. (ed.) (2000): *Adoption et fosterage*. Paris.

Corbier, M. (2001): 'Child Exposure and Abandonment', in S. Dixon (ed.), *Childhood, Class and Kin in the Roman World*, 52-73. London and New York.

---

[16] The bibliography in this volume contains all the articles referenced above, but for a full and updated bibliography of Roman childhood see Vuolanto 2007.

Coulon, G. (1994): *L' enfant en Gaule romaine* (Collection des Hespérides: archéologie, histoire). Paris.

Coulon, G. (2004): 'Images et imaginaire de la naissance dans l'Occident romain', in V. Dasen (ed.), *Naissance et petite enfance dans l'Antiquité. Actes du colloque de Fribourg 28 novembre – 1er décembre 2001* (Orbis Biblicus et Orientalis 203): 209-26. Fribourg.

Cribriore, R. (1996): *Writing, teachers and students in Graeco-Roman Egypt.* American Studies in Papyrology 36. Atlanta.

Crifo, G. (1964): 'Sul Problema della donna tutrice.' *Bollettino dell'istituto di diritto romano* 67: 87-166.

Currie, S. (1996): 'The empire of adults: the representation of children on Trajan''s arch at Beneventum', in J. Elsner (ed.), *Art and Text in Roman Culture*, 153-181. Cambridge and New York.

Dasen, V. (1997): 'Multiple Births in Graeco-Roman Antiquity,' *Oxford Journal of Archaeology* 16: 49-63.

Dasen, V. (1999): 'L'accueil des nouveau-nés malformés dans l'Antiquité. 1. L'ancienne Egypte; 2. La Grèce archaïque et classique; 3. Le monde romain', *Revue internationale de Pédiatrie* (30) (292), 37-40; (30) (294), 50-53; (30) (297), 32-35.

Dasen, V. (2003): 'Amulettes d'enfants dans le monde grec et romain', *Latomus* 62: 275-289.

Dasen, V. (ed.) (2004): *Naissance et petite enfance dans l'Antiquité.* Actes du colloque de Fribourg, 28 novembre-1er décembre 2001 (Orbis Biblicus et Orientalis 203). Fribourg.

Dasen, V., Lett, D., Morel M.-F. and Rollet C. (2001): 'Dix ans de travaux sur l'enfance', in *Enfances, Bilan d'une décennie de recherche, Annales de la démographie historique* 2, 5-100.

Daube, D. (1969): *Roman Law: Linguistic, Social and Philosophical aspects.* Edinburgh.

DeMause, L. (1974): 'The evolution of childhood', in L. deMause (ed.), *The History of Childhood,* 1-73. New York.

Dixon, S. (1988): *The Roman Mother.* London.

Dixon, S. (1992): *The Roman Family.* Baltimore and London.

Dixon, S. (1997): 'Continuity and Change in Roman Social History: retrieving 'Family Feeling(s)' from Roman law and Literature' in M. Golden and P. Toohey (eds), *Inventing Ancient Culture: Historicism, Periodization and the Ancient World,* 79-90. London and New York.

Dixon, S. (ed.) (2001): *Childhood, Class and Kin in the Roman world.* London and New York.

Engels, D. (1980): 'The Problem of Female Infanticide in the Greco-Roman World', *Classical Philology* 75: 112-120.

Evans, J.K. (1991): *War, Women and Children in Ancient Rome.* London: New York.

Eyben, E. (1993): *Restless Youth in Ancient Rome.* London.

Fayer, C. (1994): *La familia Romana, Aspetti giuridici ed antiquari.* Rome.

Fittà, M. (1997): *Giochi e giocattoli nell'antichita.* Milan.

Fossati Vanzetti, M.B. (1983): 'Vendita ed esposizione degli infanti da Costantino a Giustiniano', *Studia et Documenta Historiae et Iuris* 49: 179-224.

Foucault, M. (1990): *The History of Sexuality* Vol. 1 Harmondsworth.

French, V. (1986): 'Midwives and maternity care in the Graeco-Roman world', *Helios* 13: 69-84.

Garnsey, P. (1991): 'Child rearing in Ancient Italy', in D. Kertzer, and R. Saller (eds), *The Family in Italy from Antiquity to the Present*, 48-65. New Haven.

George, M. (2001): 'A Roman funerary monument with a mother and a daughter', in S. Dixon (ed.), *Childhood, Class and Kin in the Roman World,* 178-189. London and New York.

George, M. (ed.) (2005): *The Roman Family in the Empire: Rome, Italy, and Beyond.* Oxford.

Gourevitch, D. (1984): *Le mal d'être femme. La femme et la médecine dans la Rome antique.* Paris.

Gourevitch, D. (1998): 'Biberons romains: formes et noms', in G. Sabbah (ed.), *Le latin médical. Réalités et langage de la médecine dans le monde romain,* 117-133. Centre Jean-Palerne, Saint-Étienne.

Gourevitch, D. (1991): 'Au temps des lois Julia et Papia Poppaea, la naissance d'un enfant handicapé est-elle une affaire publique ou privée?' *Ktema* 23: 459-473.

Gowland, R. (2001): 'Playing Dead', in G. Davies, A. Gardner and K. Lockyear. *TRAC 2000. Proceedings of the Tenth Annual Theoretical Roman Archaeology Conference,* 152-68. Oxford.

Hanawalt, B. (1977): 'Childrearing among the lower classes of Late Medieval England', *Journal of Interdisciplinary History* 8: 1-21.

Hanson, A.E. (1994): 'A division of labour. Roles for men in Greek and Roman births', *Thamyris* 1: 157-202.

Harlow, M. and Laurence, R. (2002): *Growing Up and Growing Old in Ancient Rome: A Life Course Approach.* London and New York.

Harris, W.V. (1982): 'The Theoretical Possibility of Extensive Infanticide in the Graeco-Roman World', *Classical Quarterly* 32: 114-116.

Harris, W.V. (1994): 'Child-exposure in the Roman empire', *Journal of Roman Studies* 84: 1-22.

Harris, W.V. (1999): 'Demography, Geography and the Sources of Roman Slaves', *Journal of Roman Studies* 89: 62-75.

Huskinson, J.A.R. (1996): *Roman Children's Sarcophagi. Their Decoration and Social Significance.* Oxford.

Kapparis, K. (2002): *Abortion in the Ancient World.* London.

Kehoe, D. (1997): *Investment, Profit, and Tenancy: The Jurists and the Roman Agrarian Economy.* Ann Arbor, Michigan.

Köves-Zulauf, Th. (1990): *Römische Geburtsriten.* Munich.

Laes, C. (2004): 'Children and accidents in Roman antiquity', *Ancient Society* 34: 153-70.

Laslett, P. and Wall, R. (eds) (1972): *Household and Family in Past Time.* London.

Laurence, R. (2005): 'Health and the life course at Herculaneum and Pompeii', in H. King (ed.), *Health in Antiquity*, 83-96. London.

Lee, K.A. (1994): 'Attitudes and prejudices towards infanticide: Carthage, Rome and today', *Archaeological Review from Cambridge* 13(2): 21-34.

Lindsay, H. (2001): 'Adoption and its function in cross-cultural contexts,' in S. Dixon (ed.), *Childhood, Class and Kin in the Roman world*, 190-204. London and New York.

Macfarlane, A. (1986): *Marriage and Love in England 1300-1840*. Oxford.

Manson, M. (1983): 'The emergence of the small child in Rome (third century BC - first century AD)', *History of Education* 12: 149-159.

Markus, A. (1989): *Tutela Impuberis. Einfluss des Volksrechts auf das klassische römische Vormundshaftsrecht unter besonderer Berücksichtigung der Gräko-ägyptischen Papyri*. Inaugural Dissertation, Philipps-Universität (Marburg), Marburg.

Martin, D.B. (1996): 'The Construction of the Ancient Family: Methodological Considerations', *Journal of Roman Studies* 86: 40–60.

Mays, S. (1993): 'Infanticide in Roman Britain', *Antiquity* 67: 883-888.

Memmer, M. (1991): 'Ad servitutem aut ad lupanar... Ein Beitrag zur Rechtsstellung von Findelkindern nach römischen Recht - Unter besonderer Berücksichtigung von §§ 77, 98 Sententiae Syriaca', *Zeitschrift der Savigny-Stiftung für Rechtsgeschichte, Romanistische Abteilung* 108: 21-93.

Meskell, L. (1994): 'Dying young: the experience of death at Deir-el-Medina', *Archaeological Review from Cambridge* 13(2): 35-46.

Morgan, T. (1998): *Literate Education in the Hellenistic and Roman Worlds*. Cambridge.

Moxnes, H. (ed.) (1997): *Constructing early Christian families. Family as social reality and metaphor*. London.

Nathan, G. (2000): *The Family in Late Antiquity. The Rise of Christianity and the Endurance of Tradition*. New York & London.

Neraudau, J.-P. (1984): *Etre enfant à Rome*. Paris.

Nielsen, H.S. (1987): 'Alumnus: A term of relation denoting quasi-adoption', *Classica et Mediaevalia* 38: 141–188.

Norman, N.J. (2003): 'Death and burial of Roman children: the case of the Yasmina Cemetery at Carthage – Part II, The archaeological evidence', *Mortality* 8(1): 36-47.

Oldenziel, R. (1987): 'The historiography of infanticide in Antiquity. A literature stillborn,' in J. Blok and P. Mason (eds*), Sexual asymmetry. Studies in ancient society*, 87-107. Amsterdam.

O'Roark, D. (1999): 'Parenthood in Late Antiquity: The Evidence of Chrysostom', *Greek, Roman and Byzantine Studies* 40: 53-81.

Parkin, T. (1994): review of the recent work on the Roman family, *Journal of Roman Studies* 84: 178-85.

Parkin, T. (1992): *Demography and Roman Society*. Baltimore and London.

Petermandl, W. (1997): 'Kinderarbeit im Italien der Prinzipatzeit. Ein Beitrag zur Sozialgeschichte des Kindes', *Laverna* 8: 113-136.

Pollock, L. (1983): *Forgotten Children – Parent: Child relations from 1500-1900*. Cambridge.

Rawson, B. (1966): 'Family life among the lower classes at Rome in the first two centuries of the empire', *Classical Philology* 61: 71-83.

Rawson, B. (ed) (1986a): *The Family in Ancient Rome: New Perspectives*, London.

Rawson, B. (1986b): 'Children in the Roman familia', in B. Rawson (ed.), *The Family in Ancient Rome: New Perspectives*, 170-200. London.

Rawson, B. (ed.) (1991): *Marriage, Divorce and Children in Ancient Rome*. Oxford.

Rawson, B. (1997): 'Representations of Roman children and childhood', *Antichthon* 31: 74-95.

Rawson, B. (2003): *Children and Childhood in Roman Italy*. Oxford.

Rawson, B. (2005): 'The future of childhood studies in classics and ancient history', in K. Mustakallio, J. Hanska, H.-L. Sainio and V. Vuolanto (eds), *Hoping for Continuity: Childhood, Education and Death in Antiquity and the Middle Ages*, 1-11. Acta Instituti Romani Finlandiae 33. Rome.

Rawson B. and Weaver, P. (eds) (1997): *The Roman Family in Italy: Status, Sentiment, Space*. Oxford.

Redfern, R. (2002): 'Sex and the city: a biological investigation into female health in Roman Britain', in G. Carr, E. Swift and J. Weekes (eds), *TRAC 2002: Proceedings of the 12th Annual Theoretical Roman Archaeology Conference*, 147-70. Oxford.

Redfern, R. (2007): 'The influence of culture upon childhood: an osteological study of Iron Age and Romano-British Dorset', in M. Harlow and R. Laurence (eds), *Age and Ageing in the Roman Empire. Journal of Roman Archaeology*, Supplementary Series 65: 153-69.

Riché, P. (1962): *La Culture Médiévale. Education et culture dans l'occident barbare: VI-VIIIème siecles*. Paris.

Rousselle, A. (1983): *Porneia. De la maîtrise du corps à la privation sensorielle*. Paris.

Saller, R.P. (1984): 'Familia, domus, and the Roman concept of the family', *Phoenix* 38: 336-55.

Saller, R.P. (1987): 'Men's age at Marriage and its consequences in the Roman family', *Classical Philology* 82: 21-34.

Saller, R.P. (1994): *Patriarchy, Property and Death in the Roman Family*. Cambridge.

Saller, R.P. and Shaw, B. D. (1984): 'Tombstones and Roman family relations: soldiers, civilians and slaves', *Journal of Roman Studies* 74: 124-56.

Scheidel, W. (2001): 'Progress and Problems in Roman Demography', in W. Scheidel (ed.), *Debating Roman demography*, 1-81. Leiden.

Scheidel, W. (1997): 'Quantifying the Sources of Slaves in the Early Roman Empire', *Journal of Roman Studies* 87, 156-169.

Scott, E. (1999): *The Archaeology of Infancy and Infant Death*. Oxford.

Scott, E. (2000): 'Unpicking a myth: the infanticide of female and disabled infants in antiquity', in G. Davies, A. Gardner and K. Lockyear (eds), *Procedings of the Tenth Annual Theoretical Roman Archaeology Conference, London 2000*, 143-151. Oxford.

Shaw, B.D. (1987): 'The Age of Roman Girls at Marriage: Some Reconsiderations', *Journal of Roman Studies* 77: 30-46.

Shaw, B.D. (2001): 'Raising and killing children: two Roman myths', *Mnemosyne* 54(1): 31-77.

Shorter, E. (1975): *The making of the Modern Family*. New York.

Soren, D. and Soren N. (eds) (1999): *A Roman Villa and a Late-Roman Infant Cemetery: Excavations at Poggio Gramignano, Lugnano in Teverina*. Rome.

Strange, W.A. (1996): *Children in the Early Church*. Carlisle.

Stone, L. (1977): *The Family, Sex and Marriage in England, 1500-1800*. London.

Thomas, Y. (1986): 'Fathers as citizens of Rome, Rome as a city of fathers (second century BC - second century AD)', in A. Burguiere, S. Hanbury Tenison, R. Morris, and A. Wilson (eds), *A History of the Family, Volume I: Distant Worlds, Ancient Worlds* 1996 [orig. in French 1986], 228 - 269. Paris.

Treggiari, S. (1996): 'Social Status and Social Legislation', in A.K. Bowman, E. Champlin & A. Lintott (eds), *The Cambridge Ancient History*, second edition, volume X, *The Augustan Empire, 43 B.C. - A.D. 69*, 873-904. Cambridge.

Veyne, P. (1985): 'L'Empire romain', in P. Veyne (ed.), *Histoire de la vie privée. I. De l'Empire romain à l'an mil*, 19-224. Paris. [Trans. 'The Roman Empire,' in P. Veyne (ed.), *A History of Private Life from Pagan Rome to Byzantium*, Cambridge (Mass.) and London 1987, 5-234].

Voci, P. (1980): 'Storia della patria potestas da Augusto a Diocleziano', *Iura* 31: 37-100.

Voci, P. (1985): 'Storia della patria potestas da Costantino a Giustiniano.' *Studia et Documenta Historiae et Iuris* 51: 1-72.

Vössing, K. (1997): *Schule und Bildung im Nordafrika der römischen Kaiserzeit* (Collection Latomus). Bruxelles.

Vuolanto, V. (2003): 'Selling a Freeborn Child: Rhetoric and Social Realities in the Late Roman World', *Ancient Society* 33: 169–207.

Vuolanto, V. (2007): *Children in Ancient World. A bibliography*, University of Tampere, http://www.uta.fi/laitokset/historia/sivut/BIBChild.pdf

Wiedemann, T. (1989): *Adults and Children in the Roman Empire*. London.

Zanker, P. (2000): 'Die Frauen und Kinder der barbaren auf der markussäule', in J. Scheid and V. Huet (eds), *Autour de la colonne Aurélienne: geste et image sur la colonne de Marc Aurèle à Rome*, 163-174. Turnhout.

CHAPTER 3

THE PITTER-PATTER OF TINY FEET IN CLAY: ASPECTS OF THE LIMINALITY OF CHILDHOOD IN THE ANCIENT NEAR EAST

Alasdair Livingstone

You, Gilgamesh, may your belly be full,
You should ever rejoice, day and night!
Daily make merry,
dance and play day and night!
Let your clothes be clean!
Let your head be washed, may you bathe in water!
Gaze on the little one who holds your hand!
Let the wife take pleasure at your embrace![1]

A history of childhood in the ancient Near East remains to be written and would no doubt fill several large volumes. There is abundant evidence for the subject but it is unevenly spread over a chronological band of almost 3,000 years – much longer if one includes prehistory – and a geographical area stretching beyond the fertile-crescent into Anatolia, Arabia and Iran. The present contribution will concentrate on Mesopotamia and Northern Syria and chart aspects of childhood in the Sumerian, Babylonian, Assyrian and Neo-Hittite civilisations. Even with this restriction there is a vast chronological and geographical span, but nevertheless there existed a certain cultural unity defined by the common use of the cuneiform script and various degrees of indebtedness to the classical civilisation of the Sumerians in Southern Mesopotamia in the 3rd millennium BC (see Figs 3.1 and 3.2).

The subject of childhood has been greatly neglected in those publications attempting to provide an overview of Mesopotamian civilisation. A.L. Oppenheim's *Ancient Mesopotamia, Portrait of a Dead Civilisation* (1964), long regarded as the standard introduction to Ancient Mesopotamia, gives no information on Mesopotamian childhood beyond the training of scribes. This lack has been perpetuated since with childhood as a subject in its own right being largely ignored although certain specific aspects of it have been treated such as birth and babies (Stol 2000) or schooling (Civil 1998; Foster 2003; George 2005; Sauren 1980; Vanstiphout 1980; Waetzoldt 1986).[2] Karen Rhea Nemet-Nejat's *Daily Life in Ancient Mesopotamia* (2002) does not discuss childhood although it offers two full pages on toilets and drains. A recent 500-page compendium volume seeking to give a broad presentation of life and civilisation in the ancient Near

East (Snell 2005) has no section on childhood and neither this word nor the words 'child' or 'children' appear in the index. Children have, however, fared better in the field of iconography and a compendious treatment on the depiction of children in ancient Near Eastern art has been published by Parayre (1997). In the present contribution an overview of Mesopotamian childhood is given in such a way as to facilitate discussion of the issue of the liminality of childhood, specifically the circumstances in which children enter the historical and the archaeological record. Illustrative examples are selected from various areas and periods.

It is appropriate to commence with the first stages of the life course. Why should people want children? The nature of Mesopotamian society makes what seems like an obvious question more complicated for two reasons, one practical and one religious. People were dependant on their grown up children – especially sons – to care for them in their old age. They believed that when they were dead and in the underworld their welfare was dependant on funerary offerings made for them by their children and descendants.[3] There was also an element of the perpetuation of the memory of the deceased individual, and, as names were an integral part of the *persona*, the descendant, while performing the ritual for the funerary offering would as part of an incantation proclaim as follows: 'I have spoken your name among the ancestors; I have spoken your name in the funerary ritual' (Radner 2005: 74-9). The ritual was carried out at the end of the month during the period of invisibility of the lunar crescent and this meant that the name of the deceased was spoken at least once a month on earth and in the underworld. A passage in the *Epic of Gilgamesh* describes the condition of a man in the underworld according to the number of sons he has from one to seven. He with one son has a peg in his wall and sits and

---

[1] Lines from an Old Babylonian version of the *Epic of Gilgamesh*. See George 2003: 278-9.

[2] See further in the attached bibliography and especially on childhood illness Volk 2000; Cadelli 1997; on children in religion and law Cazelles 1985; Lebrun 1980; Limet 1980; Wunsch 2003/2004; on children's games Kilmer 1993.

[3] The cult of funerary offerings and the associated practices are discussed in detail in Tsukimoto 1985.

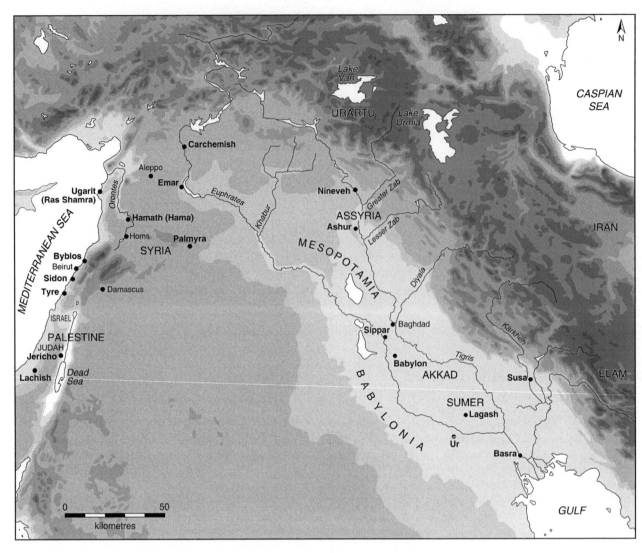

Fig. 3.1 Map of the Ancient Near East.

3000 BC	Approximate date of the beginning of literacy and history in Mesopotamia
2900 – 2300 BC	Early Dynastic Period
	c. 2500: Ur-Nanshe, ruler of Lagash
	c. 2350: Uru'inimgina, ruler of Lagash
2300 – 2100 BC	The Akkadian Empire founded by Sargon of Akkad
	c. 2200: Shar-kali-sharri, king of Akkad
2100 – 2000 BC	The Ur III Period: Sumer ruled by the 3rd dynasty of Ur
1894 – 1595 BC	The Old Babylonian Period
	Composition of the Epics of Atrahasis and Gilgamesh
1500 – 1000 BC	The Kassite Period in Babylonia
	1186-1172: Melishipak, king of Babylonia
900 – 612 BC	Neo-Assyrian Period
	8th century BC: Yariris regent in Carchemish
	680-669: Esarhaddon, king of Assyria
	668-627: Ashurbanipal, king of Assyria
600 – 539 BC	Neo-Babylonian Period
	555 – 539: Nabonidus, king of Babylonia

Fig. 3.2 Timeline.

weeps over it,[4] but at the other end of the spectrum he with seven sons is seated with the minor gods (George 2003: 733-4). For those who failed to have natural children, adopting children as a sort of old age and afterlife care policy was an option if one could afford it (Wunsch 2003-2004).

There were pregnancy tests (Reiner 1982: 124-38), the accuracy of which cannot be tested due to the difficulty in identifying some of the ingredients used. There also existed a copious ancient medical literature on pregnancy and birth (Stol 2000). Apart from this relatively 'scientific' material, conception and birth were the focus of attention in magical and mantic contexts. For example, hemerologies might specify favourable days for conception and also for birth. To be born in the second month of the year was favourable: this of course was just after the harvest, so people would be well off and able to look after the baby properly (Livingstone, forthcoming). There is also a certain amount of high jinks. If you succeeded in making a woman of the street pregnant on the 25th day of the month, the day of the festival of Ishtar of Babylon, then the goddess would reward you with riches and treasures (Livingstone 1997: 218). Birth was regarded as a miracle enacting a primeval event at which the mother goddess Mami would put magic bricks in place. This is celebrated in the *Epic of Atrahasis* as follows:

> In the house of the pregnant woman in confinement
> Let the brick be in place for seven days,
> That Belet-ili, the wise Mami, may be honoured.
> Let the midwife rejoice in the house of the woman in confinement,
> And when the pregnant woman gives birth
> Let the mother of the babe sever herself.
>
> [lacuna of uncertain length]
>
> The birth goddesses were assembled
> And Nintu [sat] counting the months.
> [At the] destined [moment] the tenth month was summoned.
> The tenth month arrived
> And the elapse of the period opened the womb.
>
> With a beaming, joyful face
> She performed the midwifery.
> She girded her loins as she pronounced the blessing,
> She drew a pattern in meal and placed the brick,
> 'I have created, my hands have made it.
> Let the midwife rejoice in the house of the wet-nurse.[5]

> Where the pregnant woman gives birth
> And the mother of the babe severs herself,
> Let the brick be in place for nine days,
> That Nintu, the birth-goddess, may be honoured
> (after Lambert & Millard 1969: 63-65).

The brick or bricks of birth are well known in ancient Mesopotamia as well as in ancient Egypt (Stol 2000: 118-22). Stol also presents modern ethnographic parallels from Palestine and Egypt.[6] The woman squats or leans on the two bricks and the midwife delivers the baby from behind. The point in the passage from the *Epic of Atrahasis* is that the practical arrangements which attended the human birth are given a mythological context. The placing of the bricks used in the birth re-enacts the mythological event in which the birth-goddess Nintu, also referred to by the hypocoristic name Mami and as Belet-ili, the 'Lady of the Gods', was believed to have attired herself suitably and carried out a ritual which included putting the birth brick in place, as set out in the passages quoted above. There existed a genre of learned Babylonian texts in which ancient scholars expounded supposed relationships of this type between what was for them contemporary ritual on the one hand, and primeval mythology on the other (Livingstone 1986, especially Chapter Five).

There was a belief in Mesopotamia that people could be somehow responsible for their illness, for example by offending their personal god or transgressing against a cultic rule or social norm. But babies were clearly innocent and another explanation for their ailments was commonly found in the Lamashtu demon, believed to be a danger to pregnant women as well as babies (Wiggerman in Stol 2000: 217-49). She is depicted with snakes in her hands and a scorpion between her legs. Fortunately there were rituals to send her away. She could be fobbed off with suckling a dog and a pig instead of babies and put on a donkey or a boat – or both – on her way back to the netherworld.

There were incantations to quiet crying babies – we would call them lullabies. An example from the Old Babylonian period is:

> Little one who dwelled in the house of darkness (the womb).
> Now you've come out and seen the light.
> Why are your tears flowing, why are you crying?
> You didn't cry before!
> You've disturbed the house god, woken the buffalo!
> Like a wine drinker,
> Like a bar regular,

---

[4] The metaphor comes from the language of real estate. Where a house has been pledged as security for a loan a peg in the wall marks the creditor's interest in the debtor's property. The man with one son laments the precariousness of his position. There is also probably an element of analogy, one son, one peg, since the man with two sons sits on two bricks while eating a piece of bread.

[5] This translation differs from that of Lambert and Millard in that the word 'prostitute' has been replaced by 'wetnurse' in agreement with the

two relevant lemmata in the *Chicago Assyrian Dictionary* and the *Akkadisches Handwörterbuch*, neither of which had appeared at the time of Lambert and Millard's writing.

[6] The word usually translated as 'stool' in the Moses birth story of Exodus 1:15ff. is in fact the dual of the ordinary Hebrew word for stone, thus 'both stones', indicating that the ancient Hebrews also had a similar birth practice.

May sweet sleep sink on the little one.
(Translation after Farber 1989: 35-9).

At this point there are instructions for a ritual, part of which involved giving the baby a dose of a potion containing beer. Here the modern parallel would be various treatments for babies with colic that included alcohol and were once sold at high street chemists.

Modern hospitals have tagging systems to identify babies. In Mesopotamia prints in wet clay of the babies' feet were sometimes made, with their names written onto the resulting clay casts, or an impression of the infant's foot made on the reverse of the legal tablet referring to it. This was done for both rich and poor children and for girls as well as boys. Three inscribed clay models of the feet of triplets, one girl and two boys, were found in the excavations at Emar, and date to the 14th century BC (Leichty 1989). The text of all three follows the same pattern: 'Foot(print) of Shanin'alanua, daughter of Satamma, son of Karbi the Satappian. Seal of Dagan-belum. Seal of Madi-Dagan. Seal of Aya-damqat.' The imprints were presumably made to avoid the substitution of changelings, for example by a wet-nurse. From the Late Babylonian period there are cases of the adoption of foundlings where it is made explicit that the foundling will be raised in close proximity with the other children but on the understanding that they would spend a life in service and possibly as slaves. The foundling was foot-printed to pre-empt possible confusion (Wunsch 2003-2004).

The classification of the stages of babyhood and childhood in Mesopotamia is a somewhat complex issue. For babies there were two stages, those still on mothers' milk and those who had been 'separated from her', weaned. Beyond babyhood the distinction between girls and boys became more important. It is possible that some Mesopotamians may have known how old their children were by lunar years and months but the most common evidence, from legal and economic records, has their growth recorded by measuring them by the half ell, about 23 cm. We find girls measuring from about two to five half ells and boys between three and six half ells. Beyond the metre-high stage many boys and girls – especially those not from elites – would in many respects be treated as adults. As will be seen below abundant attestation shows children still almost toddlers working at all sorts of jobs. The next important milestone was puberty. Even the youngest male adolescent was treated like a young man, while for women the big step was marriage. In the royal family and probably among elites the regnal years of kings could provide benchmarks for plotting the progress of the life-course. Adad-guppi, the mother of Nabonidus, charted her life from birth on as follows: 'From the 20th year of Ashurbanipal, king of Asssyria, when I was born, until the 42nd year of Ashurbanipal, the third year of his son Ashur-etil-ilani, the 21st year of Nabopolassar, the 43rd year of Nebuchadnezzar, the second year of Awel-Marduk, the fourth year of Neriglissar, during all these 95 years when I visited the temple of the moon-god Sin, he looked with favour at my good works', and so on. Adad-guppi lived to be 104, but it should be remembered that these are lunar not solar years.

Children first appear in a fully contextual and historical setting in the later Early Dynastic Period in Sumer in southern Mesopotamia, in a document which has been dubbed by modern scholarship the *Reform Texts of Uru'inimgina*. Uru'inimgina was ruler of the city-state of Lagash in Sumer in the latter half of the 24th century BC,[7] a period characterised by strife between the various polities of the land and the further development of walled cities. The reform texts, however, inscribed on a number of clay cones, a plaque and some jar fragments, tell of social turmoil and bureaucracy out of control and how this was addressed by the ruler.

The text begins and ends with records of Uru'inimgina's sacral and secular building activities, part of the inscriptional stock in trade of Mesopotamian rulers, telling of the construction of a temple for the city goddess Ba'u equipped with a pantry for regular offerings, and a canal, the 'tail' of which reached the sea. Encased within the text of the building inscriptions is an account of abuse and how wrongs were rectified. This in turn is constructed on a 'before' and 'after' model:

Since time immemorial, since life began, in those days, the head boatman appropriated boats, the livestock official appropriated asses, the livestock official appropriated sheep... when a corpse was brought for burial... when a man was brought for the reeds of Enki, then the *uhmush* official took his seven jugs of beer, his 420 loaves of bread, two *ul* of barley, one woollen garment, one bed and one chair and the *umum* took one *ul* of barley (after Cooper 1986: 70-8).

The reeds of Enki, god of wisdom and magic, probably refer to a reed coffin in which the corpse was wrapped before being lowered into the marshes and the extent of the abuse can be gauged by the figures of the commodities demanded by the funeral directors. The seven jugs would be 140 litres, and an Early Dynastic *ul* is 36 litres. The section detailing abuses ends with the comment: 'These were the conventions of former times.' Then: 'When Ningirsu,[8] warrior of Enlil,[9] granted the kingship of Lagash to Uru'inimgina, selecting him from among the myriad people, he replaced the customs of former times, carrying out the command that Ningirsu, his master, had given him.' The various officials were removed from the posts that they had abused and a fairer situation established.

---

[7] According to the widely accepted chronology proposed by Cooper (1986).
[8] The city god of Lagash.
[9] The chief deity of the Sumerian pantheon.

Children of two opposite social classes are mentioned in this text. In the period of abuse:

> The ruler's estate and ruler's fields, the estate of the woman's organisation and fields of the woman's organisation and the children's estate and children's fields all abutted one another. The bureaucracy was operating from the boundary of Ningirsu[10] to the sea (after Cooper 1986: 71).

Here, the woman is the wife of the ruler Uru'inimgina and the other estates referred to belong to their children. Uru'inimgina breaks up the accumulated build-up of real estate wealth, assigning portions of it to various temples. For individuals whom we would today categorise as children to be owning property would not of course be remarkable anywhere in the ancient world. What is remarkable here is that the children are holding estates while their father is still alive. This may be a phenomenon involving dynastic perpetuation, in that those who worked on these estates got used to the idea of the princely children being in authority, perhaps a bit like the colonial situation where grown African men were expected to address four-year old English boys as 'master'. There may, however, have been further complications involving questions that cannot yet be answered, such as the extent of the control over temple estates exercised by the palace and a delicate balance of power between the two. A text from a slightly later reign, that of Shar-kali-sharri, documents economic abuse of such power in that the king was purchasing temple estate land at a very low price and under duress (Wilcke 2003: 23).

Children from the lower social class are also mentioned in the text. Uru'inimgina cancelled the obligations of indentured families, and, in the same sentence, solemnly promised Ningirsu that he would never subjugate the waif and the widow to the powerful. Here children preserve their liminality, being a small object of focus within a much wider panorama of abuse and reform; they appear in order to highlight the magnanimous behaviour of the ruler, who has taken away from the estates of his own progeny and vowed to protect orphans. One clause in the l. reform texts stipulates the release from prison of children who had been incarcerated for theft, murder and two other crimes that are – perhaps mercifully – veiled in philological obscurity.[11] Here the impulse may have been the demand for labour. These texts are to be numbered among the first half dozen or so true historical texts in human history, and are a harbinger of what was to transpire in many later centuries of history in the region, with social inequality and attempts at social engineering and with children caught between different forces in the chaotic maelstrom of human history.

Royal children also appear in iconography in the Early Dynastic Period. These include plaques with multiple cartouches depicting a sequence of events. The plaques typically feature a hole in the middle so that they can be attached to a wall with a baked clay nail. One example shows the ruler Ur-Nanshe accompanied by his sons (Fig. 3.3); there can be no question that they are his sons as they are individually specified as such and labelled in cuneiform on the plaque.[12] In the initial scene, Ur-Nanshe carries a basket with the first bricks for the building of a temple while his sons stand with him; in the second, after the temple has been built, Ur-Nanshe drinks beer, again accompanied by his sons. Here the children appear as agents of royal propaganda: they are part of the royal family and their presence is intended to perpetuate Ur-Nanshe's dynasty. The situation is broadly comparable with a modern British monarch and consort laying the first brick for a building or cutting a string on its completion, or appearing on a ceremonial or festive occasion with their offspring on the balcony of Buckingham Palace.

Somewhat later in the Ur III Period at the end of the third millennium BC another face of ancient Mesopotamian childhood appears. Children are found as workers in factory conditions and a prominent example is the textile industry. Texts from the suburb of Gu'abba in the city-state of Lagash in the east of Sumer mention an establishment with more that 4,000 adults and 1,800 children all engaged in various phases of the textile production process (Waetzoldt 1972). This seems to be a higher proportion than in other industries and the reason may be that they were found especially useful because of their small fingers, as in parts of the carpet industry in Iran and the Indian subcontinent today.

Children in ancient Mesopotamia played an even more direct part in the economy as commodities themselves. To take just one example, an archive of commercial texts from Ur dating to the Middle Babylonian period exhibits the pattern set out below. The numeral in round brackets is the text number in the publication (Gurney 1983).

1. Redemption of a slave-girl (1)
2. Purchase of a young boy (21)
3. Purchase of a young boy (22)
4. Sale of a young boy (23)
5. Dispute arising from the purchase of a girl (24)
6. Purchase of a girl (25)
7. Settlement concerning a baby (26)
8. Purchase of a girl, with a postscript (27)

The total number of tablets in the archive is 83, which is to say that in this particular archive, which is certainly not atypical, roughly 10% of the texts concern children, all of whom are being bought and sold.

---

[10] i.e. the boundary of the city-state of Lagash.
[11] See Wilcke (2003: 22) with footnote 18.

[12] The cuneiform has been omitted from the figure as rendered here.

Fig. 3.3 Plaque showing the Sumerian ruler Ur-Nanshe and his sons at a building ceremony followed by a banquet.

More privileged children might find themselves apprenticed to a trade. An unusual example from the reign of Nabonidus in the Late Neo-Babylonian period records a young boy apprenticed to a mouse catcher (Bongenaar & Jursa 1993: 30-8). The text is as follows:

> For two years Shamash-zer-ibni, the son of Arad-Nabu, will be at the disposal of Arad-Nabu, the royal reed-mouse capturer. He will teach him the art of mice catching. Arad-Nabu will deposit 50 reed mice as products to be delivered to the (temple of) Shamash every year. He who breaks the contract will pay 1000 reed mice. Witnesses: Shamash-mudammiq, son of Nabu-ahhe-shullim, Nabu-usur, son of Arad-bel. Scribe: Arad-Bel, son of Bel-ushallim. Sippar, 30th of Elul, 7th year of Nabonidus, king of Babylon.[13]

The yearly delivery of mice to the temple of Shamash will almost certainly be because the apprentice was an indentured slave of the temple. After training he would continue to work in the service of the temple as a mouse capturer. Such contracts exist because they are a legal record of responsibilities by both parties to the apprenticeship agreed.

Children from various social groups might find themselves getting educated in the cuneiform script. A substantial amount is known about scribal education and schools, for two main reasons. One reason for this is that a very large number of school tablets with exercises written on them have been recovered, especially from the Old and Late Babylonian periods. The other reason is that there are many texts about scribes and their education because scribes were enthusiastic about writing about themselves, their work, and their experiences at school. Since the instruments used for writing were almost always made of reed they do not survive in the archaeological record. There is however on a tombstone from Marash a depiction of a boy holding a stylus in his right hand and in his left hand a bird that had presumably been his pet; next to the bird is depicted a tablet (Fig. 3.4).

A well-known text is that often referred to as 'Schooldays' (Kramer 1963: 229-48): 'When I arose in the morning I greeted my mother and said, "Give me my lunch, I want to go to school!" My mother gave me two rolls. She gave me two rolls and I went to school'. Unfortunately he was late and was beaten. He had a bad day and was beaten for almost every misdemeanour including speaking his native language, Babylonian, instead of Sumerian. At this time Sumerian was dying out and being replaced by Babylonian but was being and was

---

[13] The subject of edible mice in Mesopotamia still requires study. In the Assyrian and Babylonian literary calendar texts there were certain days of the year when mice were off the menu for reasons of taboo (Livingstone, forthcoming).

Fig. 3.4 Neo-Hittite funeral stele of a boy depicted with a writing stylus and tablet and a pet bird while standing in his mother's lap.

to be cultivated as a classical language for the next 1500 years, somewhat like Latin and Greek in the Middle Ages. Anyway, things got worse and the boy complained to his father. The father reacted cleverly, inviting the teacher to a banquet where he is given sumptuous presents. Things improved immediately for the schoolboy, who graduated with distinction and moved on to a good career.

Another literary text satirically records an oral examination in which the long-suffering student is maligned by the schoolmaster, his own father, which may supply some of the humour (Sjöberg 1975). He is questioned on all aspects of the curriculum from Sumerian to mathematics and repeatedly accused of being useless. A text recording actual teaching that survives from the Old Babylonian period has the teacher reciting Babylonian in units of five or so lines that then had to be repeated by the pupil translated into Sumerian (Civil 1998). The myriad of exercise tablets that survive often have passages written by the master on one side. The student had to write the exercise on the other side of the tablet, presumably without peeking.

The earliest lessons began with the repeated writing of single wedges, and the curriculum then passed on to simple words, phrases and personal names at quite an early stage, and then through to the more advanced subjects (Veldhuis 1997; Gesche 2001). Lessons often included something boring such as legal phraseology together with something interesting like a joke or proverb. The conjugation of the Sumerian verb was illustrated by ringing the changes of the verb *durdu*, 'fart': 'I fart, you fart, he farts', no doubt to the amusement of the young scholars. Scribes occur frequently in the various proverb collections that were made in the Old Babylonian period (Alster 1997). Being recorded by scribes themselves, the proverbs concerning scribes differ from other proverbs in usually presenting their activities in a positive light. In some areas and periods girls were educated as scribes specifically so that they could be available to keep accounts and write letters for noble ladies in parts of the palace establishments that were out of bounds to men (Harris 1990). The satirical text recording an oral examination lists several musical instruments in a broken context and it is unclear whether the boys would learn to play them. It is perhaps more likely that they were expected to know something of musical terminology. There is however an example of a royal daughter learning music (Fig. 3.5). She is shown with her father, the Kassite King Melishipak, holding a musical instrument.

The orthostat reliefs that were produced at the command of Neo-Assyrian kings and that decorated their palaces were a form of royal propaganda, and here children appear as propaganda tools. They frequently illustrated the events of war recounted in the royal annals that were inscribed on the same reliefs. Here children are used as part of the message to foreign rulers who had come to

Fig. 3.5 The Babylonian Kassite ruler Melishipak presents to a seated deity his daughter, who is holding a musical instrument.

Assyria to bring tribute or confirm their vassalage, warning them of what would happen to their own subjects were they neglectful of their duties to the king of Assyria or refused to do his bidding. The scenes often have great piquancy with provocatively stinging messages. Soldiers systematically destroy a city and carry away the people's possessions as booty while some sort of life goes on: women and children are shown sitting picnicking outside the ruins of their city. Soon they were likely to be joined to the booty and to be doled out as slaves and concubines to the wealthy citizens of Assyria, or assigned to temples as slave workers. A scene shows scribes counting booty while children sit on an ox cart. In one scene a woman is shown giving a drink to a child from a water skin.

Radner (1997:126-8) has engaged with this material and cites Philippe Ariès' opinion that until the 17th century AD childhood as an intermediate stage between that of babies and toddlers on the one hand and adults on the other was not recognised, the main argument being that children are depicted in art as miniature adults. Radner regards the Neo-Assyrian reliefs as confirming Ariès' views, since children are shown wearing miniature adult versions of their national costumes. It is likely that what children actually wore was influenced by the dress of

adults, but the reason for the manner of their portrayal in the reliefs is probably more complicated. One could compare the fake picture of an Iraqi prisoner being supposedly abused by British servicemen while wearing a very clean tee-shirt with the Iraqi national emblem emblazoned on it that were publicised in the English popular press. Here the dress is to identify the nationality of the prisoner. In the same way the clothing of the children on the reliefs serves the propaganda purpose of identifying them as victims of their own national catastrophes brought on by their countries' failure to obey Assyria.[14]

Sickness was widespread in the ancient Near East and child mortality rife, especially in the earlier years of life. This was of course in spite of the rituals and incantation referred to above intended to ward off the unwelcome attentions of the Lamashtu demon. One of the most common afflictions was eye infection, often leading to

---

[14] Wäfler (1975) demonstrates that in the Neo-Assyrian palace reliefs 21 foreign peoples are with certainty both marked out as being foreign by their dress and identified by nationality in accompanying inscriptions. They are inhabitants of the lands or cities of Pilishtu, Judaea, Israel, Phoenicia, Damascus, Hama, Arabia, Hattina (Unqi), Egypt, Sam'al (Que), Mushki, Bit-Agushi, Bit-Adini, Carchemish, Bit-Iahiri, Elam (Hindanu), Suhu, Shubria, Urartu, Gilzanu and the Zagros mountains.

blindness. Generally however, sickness is an area where, although there were certainly a lot of sick children, sometimes referred to in every day correspondence, the therapeutic literature of the doctors and diviners is with few exceptions confined to adults, and to men unless gynaecological ailments are involved. The few exceptions, such as for example a line from the 40th tablet of the medical tractate *Sakikku*, 'sick sinews' which reads: 'If a baby does not have fever but shivers, it is the hand of (the moon god) Sin', leave us no closer to a medical diagnosis (Volk 1999: 19). Diseases mentioned with reference to children in the same tractate that do seem to be identifiable include cramp, diarrhoea, constipation, and jaundice. Apart from blindness, other disabilities are mentioned, whether acquired in life or defects since birth, including lameness and deafness. According to the myth 'Enki and Ninmah', disability, unlike disease, was not regarded as a punishment of humans by the gods, but simply of divine hubris, going back to a drinking party in primeval times. The wisdom god Enki and the mother goddess Ninmah, deep in their cups, created seven beings of which one was blind and fated to become a musician and singer, and one lame of foot, decreed to be a goldsmith (Benito 1969). Here there is also an aetiological slant.

The royal correspondence of the kings Esarhaddon and Ashurbanipal shows a great concern for royal children who had become ill, including very young children. Messages passed between the kings and the physicians and magicians who were called to attend on the sick child. Apotropaic measures were in use, including dogs buried under the threshold of the doors to the childrens' rooms, to fend off the evil demons. The dogs had names such as 'Don't think, bite!' (Curtis & Reade 1995: 116-17).

A broad typology of toys and games has been established by Caillois (1958), who distinguishes four principal categories, namely, *Agôn*, competitive sporty games, *Alea*, games of chance involving the casting of knucklebones or similar objects, *Mimicry*, including games utilising models (dolls, animals, wagons) and *Ilinx*, games involving non-competitive movement. A wide variety of toys were in use in Mesopotamia and each of these four categories are attested, usually in several varieties (Kilmer 1993: 359-64). The first category is best represented by games certainly attested in literature if not by finds of the relevant artefacts or parts of them. These include a game called *pukku* and *mekkû*, 'ball and stick'.

The second category, games of chance, is well represented by board games, attested from the Early Dynastic Period onwards. Most fall into one of two categories, the game of 20 squares, and the game of 58 holes. Four examples of the 20 square type were excavated by Sir Leonard Woolley at the Royal Tombs at Ur. A tablet written in the Hellenistic period and now under study in the British Museum gives a description of the 20 square version of the game. An adulatory literary letter to Ashurbanipal purportedly from his son and successor uses gaming terminology to describe the former's success on the battlefield, speaking of 'moving from the fifth through the sixth to the seventh house (square) and then going out alone to the border' (Livingstone 1989; 56-7). It is as if in the 7th century BC the wars in Elam were won on the palace playing boards of Nineveh. Toys and games cross social boundaries; there are palace gate bull colossi from Nineveh on the bases of which bored palace guards scratched game boards.

Within the typology dubbed *Mimicry* especially popular were clay chariots, which would of course be pulled by traction animals, usually oxen, also modelled of clay. It is interesting to note that the chariot wheels, revolving on a reed axle, are usually interchangeable with loom wheels: 'Mummy, I need more wheels for my chariot!'. Action games also included painted model animals on bases with four wheels, the most elaborate examples being a lion and hedgehog excavated at the temple of Inshushinak at Susa. The presence of these in a temple could be explained in various ways. One could at least observe that gods had children and they might have had expensive toys. *Ilinx* type games are attested in the cult of the youthful goddess Ishtar and include hide and seek and skipping with a rope as well as whirling and dancing (Kilmer 1993).

An interesting and unusual situation involving royal children existed at Carchemish in the 8th century BC. Carchemish was one of a number of flourishing city states in northern Syrian belonging to the Neo-Hittite civilisation that was a sort of afterglow of the Hittite Empire following its demise in the 12th century BC. The ruler of Carchemish had died and as the eldest son and heir to the throne, Kamanis, was still a child, a regent by the name of Yariris had temporarily come to power. One might have cynically thought that Yariris would have seized power and established his own dynasty but in his inscriptions he describes in detail his care and concern for his wards and he was no doubt responsible for the orthostat relief (see Fig. 3.6) accompanying those inscriptions that shows the young royals and that was part of the fabric of the palace built by Yariris for Kamanis. The salient passage reads as follows:

> I am Yariris, the ruler, ... the prince reputed from the West and the East, the beloved of the gods. ... The gods caused my name to pass abroad and men heard it for me in Egypt and on the other hand they heard it in Babylon. ... And when I built this seat for my lord's son Kamanis he used to run to this precinct. I seated him on high. ... If this seat should pass down to any king... who shall erase my name, or who shall take away ... (a child) from the children,... may the dogs of Nikarawas eat his head! (After Hawkins 2000: 124f.).

Fig. 3.6 Neo-Hittite relief from Carchemish depicting the regent Yariris and the prince Kamanis accompanied by the other royal children. Courtesy of the Department of the Ancient Near East, The British Museum.

Elsewhere in the inscription the names of the children are listed as follows:

This is Kamanis and these are his younger brothers. Here I took him by the hand and established him over the temple, though he was a child. This is the image of Yariris. This is Malitispas and this is Astitarhunzas and this is Tarnitispas. This is Isikaritispas, this is Sikaras, this is Halpawaris, this is Yahilatispas and this is Tuwarsais, the desired one of the ruler, the prince proclaimed for prominence (after Hawkins 2000: 129).

As one might have expected and as can be seen from Fig. 3.6 the children are of different age groups. The youngest, to the far right of the orthostat relief, is a baby in the arms of a woman leading a calf on a leash. The hieroglyphic inscription to the right of the baby's head identifies it with the lines 'Tuwarsais, the desired one of the ruler, the prince proclaimed for prominence'. The woman is not identified by name and is therefore most likely to be a servant and not a member of the royal family, and, in view of the overall subject matter of the orthostat, the calf is most likely to be a pet. On the far left as if in procession stand Kamanis and Yariris, both holding staffs. This leaves then a total of seven names but eight remaining children, a discrepancy that remains unexplained. Seven of the eight children have their names inscribed in hieroglyphic next to their heads and one, to the far left of the lower register, does not. The eighth child may be a family acquaintance or perhaps more likely a space filler added by the sculptor for symmetry.

What is important here is that the orthostat serves as an illustration of the existence of childhood more or less as understood today in the context of elites in the 8th century BC. Apart from the baby, the youngest is a naked

toddler in the upper central register learning to walk with the aid of a stick. The stick itself takes on the form of a toy, since it is embellished with a carved bird at the top. Ahead of the toddler are three boys with similar hair styles. The boy in front carries in his right hand a whorl for a top and in his left hand an object that is probably the top itself. The other two boys in this register are carrying objects that remain somewhat enigmatic. One can observe, however, that both carry in their left hands some small objects; these have been thought to be knucklebones. At any rate, while the boy on the right places his hand on his brother's shoulder, the boy on the left carries in his right hand an object hanging from a piece of string. One might think that these two boys share a game that involves the small objects and the further object hanging from the string. The two standing boys in the lower register each carry spindle whorls in their right hands and a top in their left. The two seated boys in the same register appear to be older, have a more sophisticated hairstyle, and are playing a board game.

It has been noted that there is a contrast between the left, right, and upper registers of the orthostat on the one hand and the lower middle register on the other. This discussion, summarised by Canby (1986: 61-2), centres on the fact that the four figures in the lower middle register face each other as they busy themselves with their toys and games, oblivious to what seems to be a procession of the other figures, all, including the baby and the toddler, facing in the same direction behind Kamanis and Yariris. Kamanis is at the front, holding a staff in his right hand, while Yariris clasps his left forearm with his own right hand. Although the elder boys in this procession are holding toys, unlike the seated boys in the lower register they are not actually playing with them. There has been the suggestion that the standing figures have a different status, perhaps as sons of the first or chief wife, and that this status is being starkly emphasised in the artistic concept of the relief. What is of course most remarkable about the Yariris relief is that it not only engages directly with the issue of childhood within a royal family, but that it distinguishes different categories of childhood, belying Ariès.

Despite the wide chronological and geographical range of the social history that has been adduced here, some conclusions can be drawn. Of these the most salient is the wide gulf separating elites – royals and the nobility – and the moderately well-off – merchants and those engaged in various kinds of business – on the one hand from the poor and indigent on the other. Examples ranging from the Yariris stele to the much earlier Sumerian schooldays texts show children from the first category enjoying a childhood comparable in many respects to the modern notion of childhood, while children from the latter category might easily find themselves working alongside adults, and in times of stress being sold off as slaves by their own parents. In a variety of contexts the treatment of children reflects adult anxieties and aspirations. Worry about care in old age and concern motivated by widely-held belief in the need for funerary offerings in the afterlife led to the adoption of many poor and indigent children. In the Neo-Assyrian palace reliefs a different kind of male adult anxiety, this time involving foreigners, is played upon: pay homage to Assyria lest the like of this happen to your women and children.

Apart from the all-embracing dichotomy separating the rich and fairly well-off from the rest a further general observation can be made. In the evidence that we have from the ancient Near East a frequent reason why children emerge from the shadows of their liminality is that they are being used by adults in some way. In all periods children functioned as insurance measures for old age and the afterlife. In inscriptions of an Early Dynastic period ruler children of elites are cited in probably dodgy property transfers while poor children appear in the same ruler's inscriptions to emphasise his power (release of children from prison) and magnanimity (protection of orphans). In the same period children appear on inscribed stelae that can be interpreted as being intended to promote dynastic succession. This was to be the beginning of a long history of children being included in iconography in order to make a point. Whether as factory workers or in schooling children are being used in some way to promote the interests of adults, boosting the income of poor families, or in the case of schooling being prepared for more lucrative work in the future.

It has thus been possible to provide what is at least an impression of childhood in the ancient Near East, provided by texts and images drawn across a wide canvas. There is still great need – and scope – for more detailed study of children as they are represented in both these media. For iconography a valiant start has been made by Parayre (1997) with his very many examples from the whole corpus of ancient Near Eastern art, but there is still no single study dedicated to the treatment of children in that art, the roles they play and the manner of their depiction. With regard to the textual evidence the way is open for further research. For most areas and periods there are copious archives of letters and documents in which children are more than sporadically mentioned and the work of extracting and analysing the relevant information has only just begun.

Bibliography

Alster, B. (1997): *Proverbs of Ancient Sumer. The World's Earliest Proverb Collections*. Bethesda, Maryland.

Benito, C.A. (1969): *"Enki and Ninmah" and "Enki and the World Order"*. Ann Arbor, Michigan.

Biga, M.G. (1997): 'Enfants et nourrices à Ebla', *Ktema* 22: 35-44.

Bongenaar, A.C.V.M. and Jursa, M. (1993): 'Ein babylonischer Mäusefänger', *Wiener Zeitschrift für die Kunde des Morgenlandes* 83: 31-38.

Cadelli, D. (1997): 'Lorsque l'enfant paraît ... malade', *Ktema* 22: 11-33.

Caillois, R. (1958): *Les jeux et les hommes (Le masque et le vertige)*. Paris.

Canby, J.V. (1986): 'The Child in Hittite Iconography', in J.V. Canby, E. Porada, B.S. Ridgway and T. Stech (eds), *Ancient Anatolia: Aspects of Change and Cultural Development. Essays in Honor of Machteld J. Mellink*, 54-69. Madison, Wisconsin.

Cavigneaux, A. (1999): 'Nabû ša harê und die Kinder von Babylon', in J. Renger (ed.), *Babylon: Focus mesopotamischer Geschichte, Wiege früher Gelehrsamkeit, Mythos in der Moderne. 2. Internationales Colloquium der Deutschen Orient-Gesellschaft, 24.-26. März 1998 in Berlin*, 385-391. Saarbrücken.

Cazelles, H. (1985): 'Consécrations d'enfants et de femmes', in J.-M. Durand and J.R. Kupper (eds), *Miscellanea Babylonica: Mélanges offerts à Maurice Birot*, 45-49. Paris.

Civil, M. (1985): 'Sur les "livres d'écolier" à l'époque paléo-babylonienne', in J.-M. Durand and J.R. Kupper (eds), *Miscellanea Babylonica: Mélanges offerts à Maurice Birot*, 67-78. Paris.

Civil, M. (1998): 'Bilingual Teaching', in S.M. Maul (ed.), *Festschrift für Rykle Borger zu seinem 65. Geburtstag am 24. Mai 1994: tikip santakki mala bašmu*, 1-7. Groningen.

Cooper, J.S. (1986): *Presargonic Inscriptions*. New Haven, Connecticut.

Curtis, J.E. and Reade, J.E. (eds) (1995): *Art and Empire. Treasures from Assyria in the British Museum*. London.

Farber, W. (1989): *Schlaf, Kindchen, Schlaf! Mesopotamische Baby-Beschwörungen und -Rituale*. Winona Lake, Indiana.

Foster, B.R. (2003): 'Late Babylonian Schooldays: An Archaizing Cylinder', in G.J. Selz (ed.), *Festschrift für Burkhard Kienast zu seinem 70. Geburtstag dargebracht von Freunden, Schülern und Kollegen*, 79-87. Münster.

Gehlken, E. (2005): 'Childhood and youth, work and old age in Babylonia – a statistical analysis', in H.D. Baker and M. Jursa (eds), *Approaching the Babylonian Economy. Proceedings of the START Project Symposium Held in Vienna, 1-3 July 2004*, 89-120. Münster.

George, A.R. (2003): *The Babylonian Gilgamesh Epic: Introduction, Critical Edition and Cuneiform Texts*. Oxford / New York.

George, A.R. (2005): 'In Search of the é.dub.ba.a: The Ancient Mesopotamian School in Literature and Reality', in Y. Sefati, P. Artzi, C. Cohen, B.L. Eichler and V.A. Hurowitz (eds), *"An Experienced Scribe Who Neglects Nothing": Ancient Near Eastern Studies in Honor of Jacob Klein*, 127-137. Bethesda, Maryland.

Gesche, P.D. (2001): *Schulunterricht in Babylonien im ersten Jahrtausend v. Chr.* Münster.

Gurney, O.R. (1983): *The Middle Babylonian Legal and Economic Texts from Ur*. Oxford.

Harris, R. (1990): 'The Female "Sage" in Mesopotamian Literature', in J.G. Gammie and L.G. Perdue, (eds), *The Sage in Israel and the Ancient Near East*. Winona Lake, Indiana.

Hawkins, J.D. (2000): *Corpus of Hieroglyphic Luwian Inscriptions. Volume I: Inscriptions of the Iron Age*. Berlin / New York.

Joannès, F. (1997): 'La mention des enfants dans les texts néo-babyloniens', *Ktema* 22: 119-133.

Kilmer, A. Draffkorn (1993): 'Games and Toys in Ancient Mesopotamia', in J. Pavúk (ed.), *Actes du XIIᵉ Congrès International des Sciences Préhistoriques et Protohistoriques, Bratislava, 1-7 septembre 1991*, 359-364. Bratislava.

Kramer, S. N. (1970): *The Sumerians. Their History, Culture, and Character*. Chicago / London.

Lambert, W.G. and Millard, A.R. (1969): *Atra-hasīs. The Babylonian Story of the Flood*. Oxford.

Lebrun, R. (1980): 'Notes sur la terminologie et le statut de l'enfant hittite', in A. Théodoridès, P. Naster and J. Ries (eds), *L'enfant dans les civilisations orientales/Het kind in de oosterse beschavingen*, 43-58. Leuven.

Leichty, E. (1989): 'Feet of clay' in H. Behrens, D. Loding and M.T. Roth (eds), *DUMU-E₂-DUB-BA-A. Studies in Honor of Åke W. Sjöberg*, 349-356. Philadelphia.

Limet, H. (1980): 'La condition de l'enfant en Mésopotamie autour de l'an 2000 av. J.-C.', in A. Théodoridès, P. Naster and J. Ries (eds), *L'enfant dans les civilisations orientales/Het kind in de oosterse beschavingen*, 5-17. Leuven.

Lion, B. (1997): 'Les enfants des familles déportées de Mésopotamie du nord à Mari en ZL 11', *Ktema* 22, 109-118.

Livingstone, A. (1986): *Mystical and Mythological Explanatory Works of Assyrian and Babylonian Scholars*. Oxford.

Livingstone, A. (1989): *Court Poetry and Literary Miscellanea*. Helsinki.

Livingstone, A. (1997): 'How the common man influences the gods of Sumer', in I.L. Finkel and M.J. Geller (eds), *Sumerian Gods and Their Representations*, 215-220. Groningen.

Livingstone, A. (forthcoming): *Hemerologies and Menologies of Assyrian and Babylonian Scholars*.

Meijer, D.J.W. (2004): 'A scribal quarter?', in J.G. Dercksen (ed.), *Assyria and Beyond: Studies Presented to Mogens Trolle Larsen*, 387-393. Leiden.

Michel, C. (1997): 'Les enfants des marchands de Kaniš', *Ktema* 22: 91-108.

Nemet-Nejat, K.R. (2002): *Daily Life in Ancient Mesopotamia*. Peabody, Massachusetts.

Oppenheim, A. L. (1977): *Ancient Mesopotamia. Portrait of a Dead Civilization*. Chicago / London.

Parayre, D. (1997): 'Les âges de la vie dans le répertoire figuratif oriental', *Ktema* 22: 59-89.

Radner, K. (1997): *Die neuassyrischen Privatrechtsurkunden als Quelle für Mensch und Umwelt*. Helsinki.

Radner, K. (2005): *Die Macht des Namens. Altorientalische Strategien zur Selbsterhaltung*. Wiesbaden.

Reiner, E. (1982): 'Babylonian Birth Prognoses', *Zeitschrift für Assyriologie und Vorderasiatische Archäologie* 72: 124-138.

Roth, M.T. (1997): *Law Collections from Mesopotamia and Asia Minor*. Atlanta, Georgia.

Roth, M.T. (2000): 'Tašmētu-damqat and Daughters', in J. Marzahn and H. Neumann (eds), *Assyriologica et Semitica. Festschrift für Joachim Oelsner anläßlich seines 65. Geburtstages am 18. Februar 1997*, 387-400. Münster.

Sauren, H. (1980): 'Het examenreglement van de Sumerische school', in A. Théodoridès, P. Naster and J. Ries (eds), *L'enfant dans les civilisations orientales/Het kind in de oosterse beschavingen*, 59-64. Leuven.

Sauvage, M. (1997): 'Tombes d'enfants du Bronze Récent en Haute-Mésopotamie. Étude de cas', *Ktema* 22: 161-170.

Sjöberg, Å.W. (1975): 'Der Examenstext A', *Zeitschrift für Assyriologie und Vorderasiatische Archäologie* 64: 137-176.

Snell, D. (ed.) (2005): *A Companion to the Ancient Near East*. Oxford.

Stol, M. (2000): *Birth in Babylonia and the Bible: Its Mediterranean Setting*. Groningen.

Tsukimoto, A. (1985): *Untersuchungen zur Totenpflege (kispum) im alten Mesopotamien*. Kevelaer / Neukirchen-Vluyn.

Vanstiphout, H. (1979): 'How Did They Learn Sumerian?', *Journal of Cuneiform Studies* 31: 118-126.

Vanstiphout, H. (1980): 'Over het vak "Sumerisch" aan de Oudbabylonische scholen', in A. Théodoridès, P. Naster and J. Ries (eds), *L'enfant dans les civilisations orientales/Het kind in de oosterse beschavingen*, 29-42. Leuven.

Veldhuis, N.C. (1997): *Elementary Education at Nippur. The Lists of Trees and Wooden Objects*. Groningen.

Volk, K. (1996): 'Methoden altmesopotamischer Erziehung nach Quellen der altbabylonischen Zeit', *Saeculum* 47: 178-216.

Volk, K. (1999): 'Kinderkrankheiten nach der Darstellung babylonisch-assyrischer Keilschrifttexte', *Orientalia* 68: 1-30.

Volk, K. (2000): 'Edubba'a und Edubba'a-Literatur: Rätsel und Lösungen', *Zeitschrift für Assyriologie und Vorderasiatische Archäologie* 90: 1-30.

Volk, K. (2004): 'Vom Dunkel in die Helligkeit: Schwangerschaft, Geburt und frühe Kindheit in Babylonien und Assyrien', in Véronique Dasen (ed.), *Naissance et petite enfance dans l'Antiquité*, 71-92. Fribourg / Göttingen.

Waetzold, H. (1972): *Untersuchungen zur neusumerischen Textilindustrie*. Rome.

Waetzoldt, H. (1986): 'Keilschrift und Schulen in Mesopotamien und Ebla', in L. Kriss-Rettenbeck and M. Liedtke (eds), *Erziehungs- und Unterrichtsmethoden im historischen Wandel*, 36-49. Bad Heilbrunn.

Waetzoldt, H. (1988): 'Die Situation der Frauen und Kinder anhand ihrer Einkommensverhältnisse zur Zeit der III. Dynastie von Ur', *Altorientalische Forschungen* 15: 30-44.

Wäfler, M. (1975): *Nicht-Assyrer neuassyrischer Darstellungen*. Kevelaer / Neukirchen-Vluyn.

Westbrook, R. (ed.) (2003): *A History of Ancient Near Eastern Law*. Leiden / Boston.

Wilcke, C. (2003): *Early Ancient Near Eastern Law: A History of its Beginnings. The Early Dynastic and Sargonic Periods*. Munich.

Wunsch, C. (2003/2004): 'Findelkinder und Adoption nach neubabylonischen Quellen', *Archiv für Orientforschung* 50: 174-244.

Ziegler, N. (1997): 'Les enfants du palais', *Ktema* 22: 45-57.

CHAPTER 4

THE CHILD'S CACHE AT ASSIROS TOUMBA, MACEDONIA

Diana Wardle and K.A. Wardle

As in many periods, young children are largely invisible in later Greek prehistory (cf. Nordquist & Ingvarsson-Sundström 2005; Rutter 2003; Polychronakou-Sgouritsa 1994; Gates 1992). Child burials, for example, are far less common than those of adults and rarely have a distinctive range of grave goods. Illustrations of children are few and far between, while there is no consensus about which objects were created specifically for, or used by, children (i.e. toys) and which belong to the equally speculative category of cult equipment. To judge from the number of discussions of figurines or 'miniature' objects, children's playthings were non-existent. Most scholars automatically favour the cult or ritual interpretation. Common sense and the observation of children suggest the reverse: either there were no children in antiquity, or many objects, utilitarian or otherwise, were, or became, children's playthings.[1]

In this setting, the discovery of a remarkable group of assorted objects – figurines, miniature vessels, animal bones and other items – in a very early, Early Iron Age context at Assiros Toumba in Greek Central Macedonia (Phase 4: cf. Wardle 1989: 454-5; Wardle & Wardle forthcoming) provides unique evidence for the activities of children at this period. This paper argues that the most obvious interpretation of the assemblage is that of a 'cache' of a child's favourite playthings, rather than a group of ritual or magical objects. These were either made specifically for, or collected by, that child. To an adult this appears a random selection of disparate items, to a child, a treasured collection, each with its own meanings and associations. Today the same role is played by bottle tops, clothes pegs, limbless plastic figures, stones and shells, however much the parents have spent on trendy, manufactured, educational toys.

The account which follows of the representation of children in later Greek prehistory, or of objects which may perhaps be associated with them, is not intended to be comprehensive. Equally there is no space to explore such issues as the place of children in society during this long period or the theoretical aspects of which children received burial rites alongside adults and which were treated in some other way, as discussed in detail by Paul Garwood in this volume. The account is, rather, intended to illustrate the kinds of evidence available as a general background to the discovery of the Assiros cache.

Children in later Greek Prehistory

The Late Bronze Age in Southern Greece

Burials: the majority of burials in the Greek Late Bronze Age (LBA) are multiple and extramural. For example, in the typical rock-cut chamber tombs (Cavanagh & Mee 1998: 48-9, 65-9, 71-6) it is not often possible to relate the objects to specific skeletal remains. Thus, even where child bones are identified in such a grave, any connection between the children and the objects, whether they were offerings or toys, is rarely more than speculative. Separate child burials with offerings other than pottery vessels are extremely unusual. Even where there are pottery vessels, these are not necessarily designed specifically for children (see below). As far as we can tell, children are not, in general, treated differently from adults – assuming that they were buried with any ceremony at all – and are found in every type of grave (Cavanagh & Mee 1998: 128-30). Some burials of children have no offerings at all while the needs of the afterlife of others were lavishly endowed. Schliemann's discovery at Mycenae in Shaft Grave III of gold sheets shaped to cover the face, body, arms and legs of two children remains exceptional – both in the use of such sheets and in the fact they were fitted to a child (Karo 1930-3: 62, pl. 53). However, burials of children elsewhere were occasionally better equipped than those of the average adult (Polychronakou-Sgouritsa 1994: 24-6).

Figurines, small and miniature pottery vessels and pottery feeding bottles are often assumed to be typical of, but not exclusive to, child burials (Blegen 1937: 255-6; Gates 1992: 167; Polychronakou-Sgouritsa 1994: 23). Blegen, for example, in his account of the burials at Prosymna reports a total of 19 burials with the remains of children's bones. Child-related objects, such as terracotta figurines, small spouted 'feeding bottles' or, occasionally, terracotta chariots, were found in 19 cases but only 11 of these burials have both the children's bones and child-related objects.

One of the most striking groups of child-related objects comes from Tomb XXII at Prosymna. This contained four animal figurines, a model chariot with horse/s and two tiny spouted feeding bottles placed close to an adult skeleton while four more figurines, a chariot, three spouted feeding bottles, an *askos* and a small stirrup jar

---

[1] By children in this context, we mean roughly those below the ages of 8-10, by which age children, in many societies, have become significant contributors to the household economy, even if this is well before adolescence and the onset of puberty, which is widely regarded as the start of adulthood (Arnett 2007).

were found further away in the same tomb but without any associated bones (Blegen 1937: 65-8, fig. 132-3). It would be natural to conclude that a beloved child was buried here but not a single child's bone was recovered. Both adult and children's bones are reasonably well preserved at Prosymna and it would be surprising but not impossible that all trace of a child's skeleton has disappeared.

As a further indicator of child burials, it has often been asserted that jewellery was a favoured grave gift (Gates 1992: 164), but this is an over simplification since all forms of jewellery are also common with adult burials.

Lewartowski's study (2000) of around 1000 'simple' graves from all over Mycenaean Greece has added an important quantitative dimension to our understanding of Mycenaean burial customs, since the majority of these graves are single burials and there is no problem in associating the grave goods with specific burials. About 30% of those, where the age is reported, are children's graves (214 examples, Lewartowski 2000: table 15). He is, however, cautious in suggesting that his findings can be applied to communal burials, such as those in chamber tombs. Single burials in the 'simple' graves may reflect different traditions or different social strata. In addition, few of these 'simple' graves have more than a small number of offerings, so the potential for significant associations is somewhat reduced.

Lewartowski reports 25 figurines from burials of this type, of which 11 are associated with burials of children and none with those of adults, where information about age has been recorded (Lewartowski 2000: 39, table 42). There seems to be a clear association in 'simple' graves of children with such pottery types as miniature vessels (23 with children, three with adults, Lewartowski 2000: 28), 'cultic' vases such as askoi and compound vessels (Lewartowski 2000: 30) and feeding bottles. He concludes that beads and necklaces are also typical of, but not exclusive to, child burials (Lewartowski 2000: 35).

While the size of Lewartowski's sample is quite small, it nevertheless provides some indication of the kind of objects which might be associated with children in life as well as in death. However, in Mycenaean Greece, the number of instances of child burial is considerably smaller than demography would indicate: the mortality rate for children up to the age of 10 may well have been as much as 50% while children only account for some 25% of skeletons reported in all types of Late Hellenic III cemeteries over a period of some 400 years (Cavanagh & Mee 1998: 128-9). Part of the explanation may lie with the fragility of the bones of children of this age group. They may simply not survive.

It may also be that infants and young children were treated differently from adults – over 70% of instances of intramural burial in the Greek Late Bronze Age are those of young children in 'simple' graves (87 examples, Lewartowski 2000: 54, table 15). Offerings, however, are rare: an Early Mycenaean intramural grave at Lefkandi contained the remains of five young children accompanied by a single miniature goblet (Popham & Sackett 1968: 5). It should perhaps be emphasised in this context that it is impossible to tell what proportion of the Mycenaean population as a whole did not receive formal burial (cf. Cavanagh and Mee 1998: 78-9 with reference to Prosymna). Despite the extensive information about Mycenaean burial customs, there are still large parts of the community which remain invisible to us.

Illustrations of children: despite the wealth of figurative art in the LBA Aegean, young children are rarely depicted. The only explicit three-dimensional representations of young children survive in ivory or bronze. Ivories include a seated, naked, male child at play from Palaikastro in Crete (Marinatos & Hirmer 1960: fig. 109; Rutter 2003: fig. 8), a standing, naked, male child, from the same site (Rutter 2003: fig. 9) and the clothed child wearing a bead necklace, part of the Ivory Trio found close to the Palace at Mycenae (Wace 1961; Marinatos & Hirmer 1960: fig. 218-9; French 2002; Wardle & Wardle 1997: fig. 24). Here a delicately carved child (opinions are divided as to sex) leans across the laps of two elegantly attired women – one of the great treasures of Mycenaean art. A crawling baby in bronze was a gift by Sir Arthur Evans to the Ashmolean Museum and is said to have been found in the Psychro cave (Ashmolean Museum Cat. No. 1938.1162; Rutter 2003: 37, lower). These are remarkably realistic representations of young children without any trace of the tendency, sometimes seen in Classical art, of representing children simply as small adults (Beaumont 2003: 62).

Other illustrations show older children. These include the three boys of different ages who can be seen in the wall painting found in house Xeste 3 at Akrotiri (Doumas 1992: 146-51, figs. 109-15). The oldest holds a striped length of cloth, another, younger, a bronze or gold one-handled bowl and the youngest a rock crystal vessel. The artist(s) who created this wall painting took great care to convey age by physical characteristics rather than simply by size. The boys are lithe and slender in complete contrast to the well-bellied, mature man in the same scene. The different styles of hair shown on these youths, as well as in the companion scene of girls gathering crocus flowers, seem to indicate developing maturity and status (cf. Doumas 1983: 78; Rutter 2003: 44-6). The boxers from room Beta 1 at the same site are equally realistically depicted and also have elaborated hair styles which suggest status (Doumas 1992: 110, fig. 112-5). Although they are always called boys on the basis of their red skin colour, one of the pair has hoop earrings (like the crocus-gathering girls), a necklace and bead bracelets on both ankles and one arm. The other figure is not complete enough to determine whether s/he also wore jewellery.

Small figures are sometimes seen in the miniature scenes on gold rings (e.g. Marinatos & Hirmer 1960: fig. 207) and seal stones, but these are usually interpreted as figures in the distance, or simply small in order to fit the space. The detail in these is insufficient to determine age rather than size.

Children in Linear B: the Linear B archives from Pylos and Knossos (Ventris & Chadwick 1956: 155-65) make it clear that children were regularly provided for in the ration lists, with half the adult ration, but it seems likely that these records relate to contributing members of the workforce rather than to younger children as family members. In practical terms, this could mean children as young as seven or eight, if we consider historical or ethnographic parallels for child labour (in Victorian England, for example, the Coal Mines Act of 1842 prohibited the employment of children under ten in the mines for the first time). Moreover the general context of these records seems to relate to foreign women as workers of different kinds who are often assumed to be captured slaves, accompanied by younger children, both boys and girls, in almost equal numbers (Chadwick 1976: 78-83) and it may well be that there is nothing in the archives which related to the children of 'free citizens'.

Pottery: the later Mycenaean pottery repertoire (LH IIIA – LH IIIC, c. 1400-1100 BC) includes several shapes of vessel, which are regularly associated with the feeding of infants and small children. These include small jugs with a spout set on the shoulder at 90° to the vertical handle (feeding bottles: FS155-63 = Furumark shapes 155-63, see Furumark 1941: 608-10; Mountjoy 1986: 60-1, 77, 104-5, 144-5, 188), spouted cups FS248-53 (Furumark 1941: 626-7; Mountjoy 1986: 87-8, 113, 148) or, more rarely bowls FS298-302 (Furumark 1941: 637; Mountjoy 1986: 118-9) or simple small 'pap boats' – bowls with a slight spout to feed semi-liquid foods. There are also askoi made by squeezing together the sides of a bowl to leave an opening at either end as a spout (FS194-5, Furumark 1941: 617; Mountjoy 1986: 81, 108). Some caution should, however, be exercised in the automatic association of these kinds of pottery vessel solely with the feeding of infants since they are usually rough surfaced and porous. They would thus not be very comfortable to drink from (any kind of cloth or leather 'teat' would long since have disappeared) and impossible to clean. Milk products would be especially prone to contamination or souring. In a hot climate they could well have been used for water rather than milk.

A second group includes small wheel-made versions of standard Mycenaean shapes such as kylikes, bowls, jugs or flasks which are decorated with a simplified form of the standard decoration. Most reported examples are tomb offerings (such as those from Prosymna: Blegen 1937: 255-6) and some are specifically associated with child burials (e.g. a flask from a child's grave at Agios Stephanos in Lakonia: Mountjoy 1999: 269:98, fig. 98).

A third group comprises small hand-made jugs and jars with more or less globular bodies (FS126, Furumark 1941: 604) or bowls and, less commonly, other shapes imitating standard Mycenaean types such as the kylix (Wardle 1969: 277-8; Mountjoy 1986: 101, fig. 123, 126, fig. 153). These are usually termed miniatures but their size is less distinctive than their decoration. On these handmade vessels the decoration is rarely the equivalent of that on the full size versions. They are usually painted with vertical or horizontal wavy lines in a very similar manner to those on female or animal figurines (French 1971: 109, fig. 1, 151).

The function of the hand-made 'miniatures' remains debatable. Most fragments are found in domestic rubbish contexts of LH IIIB date (e.g. at Mycenae: Wardle 1969: 277-88, cat. nos. 58-66; 1973, 319 cat. nos. 96-101; Mountjoy: 1976, 93) while far fewer are associated with burials as at Prosymna (see above). They do not appear to have any particular association with cult sites. At Mycenae, for example, there are none among the vessels from the Temple complex (Moore & Taylour 2000) and few among those from the Room with the Fresco Complex (Moore & Taylour forthcoming). This contrasts with the later practice of the Late Geometric, Archaic and Hellenistic periods when they are typical offerings in sanctuary deposits (Coldstream 1977: 332).

Figurines or toys? Small clay figurines are a regular part of the Mycenaean repertoire in settlements, tombs and cult contexts (French 1971: 102-8, including references to discussions of function; French 1985: 231-5, 252-76). The most typical are female figures in the forms known as Ψ, Φ and T from their schematic shapes. Some are modelled to include one or two infants at the breast or on the back (kourotrophoi: French 1971: 142-4; Demakopoulou 1988: 190, fig. 165). It has been suggested that this figurine type intentionally reflects the role of women in Mycenaean society (in contrast to Minoan) as child-nurturers (Olsen 1998: 384-8). This is surely to read too much into the evidence, especially since, if they are symbolic in intention, we do not know whether they represent the human or divine.

Schematic bull figures with short curving horns are also frequent, together with rarer examples of other animals such as a hedgehog rhyton from Prosymna (Demakopoulou 1988: 224-5, fig. 214; French 1971: 151-64) or composites representing chariots, men riding on horses, or on bulls (which have been interpreted as plough oxen: French 1971: 164-7; Konsolaki-Yannopoulou 2003). A further category includes items of furniture such as tables, beds, chairs and three-legged 'thrones' with curved backs and sometimes an added seated figure as well as other types such as birds or boats (French 1971: 167-73). Exceptionally elaborate items include an occupied chariot with moving wheels and two camel-like horses from a chamber tomb at Megalo Monastiri in Thessaly (Theocharis 1964: 256, pl. 292e; Hourmouziades 1982: 85, fig. 55). Although no evidence is cited, the excavator suggests that several children were buried in this tomb.

The discovery of a Mycenaean sanctuary at Agios Konstantinos on the Methana peninsula with numerous animal figurines (single animals or compound chariot or driven oxen groups: Konsolaki-Yannopoulou 1999: 2002, 2003) is the first direct association between cult activity and figurines in Late Bronze Age Greece. This is in contrast to the use of large figures in the Cult Centre at Mycenae (Moore & Taylour 2000), the shrines at Phylakopi (French 1985: 211-30, 236-52) and Tiryns (Kilian 1981).

There are several important groups of Mycenaean figurines from later cult contexts such as the Marmaria at Delphi (Nicholls 1970: 3), Amyklae near Sparta (Demakopoulou 1982), the vicinity of the Aphaia temple on Aegina (Pilafides-Williams 1987) and the Apollo Maleatas sanctuary above Epidaurus (Lambrinoudakis 1981). These are generally assumed to reflect Mycenaean cult activity at these sites, and to indicate cult continuity between the Mycenaean and Archaic periods.

Even though it is highly probable that these groups are cult-related because of their cult associations, it is not necessarily the case that all figurines and models are exclusively cult-related. The numbers found, both whole and as fragments, in almost all domestic rubbish contexts at sites such Mycenae (Wardle 1969: 294; 1973: 337) or Tiryns (Kilian 1981, Weber-Heden 1990) suggest they were also in everyday use for some purpose. If their use was in some kind of domestic shrine or shrines (a use for which there is in fact no evidence), it would be surprising to find them treated with such casual indifference when discarded.

All these figurines would, however, make excellent children's toys, although, as already mentioned, few direct associations with children can be made from burial evidence. If this is the case, it must either be assumed that the figurines served both functions (whether by intention or by accident) or that their presence at cult sites is child-related, perhaps as dedications by or on behalf of children.

The practice in a later period at the Brauronia in Attica, of the dedication of playthings by girls who had reached 'adulthood', is perhaps the best-known example from Greece of children's dedications accompanying rites of passage as recorded in one of the poems in the *Anthologia Palatina* (VI:280):

> Timareta, before her marriage, dedicated her drums, her lovely ball ... her dolls and their dresses to Artemis, a fitting gift from a virgin to a virgin ...

Similarly, at the sanctuary of Apollo Thermios in Aetolia there are many small pyramidal clay loom weights among the numerous unpublished items on display in the Museum: these are from the excavations of Sotiriades and Rhomaios over 90 years ago and have no specific context or association (as is true of most objects from sanctuary sites). Each is a singleton, not part of a set, and differently decorated before firing, identifying its owner or donor. The date of some is assured by the impressions on them, of the typical head-loops of Archaic double bronze pins (c. 700-550 BC); another is impressed with a figured seal stone and is perhaps Hellenistic. They are presumably dedications by women at a significant point in their lives. Is it possible that they are the tangible evidence of similar rites of passage for young girls as recorded for Brauron?

The Early Iron Age in Southern Greece

The substantial social and economic changes which accompanied the transition to the Iron Age resulted in the loss, on the one hand, of typical Mycenaean characteristics such as the figurines and, on the other, in the change of burial practices from multiple to individual burial (Desborough 1964: 36-8; Dickinson 2006: 178-84). In some respects, therefore, it is easier to identify items associated with children in this period than previously. At the same time, however, the character of the settlements changed in such a way that these became virtually invisible archaeologically. Thus the archaeology of the early stages of the Greek Iron Age effectively provides the history of death rather than of life. Two dimensional representations are very rare until the end of the Geometric period and even then the depiction of children is unusual or debatable (Beaumont 2003: 61).

Burials: the single burials of this period may be either cremations or inhumations and, where the age of the deceased is determinable, offer the best chances of identifying objects with specific associations with children. Even so, identified child burials remain almost as unusual as in the Bronze Age, a fact which invites speculation about the status of infants and children within the societies of the period, and there is little consistency about the treatment they received from region to region (Lemos 2002: 189). Well-published cemeteries with graves of the 11th to 8th centuries BC (Protogeometric to Late Geometric) include those at Knossos in Crete (Coldstream & Catling 1996), Lefkandi in Euboea (Popham & Sackett 1980) and the Kerameikos in Athens (Kraiker & Kübler 1939; Kübler 1943). Some of the richest graves in these cemeteries seem to be those of children and contain gold attachments and exotic objects of faience which are rare by any standards in prehistoric Greek cemeteries (Lefkandi: T5, T22, T36: Popham & Sackett 1980, 205). If we may assume that the children's bone and tooth fragments in these graves represent the only occupants (and in the case of cremated remains this is difficult to determine) then we must assume that rich adult style grave goods were sometimes lavished on a deceased and much lamented child.

In general, however, as Morris has noted, it is only towards the end of the Geometric period that children become visible regularly in the funerary record (Morris 1989: fig. 22).

Figurines: Mycenaean style figurines went out of fashion at the end of the Bronze Age and the limited number of settlements excavated provides little evidence for the use of any other types. A few dolls or puppets are known from burials, and these are usually handmade and burnished and decorated with patterns executed in pointillée (Desborough 1972: 142-4: Snodgrass 1971: 96-7). Several are bell-shaped and some have separate jointed legs (e.g from Nea Ionia: Smithson 1961: 172, no. 54, pl. 30). They seem so different from other objects in the graves in the Kerameikos, Lefkandi and other sites where they have been found that they have regularly been regarded as 'northern' imports. In part this is because of their similarities to the bird ornamented clay wagon models of Central Europe of which the best known are the pair from Dupljaja (Forrer 1932: figs 9, 10; cf. Pare 1989: figs 4, 10, 16).

While these 'figures' have many of the characteristics of playthings, resembling dolls or puppets, they have no exclusive association with the burials of young children. At Lefkandi, for example, there is no indication of the age or sex of the occupant of the grave containing a figure of this type, although it also contained a bird askos (P22: Popham and Sackett 1980: 149-51, pl. 137). In Athens, they have been found with both female and child burials (Desborough 1972: 143).

A few elaborate animal figures are known from the Protogeometric period (Desborough 1972: 146, pl. 26) but only in the later part of the Geometric period when large numbers of offerings and dedications were made at sanctuary sites such as Olympia, Delphi, the Heraion at Perachora, Artemis Orthia at Sparta, or Aetos on Ithaka, do human and animal figurines, especially warriors and horses, become at all frequent (Coldstream 1977: 332-3) but there is nothing to connect the vast majority of these with any specific age group.

Playthings: other items from Attic tombs in the same incised ware as the figurines include small bowls, spindle whorls, beads and hollow balls which could easily be understood as playthings. Intriguingly Desborough almost laboriously avoids using the word 'toys' for these objects (Desborough 1972: 143) while Snodgrass has no hesitation in so doing (Snodgrass 1971: 96). Does this difference reflect the different attitudes of two generations of scholars?

To our knowledge, only one Early Iron Age child's tomb has been reported from outside Attica which contains playthings (we are grateful to Dr. E. B. French who excavated this tomb, first identified the objects and drew it to our attention). This is a small cist grave measuring 0.79 x 0.42m found dug into the House of the Sphinxes at Mycenae (Desborough 1956; Mycenae Archive trench notebook x059, 23 August: E. B. Wace's account of grave above Room 12). The skeleton of a child was laid in it in a crouched position and accompanied by a small late Protogeometric jug and two bronze rings. Three stone slabs were then placed over the body and immediately afterwards a group of pottery vessels was placed on top of these slabs as an offering. First was an amphora of 'pie ware' whose mouth was closed by a small saucer of the same ware. Inside the saucer was a small spouted bowl which could, according to Desborough, have been a lamp while inside the amphora itself was a small burnt hand-made jug, 23 small pebbles and one large one (Desborough 1956: pl. 34b). These pebbles are best interpreted as 'jacks' for the kind of games often played in the Classical world with knucklebones (astragaloi: Neils and Oakley 2003: 276-9) or stones. No indication is given in the report of the age of this child, but the size of the cist grave and the photograph of the remains in situ (Desborough 1956: pl. 33c) suggests a juvenile rather than an infant.

Pottery: spouted clay feeding bottles are well represented at Lefkandi, for example, mostly in smaller graves presumed to be those of children and in one case only with the tooth fragments of a child (T36: Popham and Sackett 1980: 190-2, 236-7). Miniature vessels, principally small versions of jugs, are also associated with the smaller tombs and presumed to be child-related (Popham and Sackett 1980: 203-5).

The Late Bronze and Early Iron Age in Macedonia and Northern Greece

Burials: burials are not well represented in Bronze Age Macedonia and none are obviously those of children. Although numerous Iron Age cemeteries have been excavated, only those at Torone (Papadopoulos 2005) and Vergina have been published in detail and, at the latter, the soil conditions prevented the survival of skeletal remains (Andronikos 1969: 161-3). At Torone, it has been observed that, just as in Southern Greece in the Bronze Age, children were under-represented among the burials (here 4% of the total). In these graves offerings were rather sparse – chiefly small hand-made pottery vessels (Papadopoulos 2005: 377-80).

It may be surmised that the pithos burials at Vergina and elsewhere were frequently those of children but the evidence is generally inconclusive. At Assiros Toumba itself a burial pithos set into the debris of the earlier Iron Age settlements (Phases 4-1.5) contained a few infant bones as well as those of an older female, probably added a little later as the infant bones had been pushed to one side (Wardle 1989: 449).

Pottery: little of the normal range of prehistoric Macedonian pottery has characteristics which would suggest it was used by or for children. Side-spouted vessels, for example, are not part of the repertoire of either Bronze Age or Iron Age Macedonia. The only exceptions are the miniature vessels (such as those found in the cache), which only came into fashion at Assiros at the start of the Iron Age. Most of these are simple jars or bowls of very small size, though versions of many larger vessels such as the one-handled cooking pot, wishbone-handled bowl or double vessel are also known. At Kastanas such vessels are very much rarer (Hochstetter 1984: 179).

Figurines: in contrast to Mycenaean Greece, figurines are not part of the Macedonian Late Bronze Age repertoire of settlement finds. Those figurines of Mycenaean style known from Agios Mamas (Heurtley 1939: 101, fig. 104y) and Aiani (Karamitrou-Mentesidi 1993: 121, fig. 71) stand out by virtue of their rarity. Figurines are equally exceptional in the Iron Age. No certain examples were found at Kastanas: Hochstetter (1984: fig. 110:10-11) illustrates two clay legs she regards as from a pottery vessel, perhaps a bird askos. Fragments from large bird askoi have been found at Assiros in both Bronze and Iron Age levels.

Another object from Kastanas tentatively interpreted as a model shoe remains enigmatic (Hochstetter 1987: fig. 19.6). The only figurines from Assiros were found in the cache described below. Only with the child burials of the Archaic period such as those at Sindos to the west of Thessaloniki (Vokotopoulou et al. 1985: no. 157, 224, 295 etc.), or, in the 5th century, in the children's graves at Michalitsi near Preveza (Catling 1974: 24, fig. 46; Vokotopoulou 1972: 450-2, pl. 382b-e) do models reappear in burials, most notably of carts or wagons in bronze or iron with draught animals in clay. At Sindos, there are also tables and chairs (Vokotopoulou et al. 1985: no. 226, 227, 276, 277 etc., some illustrated by Koliopoulos 2007) which appear to belong to children's burials, as confirmed by the use of small size face masks in some cases.

Assiros Toumba in the Early Iron Age

The settlement of Assiros Toumba is situated in the north-west end of the Langadas basin some 23km north of Thessaloniki on a main route leading from the coast, through the basin and on towards the Strymon valley, one of the main routes into the Balkan interior (Fig. 4.1). It was continuously occupied from c. 2000 BC in the Middle Bronze Age to c. 900 BC in the Early Iron Age with no sign of major cultural changes during this period (Wardle & Wardle 2007). Most structures of the 14 major building phases identified were of mudbrick with timber framing. The debris from the collapse of each successive phase was left in place. The defensive banks surrounding the settlement were regularly renewed and ensured that the Toumba (mound) steadily built up to reach a height of 14m above the level of the surrounding plain towards the end of the Bronze Age.

At this time, there was a small village community with a population of around 150-300 at the most, living on the summit of the mound. The houses were arranged in regular blocks of 'rooms' separated by parallel streets in a remarkable example of early town planning. The pottery which characterises this settlement is handmade and burnished in contrast to the wheel-made painted Mycenaean pottery imported from southern Greece or, more commonly at this period, made in workshops in Macedonia (Buxeda i Garrigós et al. 2003). Pottery of this kind is found in the lowland area stretching from the Veria plain in the west to the Strymon valley in the east.

Given the 100 year discrepancy between the conventional dates for this period, provided by Mycenaean pottery, and the new dendrochronologically wiggle-matched C14 dates obtained from charred timbers, dates given here for Assiros are cited with a wide margin (Newton, Wardle & Kuniholm 2005a, 2005b; Wardle, Newton & Kuniholm 2007).

Following a devastating fire dated around 1200-1150 BC, the settlement was rebuilt (Phase 5), only to be burnt again quite soon afterwards. This level sees the last use of Mycenaean style pottery and the following Phase 4 (1100-1000 BC) sees the introduction of the first recognisable Iron Age elements. These elements reflect changes in technology and detail of decoration rather than major shifts in the shapes and function of the pottery vessels (Wardle 1998).

This transition, however, seems to mark a low point in the prosperity of the settlement, because the first Iron Age structures are less densely packed and less substantial than those of previous phases. The population is likely to have been around 50 people at most, perhaps 5-8 families. The remains of the structures found are principally stone wall-footings and the debris around and over them is a soft grey fill with abundant fragments of pottery and of animal bone. In the following phases (3 & 2, 1070-950 BC) the structures are rebuilt to a more orderly plan and use the space more efficiently.

The economy of the Iron Age settlement was principally agricultural; the pottery is utilitarian and domestic; surviving tools were of stone and bone and any metal in use was retained or recycled. There is little sign of any luxury or prestigious objects. The cache of varied but individually unremarkable items in the levels of Phase 4 is perhaps the most remarkable discovery to be associated with it. There is nothing else among the finds of this phase to suggest any special function for the settlement as a whole, or for any part of it. Small children were undoubtedly present in this community and the most natural interpretation for the cache of objects is that they represent a collection of playthings.

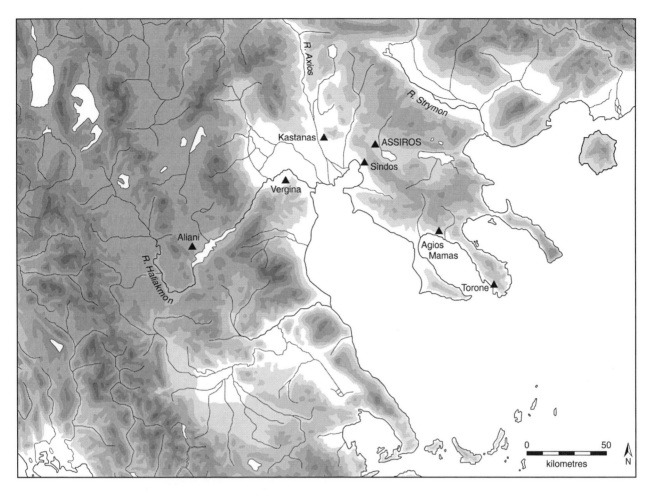

Fig. 4.1: Map of Macedonia showing sites mentioned in the text.

The cache and its contents (Figures 4.2-4.4)

The context

An extraordinary group of objects was found in a small pit some 30cm deep and 75cm in diameter cut in the deep grey levels which accumulated above the earliest Phase 4 floors in the central part of the site. Since this pit lay well below the stone footing of the wall between the Phase 3, Rooms 17 and 18, it should belong to the later stage of use of the Phase 4 structures rather than have any connection with the succeeding ones. It is not certain from the poorly preserved remains of Phase 4 walls whether this would have been an interior or exterior space.

When first encountered, it was not apparent that the objects were anything out of the ordinary. The position of each of the manufactured items was recorded as it was found (and before removal). Since several of the objects had been lifted from their original position before the existence of a group was recognised, no photograph was taken to show them all in situ. The dug earth was sieved as a matter of routine to make sure nothing escaped notice. As a result it only gradually became apparent that the objects formed a group which included 'natural' items

such as animal bones and pieces of quartz. Most of the objects were more or less worn suggesting a period of handling in some manner, as could well be the case with objects treasured by a child.

The cache included a range of complete metapodials from different animals including sheep, deer and hare (Fig. 4.2 upper) as well as two pieces of horn core and six pieces of quartz. These would have passed without remark in the normal course of excavation but quartz pebbles (Fig. 4.3 lower) were not often encountered elsewhere on the site and must have been 'brought in' specially. They are not, for example, worked further or shaped to form tools. To find a group of six such sparkling angular pebbles was particularly unusual. A pierced cowrie shell (SF1954, Fig. 4.4) is even more unusual and must ultimately have been brought from the Aegean sea some 25km away.

Three clay spindle whorls (SF1921, SF1925, SF1926, Fig. 4.2) of the bi-conical shape found in every part of the site in every level are perhaps the most familiar of the manufactured objects. Rarer but equally mundane is a clay bead (SF1922, Fig. 4.4).

Miniature clay vessels come into fashion at the beginning of the Iron Age at Assiros: all 28 are from this period and

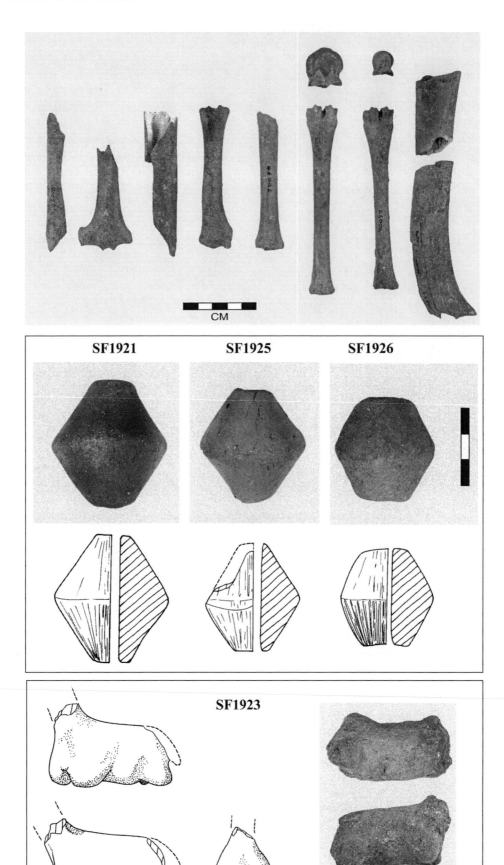

Fig. 4.2 Animal bones and horn cores, spindle whorls, animal figurine.

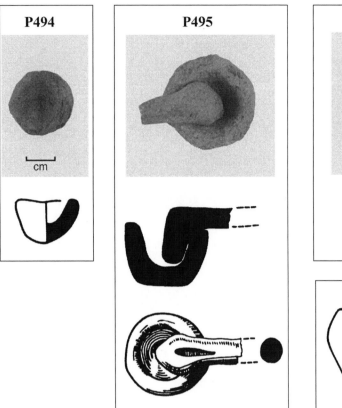

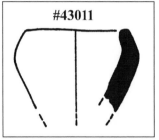

Fig. 4.3 Miniature vessels, quartz pebbles.

four come from the cache: two are 'thumb' pots – small balls of clay roughly hollowed out with the thumb (P493, P494, Fig. 4.3), the third is a unique example of a miniature mortar with a pestle fixed in it (P495, Fig. 4.3) and the fourth, a fragment of a conical bowl (#43011, Fig. 4.3).

Most remarkably this cache contains the only clay figurines found at Assiros (if one excepts the horse-head protomes found on several wishbone-handled bowls of Iron Age date). One is a very worn and damaged animal figurine (SF1923, Fig. 4.2) made in gritty clay. The second is the broken head of a snake figure (SF1927, Fig. 4.4). There was also a horse's head from another figurine or more probably the protome (SF1930, Fig. 4.4) from a wishbone handled bowl, although this protome has no exact parallels in the pottery from Assiros. Finally there were two bone awls (SF1918, SF1929, Fig. 4.4) while sherds including a Bronze Age wishbone handle probably also belonged to the cache (Fig. 4.4 lower).

It is of course impossible to know whether the cache is complete or whether it would have included objects of cloth, wood, leather or other perishable materials. All these have been exploited by children through the ages whether manufactured into objects such as rag dolls, or, often, as shreds or pieces of no particular form but with special sensory associations for a small child of touch or scent.

Interpretation

This precise significance of this group is hard to assess, especially since, as noted above, it is a unique find in Macedonia or even in the wider Aegean context already described. A few of the objects may once have been functional and others are clearly models of functional objects. The bones, quartz pebbles and the single shell do not have any obvious practical function in the form in which they were found. Nor is it easy to see how the objects in the group might relate to each other, except in so far as they were found together. Possible theoretical interpretations, other than a collection of a child's treasures, include funerary, accidental, functional or symbolic use.

Funerary: such a group of objects might conceivably have been placed in a grave but no human bones, either adult or immature, were found in the vicinity and no structure was observed which might be grave-related. Given the excellent preservation of the animal bones which formed part of the group, it is very improbable that any human bones had decayed beyond the point of recognition.

Accidental: it is highly unlikely that such an eclectic and varied group of objects came to be associated by chance. At Assiros the figurines, as already noted, are unique to the cache and the quartz pebbles and the cowrie shell are very rare. The pebbles probably came from one of the ravine beds in the district which are so rich in different types of stone. The variety of species represented by the same animal body part reinforces the concept of deliberate collection rather than accidental inclusion. There can be little doubt that the collection of items was purposeful.

Functional: only the spindle whorls can be said to have a function, either for use in spinning wool, as beads or as fastenings. While the bones and quartz pebbles could have been collected as raw materials, there is no evidence for objects made from quartz or for quartz being intentionally added to an object at Assiros. The miniature vessels are too small to have any practical purpose though both they and the animal figurine could have a symbolic one. It is not clear whether the snake head was a decorative element on some larger object although the horse head protome probably was. There are other protomes which could be horseheads on bowl handles at Assiros but this is the most detailed and delicate, and certainly represents a horse. There is nothing about the group as a whole which suggests a practical function in the everyday life of the adult inhabitants of Assiros Toumba.

Symbolic: the possibility that this group of objects were part of a foundation deposit or had a role in ceremonial, ritual or magical/shamanistic activities cannot be entirely ruled out but can only be explored through rather tenuous archaeological and anthropological parallels.

Foundation deposits are known from various Egyptian contexts where they often include prestige items with religious connotations (Weinstein 1973; Letellier 1977) but have not yet been recognised on Aegean sites. In later periods they are sometimes associated with religious or public buildings but the objects are generally new and of some intrinsic or obviously symbolic value. The concept of a 'time capsule' to be discovered at some point in the future is relatively modern, first used for the World Fair in 1939 (Jarvis 2002). Although the cache at Assiros was found beneath the level of later walls, these were only constructed after a debris level some 20cm deep had accumulated and which in any case did not run directly over the shallow pit. No direct relationship can be established to suggest that these items belong to such a foundation deposit.

None of these objects have any intrinsic value or suggest prestige items. Although the figurine is unique, the poor quality of the material used (gritty clay) and the worn condition seem to rule out any value except to its owner. Thus it seems rather improbable that they could serve in any kind of public or ceremonial activity where ostentation and display might naturally be expected. In the same way, use in some cult activity would be more plausible if any other aspects of the context or nearby structures pointed in this direction.

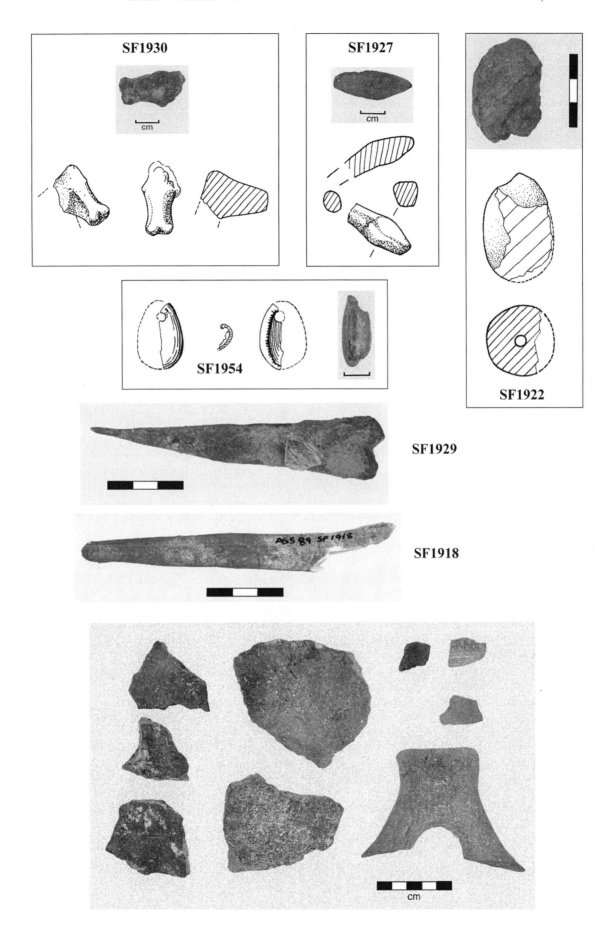

Fig. 4.4. Horse head protome, snake head, bead, cowrie shell, bone tools, sherds.

Another possibility of symbolic use which may be entertained is that these objects were seen to be possessed of, or endowed with, some magical power exploited in a 'shamanistic' manner. Shaman and shamanism are terms which have come to be used for similar personalities and similar practices in many different places around the world (Eliade 1972), even though they are strictly only applicable to remote parts of Siberia and Central Asia (von Stuckrad 2005) and, indeed, unknown in the Greek world (Richardson 1985: 88) or its northern periphery (Dowden 1980: 487). A number of recent studies have been made which consider the supernatural powers such shamans are seen to possess (such as their ability to bring about out-of-body experiences, and engage in divination) and their place in specific communities. In addition they have explored the iconography and equipment used by the shaman but seen from an archaeological perspective (Price 2001; Aldhouse-Green & Aldhouse-Green 2005).

Characteristics of shamans defined in this way are 'activities carried out in a special place … the use of drums … rods or other lot-casting devices, rattles or bells … wands or staffs … costumes… figurines' (Aldhouse-Green & Aldhouse-Green 2005, 10-2). Among the examples of such equipment they cite in an archaeological context are the ritual stone axes, bird bones and pebbles found in Italian Neolithic cult caves or, in a modern anthropological context, the use of quartz crystals or nodules, which have a powerful significance for the Tukanoan 'shamans' of the Amazon basin (Aldhouse-Green & Aldhouse-Green 2005: 67, 142-5). Among the Inuit of the Thule culture there was a strong but not exclusive correlation between miniature objects and shamanistic equipment (Park 1998: 275).

In a southern Balkan context, in the 19th and early 20th centuries mummers would tour the villages, especially those of the Vlach communities, in the days immediately after Christmas, to drive away evil spirits and perform a traditional play of death and 'resurrection'. Their practices and equipment also engage with the supernatural. Costumes and horned masks of skins hung with bells were characteristic and they carried rods and staffs (Wace & Thompson 1914: 137-41, pl. 1).

Other practices from the same region recorded in the last hundred years which border on magic or shamanism relate to the Sarakatsani shepherds. This nomadic people held the hearth within their conical hut as a place of considerable supernatural importance and a source of life: women would give birth beside it, while aborted foetuses, the afterbirth of the living, or after an interval the stillborn, would be buried beneath one of the stones which encircled the hearth (Hatzimichali 1957: ρμη´-ρνα´, ρξζ´; Leigh Fermor 1966: 41). Phylakteries of different kinds (including viper's heads sanctified by the celebration of 40 liturgies period in a church and buried in the sheepfold: Hatzimichali 1957: ρμβ´; Campbell 1964: 334) or amulets to ward off evil spirits were commonplace (Hatzimichali 1957: ρλθ´) but divination

did not require any specific equipment beyond the examination of the livers or shoulder blades of slaughtered animals or the flight of birds (Hatzimichali 1957: ρμδ´). Similar use of amulets was still widespread in the 19th century (Rennell Rodd 1892: 162).

Although some of the items from the Assiros cache – the bones, the quartz pebbles, the miniatures and the figurines – could conceivably serve as equipment for shamanistic or divinatory practices, the lack of any distinctive context for the collection (such as the corner of a room, a hearth or doorstep) suggests that this explanation for the cache is improbable, though, as with most archaeological interpretations, it cannot be ruled out absolutely. The parallels are all remote in time and space and practices akin to shamanism have not yet been demonstrated for prehistoric or historic Greece.

Toys and playthings?

All round the world, although parents are usually the closest observers of the activity of children, it is left to the anthropologists and sociologists to articulate these observations in accounts which attempt to rationalise the behaviour of children at play (Goldman 1998; Sutton-Smith 1986). This play is discussed in terms of learning adult behaviour, of role playing or of make-believe. The focus is, however, usually on the activity rather than the 'equipment' which a child incorporates into this activity. Such equipment may include 'toys' manufactured for or by the child (Rossie 2003: fig. 6) and 'playthings' – often literally objets trouvées which are adapted for, or adopted into, different kinds of play. These objects can be themselves or, with the aid of fertile imaginations, they can be used to represent a wide range of animate or inanimate entities. The behaviour of a child at play is only 'childish' in the sense that it is inexplicable to the adult: it is often complex, imaginative and rational, albeit with different parameters of reality from those of the adult.

Over the years, first hand observations of children make clear that even in the materially advanced societies of Western Europe, the sophisticated products of adult minds (dolls with changes of clothing and accessories, construction kits, or sets of characters) are often abandoned by young children in favour of simple almost formless objects (shells, stones, twigs or abandoned cardboard boxes). These objects can perhaps be better imagined with active or passive roles in a wide variety of types of play than those which adults have already characterised with a specific role. Value is in no way a concept alien to small children, though a very different concept to that of adults. How often have siblings had to be separated, when squabbling over some 'pointless' treasure?

Anthropologically reported observations confirm these characteristics as universals for many societies without the material wealth of the Western world (Goldman 1998;

Rossie 2003). It would be astonishing if they were not timeless universals, however much 'play' had to be subordinated to the economic imperatives of early communities whose survival depended on the contributions of members of every age group capable of contributing.

The objects found in the cache, as anyone unfamiliar with the kinds of 'ritual activity' so much discussed by anthropologists would agree, would be very appropriate for the kind of play that is developed by the child rather than directed by the adult. There is, indeed, nothing about the context in which the cache was found or the objects it contains which would preclude its creation by a small child. The earth in which it was found was soft and the excavation of a small hollow would present no difficulty. Many of the items would have been easy to acquire: the animal bones, for example, are part of the normal waste of meat consumption. The miniature vessels belong to a class which is reasonably common at Assiros in the first years of the Iron Age, and only at this period. There is no reason why these should not have been deliberately created for children rather than for some cult or shamanistic purpose. The spindle whorls and the bead are commonplace objects while only the figurines are unique to this group. The sparkly quartz pebbles were collected away from the settlement but are probably too large and heavy to serve as 'jacks' in the manner already suggested for the group of stones found in the Protogeometric grave at Mycenae.

Discussions about what constitutes a 'toy' have become more formalised in recent studies. It is important to recognise that there is no clear boundary between objects exploited by adults and non-adults: play often, but by no means always, has a formative role (Campbell 1964: 156, with reference to the children of the nomad Sarakatsani) in which the child may employ objects which have a practical adult use. Small objects may well provide an introduction to full-sized objects which are part of adult equipment (Park 1998: 274) and the association between small versions of standard objects and children is cross-culturally attested, even if never reserved exclusively for children (McLaren 2004: 298-9; Park 1998: 274-80; Lillehammer 1989: 100). Objects considered as toys are often retained or even deliberately acquired by adults for decoration and pleasure without losing their status, although these are often more elaborate, delicate or valuable than those owned by children.

Conclusion

Three thousand years have passed since this enigmatic group of objects was assembled, placed in a small pit and lost to view. We do not know whether it was intentionally buried or accidentally hidden when wind and rain washed the loose fill around the pit into it. Clearly the owner (or owners) never returned to claim a 'treasure trove' of items which were personally precious though of no intrinsic value. We have argued that these items were child-related and, while certainty will never be possible, we think of them as a collection of favourite items gathered up by a small child and, for some reason, lost from sight. Other explanations, as suggested above, do not convince.

We hope that by drawing attention here to a very unusual group of objects, we will have encouraged others to look (again?) at enigmatic collections from archaeological contexts and consider whether 'childish' activities provide a satisfactory explanation. Children, after all, were our past and will be our future.

Bibliography

Aldhouse-Green, M. & Aldhouse-Green, S. (2005): *The quest for the shaman: shape-shifters, sorcerers and spirit-healers of Ancient Europe*. London.

Andronikos M. (1969): *Vergina I: to Nekrotapheion ton Tymvon*. Athens.

Arnett J.J. (2007): *Adolescence and Emerging Adulthood: A Cultural Approach*. Upper Saddle River.

Beaumont, L. (2003): 'The changing face of childhood' in J. Neils. and J. Oakley (eds), *Coming of Age in Ancient Greece: Images of Childhood from the Classical Past*, 59-83. Yale.

Blegen C.W. (1937): *Prosymna: The Helladic Settlement preceding the Argive Heraion*. Cambridge.

Buxeda i Garrigós J., Jones R.E., Kilikoglou V., Levi S.T., Maniatis Y., Mitchell J., Vagnetti L., Andreou S. and Wardle K.A. (2003): 'Technology transfer at the periphery of the Mycenaean world: the cases of Mycenaean pottery found in central Macedonia (Greece) and the Plain of Sybaris (Italy)', *Archaeometry* 45(2): 263-284.

Campbell, J. K. (1964): *Honour, Family and Patronage*. Oxford.

Catling, H.W. (1974): *Archaeological Reports for 1973-4*, no. 20. London.

Cavanagh, W.G. and Mee, C.B. (1998): *A Private Place: Death in Prehistoric Greece: SIMA 125*. Jonsered.

Chadwick J. (1976): *The Mycenaean World*. Cambridge.

Coldstream J.N. (1977): *Geometric Greece*. London.

Coldstream J.N. and Catling H.W. (eds), (1996): *Knossos North Cemetery: Early Greek Tombs*. (British School at Athens Supplementary Volume 28). London.

Demakopoulou K. (1982): *To Mykenaiko Iero sto Amyklaio kai i YE IIIC Periodos sti Lakonia*. Athens.

Demakopoulou K. (1988): *The Mycenaean World: Five centuries of Early Greek Culture 1600-1100 BC*. Athens.

Desborough, V.R.d'A. (1956): 'Mycenae 1939-1955, Part III: Two tombs', *Annual of the British School at Athens* 51: 128-130.

Desborough, V.R.d'A. (1964): *The Last Mycenaeans and their successors*. Oxford.

Desborough, V.R.d'A. (1972): *The Greek Dark Ages*. London.

Dickinson, O.T.P.K. (2006): *The Aegean from Bronze Age to Iron Age: continuity and change between the twelfth and eighth centuries BC*. London.

Doumas, Chr. (1983): *Thera: Pompeii of the Ancient Aegean*. London.

Doumas, Chr. (1992): *The Wall Paintings of Thera*. Athens.

Dowden, K. (1980): 'Deux notes sur les Skythes et les Arimaspes', *Revue des Études Grecques* 93, 486-92.

Eliade, M. (1972): *Shamanism: Archaic Techniques of Ecstasy*, Bollingen Series 76, Princeton (Translated from the French edition, *Le Chamanisme et les techniques archaïques de l'extase*. Paris 1951).

Forrer, R. (1932): 'Les chars cultuels préhistoriques et leurs survivances aux époques historiques', *Prehistoire* 1: 19-123.

French, E.B. (1971): 'The Development of Mycenaean Terracotta Figurines', *Annual of the British School at Athens* 66: 101-187.

French, E.B. (1985): 'The Figures and Figurines' in A.C. Renfrew, *The Archaeology of Cult: the Sanctuary at Phylakopi,* (British School at Athens Supplementary Volume 18): 209-80. London.

French, E.B. (2002): *Mycenae: Agamemnon's Capital*. Stroud.

Furumark, A. (1941): *The Mycenaean Pottery: Analysis and Classification*. Stockholm.

Gates C. (1992): 'Art for Children in Mycenaean Greece', in R. Laffineur and J.L. Crowley (eds), *Aegean Bronze Age iconography: shaping a methodology : proceedings of the 4th International Aegean Conference, University of Tasmania, Hobart, Australia, 6-9 April 1992* (*Aegaeum* 8): 161-171. Liège.

Goldman, L.R. (1998): *Myth, mimesis and make-believe*. Oxford

Hatzimichali, A. (1957): *Sarakatsanoi*. Athens.

Heurtley, W.A. (1939): *Prehistoric Macedonia*. Cambridge.

Hochstetter, A. (1984): *Kastanas: Die handgemachte Keramik* (Prähistorische Archäologie in Südosteuropa 3). Berlin.

Hochstetter, A. (1987): *Kastanas: Die Kleinfunde* (Prähistorische Archäologie in Südosteuropa 6). Berlin.

Hourmouziades, G. (1982): 'Ancient Magnesia' in M. & R. Capon. (eds), *Magnesia: The Story of a Civilization,* 10-103.

Jarvis, W.E. (2002): *Time Capsules: A Cultural History*. Jefferson.

Karamitrou-Mentesidi, G. (1993): 'I Ano Makedonia stin Ysteri epochi tou Chalkou kai stin Proimi epochi tou Siderou' in I. Vokotopoulou (ed.), *Ellinikos Politismos: Macedonia to Basilieio tou Megalou Alexandrou. Marché Bonsecours, Montreal 7th May–19th September 1993*: 116-21. Athens.

Karo, G. (1930, 1933): *Die Schachtgräber von Mykenai.* München.

Kilian, K. (1981): 'Zeugnisse mykenische Kultausübung in Tiryns', in R. Hägg and N. Marinatos (eds), *Sanctuaries and Cults in the Aegean Bronze Age,* 49-58, Stockholm.

Kraiker, W.A. and Kübler, K. (1939): *Kerameikos: Ergebnisse der Ausgrabungen I.* Berlin.

Koliopoulos, J.S. (2007): *Ancient Thessaloniki* http://www.eng.auth.gr/macedonia/36.html, accessed 070707.

Konsolaki-Yannopoulou, E. (1999): 'A group of new Mycenaean horseman from Methana' in P. Betancourt, V. Karageorghis, R. Laffineur and W.D. Niemeier (eds), *Meletemata, Studies in Aegean Archaeology presented to Malcolm H. Wiener as he enters his 65th year* (*Aegaeum* 20): 427-33. Liège.

Konsolaki-Yannopoulou, E. (2002): 'A Mycenaean sanctuary on Methana' in R. Hägg (ed.), *Peloponnesian Sanctuaries and Cults. Proceedings of the Ninth International Symposium at the Swedish Institute at Athens, 11-13 June 1994,* 25-36. Stockholm.

Konsolaki-Yannopoulou, E. (2003): 'Ta Mykinaika Eidolia apo ton Agio Konstantino Methanon' in E. Konsolaki-Yannopoulou (ed.), *Argosaronikos: Praktika 1ou Diethnous Synedriou Istorias kai Archaiologias tou Argosaronikou, Poros, 26-29 Iouniou 1998, A: I Proistoriki Periodos*, 375-406. Athens.

Kübler K. (1943): *Kerameikos: Ergebnisse der Ausgrabungen IV.* Berlin.

Lambrinoudakis, V. (1981): 'Remains of the Mycenaean period in the Sanctuary of Apollo Maleatas', in R. Hägg and N. Marinatos (eds), *Sanctuaries and Cults in the Aegean Bronze Age* (Skrifter utgivna av Svenska institutet i Athen XXVIII), 59-65. Stockholm.

Leigh Fermor, P. (1966): *Roumeli: Travels in Northern Greece*. London.

Lemos, I.S. (2002): *The Protogeometric Aegean: the archaeology of the late eleventh and tenth centuries BC*. Oxford.

Letellier B. (1977): 'Gründungbeigabe' in W. Helck & W. Westendorf (eds), *Lexicon der Ägyptologie* II: 906-12. Wiesbaden.

Lewartowski, K. (2000): *Late Helladic Simple Grave.* BAR Int. Series 878. Oxford.

Lillehammer, G. (1989): 'A child is born. The child's world in an archaeological perspective', *Norwegian Archaeological Review*. 22 (2): 89-105.

Marinatos, Sp. and Hirmer, M. (1960): *Crete and Mycenae*. London.

McLaren, D. (2004): 'An Important Child's Burial from Doune, Perth and Kinross, Scotland', in A. Gibson and A. Sheridan (eds), *From Sickles to Circles: Britain and Ireland at the Time of Stonehenge*, 289-303. Stroud.

Moore A.D. and Taylour, W.D.T. (2000): *The Temple* (Well Built Mycenae Fasc. 10). Oxford.

Moore A.D. and Taylour, W.D.T. (forthcoming): *The Room with the Fresco Complex.* (Well Built Mycenae Fasc. 11).

Morris I. (1989): *Burial and ancient society: the rise of the Greek city-state*. Cambridge.

Mountjoy, P.A. (1976): 'Late Helladic IIIB 1 Pottery dating the Construction of the South House at Mycenae', *Annual of the British School at Athens* 71: 77-112.

Mountjoy, P.A. (1986): *Mycenaean Decorated Pottery: A guide to identification* (*SIMA* 73). Gothenburg.

Mountjoy, P.A. (1999): *Regional Mycenaean Decorated Pottery*. Rahden.

Newton M.W., Wardle K.A. and Kuniholm P.I. (2005a): 'Dendrochronology and Radiocarbon determinations from Assiros and the beginning of the Greek Iron Age', *Archaiologiko Ergo Makedonias Thrakis* 17 (2003): 173-190.

Newton M.W., Wardle K.A. and Kuniholm P.I. (2005b): 'A Dendrochronological ^{14}C Wiggle-Match for the Early Iron Age of north Greece: a contribution to the debate about this period in the Southern Levant', in T.E. Levy and T. Higham (eds), *The Bible and Radiocarbon Dating: Archaeology, Text and Science*, 104-113. London.

Nicholls R.V. (1970): 'Greek votive statuettes and religious continuity *ca* 1200-700BC' in B.F. Harris (ed.), *Auckland Classical Essays presented to E.M. Blaiklock*, 1-38. Oxford and Auckland.

Nordquist, G. and Ingvarsson-Sundström, A. (2005): 'Live hard, die young: mortuary remains of Middle and early Late Helladic children from the Argolid in social context', in A. Dakouri-Hild and S. Sherratt (eds), *Autochthon: papers presented to O.T.P.K. Dickinson on the occasion of his retirement* (BAR Int. Series 1432), 156-74. Oxford.

Olsen, B.A. (1998): 'Women, Children and the Family in the Late Aegean Bronze Age: Differences in Minoan and Mycenaean Constructions of Gender', *World Archaeology* 29 (3): 380-92.

Papadopoulos, J.K. (2005): *The Early Iron Age Cemetery at Torone* (Monumenta Archaeologica 24, Cotsen Institute of Archaeology). Los Angeles.

Pare, C. (1989): 'From Dupljaja to Delphi: the ceremonial use of the wagon in later prehistory', *Antiquity* 63: 80–100.

Park, R.W. (1998): 'Size counts: the miniature archaeology of childhood in Inuit societies', *Antiquity* 72: 269-81.

Pilafidis-Williams, K. (1987): *The Sanctuary of Aphaia on Aigina in the Bronze Age*. Munich.

Polychronakou-Sgouritsa, N. (1994): 'Paidikes taphes sti mykenaiki Ellada', *Archaiologikon Deltion* 42A (1987): 8-29.

Popham, M.R. and Sackett, L.H. (1968): *Excavations at Lefkandi, Euboea 1964-66*. London.

Popham, M.R. and Sackett, L.H. (1980): *Lefkandi I: The Iron Age* (British School at Athens Supplementary Volume 11). London. (Plates volume published in 1979)

Price, N.S. (ed.), (2001): *The Archaeology of Shamanism*. London.

Rennell Rodd, J. (1892): *The Customs and Lore of Modern Greece*. London.

Richardson, N. J. (1985): 'The Orphic Poems', *Classical Review* 35: 87-90.

Rossie, J-P. (2003): *Children's creativity in toys and play: examples from Morocco, the Tunisian Sahara and Peace Education*. Stockholm: web publication at http://filarkiv.sitrec.kth.se/pub2003/Hameenlinna/text Hameenlinna.htm, accessed 190707.

Rutter, J. (2003): 'Children in Aegean Prehistory', in J. Neils and J. Oakley (eds): *Coming of Age in Ancient Greece: Images of Childhood from the Classical Past*, 31-58. Yale.

Smithson, E.L. (1961): 'The Protogeometric Cemetery at Nea Ionia, 1949' *Hesperia* 30 (2): 147-178.

Snodgrass, A.M. (1971): *The Dark Age of Greece*. Edinburgh. (Reprinted with expanded introduction 2000).

Sutton-Smith, B. (1986): *Toys as Culture*. New York.

Theocharis, D.R. (1964): 'Anaskaphi mykinaikon thalamoeidon taphon para to Mega Monasteriou (Larisis)', *Archaiologikon Deltion* 19 Chr. 2: 255-8.

Vokotopoulou, I. (1972): 'Archaiotites kai Mnimeia Ipirou', *Archaiologikon Deltion* 27, Chr. 2: 441-454.

Vokotopoulou, I., Despini, A., Misalidou, B. & Tiverios, M. (1985): *Sindos: Katalogos tis Ekthesis*. Thessaloniki.

Ventris M. and Chadwick J. (1956): *Documents in Mycenaean Greek*. Cambridge.

von Stuckrad, K. (2005): 'Constructions, normativities, identities: recent studies on Shamanism and Neo-shamanism', *Religious Studies Review* 31: 123-8.

Wace, A.J.B. and Thompson, M.S. (1914): *The Nomads of the Balkans: an account of life and customs among the Vlachs of Northern Pindus*. London.

Wace, H. (1961): *Ivories from Mycenae 1939-I: The Ivory Trio*. (Privately published).

Wardle, K.A. (1969): 'A Group of LH IIIB 1 Pottery from within the Citadel at Mycenae', *Annual of the British School at Athens* 64: 261-97.

Wardle, K.A. (1973): 'A Group of LH IIIB 2 Pottery from within the Citadel at Mycenae', *Annual of the British School at Athens* 68: 297-348.

Wardle, K.A. (1989): 'Excavation at Assiros Toumba 1988: A preliminary report', *Annual of the British School at Athens* 84: 447-463.

Wardle, K.A. (1998): 'Change or Continuity: Assiros Toumba at the transition from Bronze to Iron Age', *Archaiologiko Ergo Makedonias Thrakis* 10 (1997): 443-460.

Wardle K.A., Newton M.W. and Kuniholm P.I (2007): 'Troy VIIB 2 Revisited: the Date of the Transition from Bronze to Iron Age in the Northern Aegean', in H. Todorova, M. Stefanovich and G. Ivanov (eds), *The Struma/Strymon River Valley in Prehistory. Proceedings of the International Symposium Strymon Praehistoricus, Kjustendil–Blagoevgrad (Bulgaria), Serres–Amphipolis (Greece) 27.09–01.10.2004* (In The Steps of James Harvey Gaul Volume 2), 481-497. Sofia.

43

Wardle K.A. and Wardle, D. (1997): *Cities of Legend: The Mycenaean World.* Bristol.

Wardle K.A. and Wardle, D. (2007): 'Assiros Toumba: A brief history of the settlement', in H. Todorova, M. Stefanovich and G. Ivanov (eds), *The Struma/Strymon River Valley in Prehistory. Proceedings of the International Symposium Strymon Praehistoricus, Kjustendil–Blagoevgrad (Bulgaria), Serres– Amphipolis (Greece) 27.09–01.10.2004* (In The Steps of James Harvey Gaul Volume 2), 451-79. Sofia.

Wardle K.A. and Wardle, D. (forthcoming): *Assiros I: the Iron Age Settlement.*

Weber-Hiden, I. (1990): 'Die mykenischen Terrakottafiguren aus den Syringes von Tiryns', *Tiryns* XI, 35-85. Mainz.

Weinstein, J.M. (1973): *Foundation deposits in ancient Egypt.* (Ann Arbor Xerox University Microfilms).

CHAPTER 5

TRANSITIONS TO ADULTHOOD IN EARLY ICELANDIC SOCIETY

Chris Callow

This article deals with a fundamental problem that faces anyone trying to understand childhood in societies in the remote past. It deals with how we might interpret a limited range of prescriptive and descriptive textual evidence. The case study used here is rather different from many of the others in this volume: it is of a medieval, northern European society, and one which was entirely rural. Despite the apparent difference between this study and others in this volume, many of the methodological problems are strikingly similar. We still have to ask ourselves about how we reconcile sometimes conflicting pictures of young people and the process of growing up. The shaping of gender identities in childhood is a key issue too, not least the way writers choose to represent them. It will be argued below that even, or perhaps especially, in an impoverished society like Iceland social differences in childhood were surprisingly strong represented. Historiographically, the 'legacy of Philippe Ariès' (Harlow, Laurence & Vuolanto, this volume) and that of Nicholas Orme (2001) have been keenly felt in recent specialist studies of children in medieval Iceland, but this paper will demonstrate that there is much more work which might be done on the many genres of literature which characterise the bulk of our evidence.

This study will be selective in the evidence it uses in order to look at the way children's ages and social class interact. Two forms of evidence from roughly the same milieu form the basis of that discussion: a genre of extended, anonymously-written narratives – the *Sagas of Icelanders*[1] – and the earliest body of Icelandic law (known oddly as *Grágás*, 'grey goose')[2] which dates from roughly the same period. Although the surviving texts are most likely to have been written down or significantly revised in the 13th century, there is still an issue about which historical period and to whose views they represent. The consensus is that they most likely tell us about the 13th century and not earlier, however the texts evolved. Most scholars believe that *Sagas of Icelanders* provide further problems as social historical texts because they tell stories which are set in the 9th to 11th centuries. While it is no longer contended that this genre of saga is fiction, in the modern sense of a novel, we still need to be mindful of whose views of the past these sagas represent. In many ways they read as if they

relate closely to local, native oral traditions but at the same time they were written down by anonymous Christian authors whose views of history may partly have been shaped by Christian, Latin traditions of thinking among Iceland's elite. This point pertains no less to a discussion of ideas about children and childhood than it does to any other aspect of that society.

The discussion that follows aims to demonstrate that generally neither sagas nor the laws show a great deal of interest in children, let alone explicitly consider the nature of childhood and adulthood, or differences between the two. The images of children we do have generally pertain to Iceland's wealthier peasantry and its elite. Despite this it is possible to see a range of roles and behaviours associated with children of particular chronological ages, with an emphasis on teenagers. This information is not always easy to interpret: the sagas are full of remarkably precocious children, often male heroes-in-the-making, which test modern readers' sense of what is credible. Yet a straightforward counting-up of saga references to characters of specific ages, up to the age of 20 or so, indicates some clear patterns in the way age was probably remembered and conceptualised. Both the sagas and laws pay far more attention to the lives of boys from 12 to 16 than they do for any other specified age group. For girls the evidence suggests that chronological age was nowhere near as significant for the things that they were and were not permitted to do. The sagas mention the ages of female characters so rarely that we may even question whether women were ever seen to have a meaningful transition to adulthood in the same way as men. Before we turn to more specific questions, however, some historical and historiographical background on Iceland will probably be useful contexts for students of childhood.

Iceland

Iceland was one of the many destinations for Scandinavian emigrants in the 'Viking expansion' of the 9th and 10th centuries. Iceland seems to have been empty before c. 870 AD, the date just after which both archaeology and history suggest the first colonists arrived. Men of Scandinavian origin certainly formed a significant part of the early population, but they may themselves have arrived after a spell living in the British Isles, and brought with them others, both men and women, free and unfree, from the British Isles and Scandinavia. The debate on Icelanders' origins has a long-standing significance and is now the subject of renewed interest from geneticists (Helgason et al. 2001; Sigurðsson 2000). The colonisation of Iceland probably

---

[1] 'Sagas' is used as shorthand for *Sagas of Icelanders* throughout this article. Whenever another genre of saga literature is referred to it is identified specifically, e.g. *Contemporary Sagas*.

[2] Old Icelandic/Norse personal and place names are spelled in a form to help English readers: 'th' is used for the characters ð and þ; the final 'r' in Old Icelandic personal names has also been omitted. Other Old Icelandic/Norse terms and modern Icelandic authors' names use the standard, modern Icelandic alphabet.

took place over the course of the 10th century and perhaps took even longer: sagas and other sources seem to see the colonisation as complete by the mid-10th century, although their portrayal of it is heavily schematised. Archaeology suggests that the settlers took time to adapt to the new environment – some early upland farms were abandoned or were moved after only a few decades' occupation – so that fairly soon people inhabited only the lower, coastal areas of the island. The majority of buildings were constructed out of a mixture of turf, stone and wood, just as they would be until the 20th century. These tended to be dispersed fairly evenly across lowland areas (Vésteinsson 2007).

The earliest colonists in Iceland are likely to have held non-Christian beliefs, but at some stage Iceland converted to Christianity. There do not seem to have been churches until the 11th century, while the written evidence of later centuries consistently identifies AD 1000 as the precise date of Christianity's official acceptance as part of their grand narrative. Tithe payments were introduced in 1097 and both of Iceland's bishoprics were apparently in place by 1106, one in the south of the country and one in the north. While such information may not tell us much about the realities of people's beliefs in these early centuries it seems clear that everyone was nominally Christian by the 12th century (see generally Vésteinsson 2000; Kristjánsdóttir 2004). Just as with the rest of the Christianised north of Europe, it was the Church which seems to have been instrumental in spreading the use of writing in Iceland. *Sagas of Icelanders* are generally thought not to have been written until after many other, more conventional forms of vernacular writing had been undertaken (Whaley 2000). Icelandic texts which are generally seen as predating the sagas include a short institutional history of Iceland (*Íslendingabók*), various histories of Norway, grammatical treatises, genealogies and a lengthy account of Iceland's colonisation (*Landnámabók*).

Other notable features of Iceland's early society potentially relate to what we can see in portrayals of children. It seems to have been relatively egalitarian, or at least it was missing a super-rich elite of the kind which dominated most of medieval western Europe. There was no king, save for the distant and probably intermittent influence of the Norwegian king. Icelandic chieftains seem to have had relatively weak control over the districts they lived in, to the extent that they may have had to tolerate the public opposition of wealthier farmers who lived near to them. It is not clear how many chieftains there were at any one time, but depictions of the late 12th and early 13th century, which are far clearer and more convincing than for any earlier period, suggest that the top tier of the political pyramid consisted of six to eight extended families. All of our sources stress the continued importance of the annual assembly or parliament, the Alþing, as a place for political negotiations and dispute settlement. On occasion it does appear that certain individuals could almost act like

kings, but their power was still short-lived and difficult to pass on to an heir. Some scholars have started to see more similarities between medieval Icelandic lordship and political structures and those of western Europe, but while the introduction of the structures of the Church are generally thought to have strengthened the position of the secular elite, that elite was never very strong (Vésteinsson 2000; Sigurðsson 1999; Karlsson 2004).

One key reason for medieval Iceland's relatively weak political elite was the fact that the country was materially poor. Pastoral farming supplemented by fishing was close to being a universal occupation; everyone pretty much had access to the same range of limited resources, even if those resources, such as lowland grazing, sea birds and their eggs, and beaches which tended to provide driftwood and stranded whales, varied in quality and distribution (Kristjánsson 1980-86; Thoroddsen 1911; Gelsinger 1981). Chieftains vied for control of additional, imported resources (mostly from Norway) such as grain and good quality weapons and timber. Material culture was generally poor and so it seems that it was difficult for anyone to impress others or control them effectively for very long.

At the lower end of the social scale, there was very likely a distinction between those farmers or heads of household (sing. *bóndi*, pl. *bændr*) who owned their own farm, on the one hand, and those who were tenants on the other, even if this distinction is rarely made explicit in sagas. Both groups of farmers were legally obliged to ally themselves to a chieftain of their choice if they had more than a certain level of wealth. Ties to lords were still weaker than in most contemporary western, rural situations, at least for those Icelandic farmers who owned their properties. The *Sagas of Icelanders* and *Grágás* also mention household slaves, but their numbers are difficult to estimate and they are entirely absent from the *Contemporary Sagas* which discuss 12th and 13th-century politics.[3] It is generally considered that slavery must have died out and that the laws must be anachronistic in their references to the phenomenon.

To sum up, Icelandic society was probably not so very different in demographic terms from other parts of Europe, despite its many unusual features. Even in the relatively early days of its 'Viking' colonisation it probably had a high number of children; it would be hard to imagine a pre-industrial society which did not have a significant number of children in order to be viable. The society into which these children were born was poor,

---

[3] *Contemporary Sagas* (*samtíðarsögur*) are a genre which are conventionally identified as a single group because they record 12th- and 13th-century events in Iceland and were probably written within a few decades of the events they describe. Traditionally seen as more credible as sources for political and social history, they are nonetheless demonstrably partisan, shaped by literary models and dependent on oral traditions. For a recent discussion and bibliography in English see Bragason 2005. Children are mentioned in *Contemporary Sagas* but even less often than in *Sagas of Icelanders*.

and in terms of material culture there may have been relatively little distinction between richer and poorer children. That is not to say that other evidence for children shows them as socially undifferentiated: differences in families' wealth did matter and the arrival of Christianity, for example, may have provided schooling for boys and girls among the elite (Vésteinsson 2000: 141-2, although see also Jakobsson 2005: 67-8). As will be demonstrated below, parents' status does matter for the way medieval Icelandic children are portrayed in literature and, most likely, in reality.

Issues and debates

The recent rebirth of interest in children in medieval studies generally (Shahar 1990; Crawford 1999; Orme 2001; Classen 2005) has led to a reinvigoration of the interest among historians and scholars of Old Norse literature in many aspects of childhood, especially since the 1980s. Most significantly, a paperback volume, *Miðaldabörn* (*Medieval Children*) has recently been published which is entirely dedicated to medieval children (Jakobsson & Tulinius 2005). It is rare for Icelandic publishers or historians to produce volumes dedicated to any single historical issue, let alone one which is so narrowly-defined; it says a lot about changing Icelandic academic interests (and perceived potential wider public interest) that such a book has been produced. A review of this book will provide a good idea of current thinking and the earlier scholarship which has shaped it.

The volume begins with an article which discusses early Scandinavian and Icelandic legal evidence on the provision for the care of children of slave women or poorer women. In some ways this is actually addressing a long-running debate concerning whether or not infanticide or the exposure of children actually took place in pre-Christian Scandinavia and whether or not Christianity (would have) prevented it (Mundal 2005). Infanticide is a recurring issue in studies of Viking Age Scandinavia because Christian legal texts go out of their way to say that child exposure (*barnarútburðr*) should be prohibited, while sagas mention children saved from exposure (Clover 1988). Mundal accepts the legal provisions – both in *Grágás* and mainland Scandinavian texts – as proof that child exposure did take place and that it must have been fairly common in pre-Christian society (2005: 20). Such a view is generally in line with those of some scholars who have looked at a broader range of sources (Clover 1988; Wicker 1998). The noun *barnarútburðr*, however, does not unambiguously signify infanticide and taken more literally might simply mean the 'bearing out' of children, in other words, some form of exposure or the abandonment of children to be found by someone else. It still seems difficult to me to make such a strong case for the deliberate killing of children on the basis of such late, prescriptive texts (Callow 2006). It might equally be argued that the numerous provisions for ensuring that all children were cared for actually add up

to a situation where children could rarely have been abandoned in practice, even if a mother could or would not care for a child.

Fosterage is a common phenomenon in *Sagas of Icelanders* whereby children (usually boys) are brought up in a household other than their parental home. It says something about both the narratives themselves and the secondary literature that most books on medieval Icelandic or Scandinavian society have an entry for 'fosterage' in their indices, yet none for 'children' or 'childhood'; fosterage is almost a euphemism for childhood.

Cases of fostering from the *Sagas of Icelanders* (and indeed *Contemporary Sagas*) suggest that it could take places for a number of different reasons. Sometimes there could be an arrangement made between adults who were friends and equals; it could be imposed on a weaker household by a more powerful one as a punishment for past offences; and sometimes richer households took in children from households which could not feed them (Miller 1990: 122-4, 171-4). Gunnar Karlsson's article (2005) demonstrates the wide variety of fostering relationships and the breadth of vocabulary therefore associated with it in *Sagas of Icelanders*. Karlsson's and Jakobsson's articles in the volume also address a persistent issue for Icelandic scholars concerning fosterage – to what extent the fostering-out of children reflected medieval Icelandic parents' indifference towards their children (Sigurðsson 1991). Both put forward arguments for parents' being caring: for Karlsson (2005: 55-6) the real purpose of the fostering-out of elite boys was to toughen them up, as a kind of finishing school for the harsh realities of Icelandic society where fighting and death in battle were common. Jakobsson makes the case for strong emotional bonds between foster children and the individuals identified as their foster parent(s) and foster siblings (Jakobsson 2005). Such concerns in the scholarship mirror medievalists' wider concerns as to whether medieval parents saw childhood as important.

Anna Hansen is one of the scholars to have written most extensively on medieval Icelandic childhood in recent years (Hansen 2002, 2005). In the *Miðaldabörn* volume she puts forward the view that boys and unmarried girls were especially powerless until they were 16 because they could not inherit property. On the basis of some *Sagas of Icelanders* and *Grágás*, Hansen concludes that many children were entirely dependent on parents or guardians until they were 16 years old and must have feared the death of their parents and the possibility of their inheritance being controlled by someone else (Hansen 2005). Ásdís Egilsdóttir (2005) examines the stories of male heroes in some examples of 13th- or 14th-century *Fornaldarsögur* (sagas about the distant Scandinavian past) which show the anxieties for elite males as they grew up and felt the pressures of masculine identity impinging on them; the stories concern boys being criticised for being late developers but who eventually leave home to become heroes. Án Bow-bender (*Áns saga bogsveigis*) and Göngu-Hrólfr (*Göngu-Hrólfs saga*) are two such examples – both were defective in various ways as boys (physically and socially) and unloved by their fathers. Arguments have also been put forward elsewhere about whether or not a psychological interpretation of heroes' behaviour is appropriate (Jakobsson 2003).

Egils saga Skallagrímssonar is used by Agnes S. Arnórsdóttir (2005) to remind us of the complexity of masculinity on the one hand and the disinterest of saga writers in girls on the other. *Egils saga* is inescapable in discussions of childhood in medieval Iceland. The saga focusses on the life of Egill Skallagrímsson and in particular his travels to the English and Scandinavian courts. It is unusual because of the relatively large amount of time it devotes to its hero's (troubled) childhood as well as his old age. For this reason, it is possible for Brynhildur Þórarinsdóttir (2005) to claim that the saga's author sees Egill as going through four stages in his childhood: from birth to three years; from three to seven; and then from seven to 12 but with an overlapping stage of real significance, a pre-teen phase, from ten to 12 years (2005: 113-4) while recognising *Egils saga's* unique interest in childhood (2005: 131).

This brief review of this single volume clearly shows some of the ways in which childhood is being considered by scholars in this field. *Sagas of Icelanders* form the main corpus of evidence being used, but new literary genres are starting to be investigated; Arnórsdóttir (2005: 110) also hints at the need for a reinvestigation of manuscript variants of individual texts to enable us to see whether changing ideas about childhood and gender can be identified in revisions of those texts over time. Childhood is being investigated in the light of recent publications on medieval childhood in other regions, such as those of Nicholas Orme and Shulamith Shahar already cited, but there is still room for more research which cuts across genres. The value of the legal material, meanwhile, remains a problem.

A cautionary tale

Sagas of Icelanders give a fairly detailed picture of life in medieval Iceland and one which in some respects at least may well relate more closely to a reality than legal texts. There are about 40 sagas, of varied length, which detail blood feuds, legal disputes, love affairs, ghost stories and other memorable events which tend to centre on a small number of families. Children play only a small part in the sagas, but when they do it can often be informative about writers' unconscious attitudes to children for a variety of reasons. Some sagas focus on remarkable individuals and these are of particular interest for determining what was considered typical or atypical, appropriate or inappropriate behaviour for children of different ages and social status.

Still, the more discursive accounts about specific, named individuals are unusual. One short, and in some senses more typical, episode involving a child might provide a starting point for demonstrating both the inherent interest and the general problems which saga accounts of children provide. The source of the story is *Droplaugarsona saga* which, at 15 chapters in length, is one of the shorter *Sagas of Icelanders*. *Droplaugarsona saga's* wider subject, however, is typical for the genre – a dispute set in 10th-century Iceland between two men that leads to killings and revenge. The saga says just this in the middle of one chapter:

> One day after that, Grím played a board game with a Norwegian and a boy of Thorkell and Jórunn's ran past the table and knocked over the gaming board. The Norwegian kicked out at the boy who farted. Grím roared with laughter. (*The saga of the sons of Droplaugr*: ch.13).[4]

It is fair to say that this is probably the only instance in the sagas of a child almost simultaneously running into a chess board, being physically mistreated and suffering from wind. To my knowledge it is also the only occasion where a non-Icelandic saga character hurts a child and where a child's maltreatment is a source of amusement. Yet those are the unusual features of the story. In just as many ways this story highlights how sagas do and do not deal with children. We clearly know very little about this child. We know he is a boy (*sveinn*) but it is not important for the story for us to know his name or age. We also know something about the boy's familial status but only by virtue of the fact that it makes sense for the writer to place the story in the home of the husband and wife Thorkell and Jórunn.

For the sake of a few extra words, any number of details about the boy and his actions might have been included. We could have been told his age, some physical characteristics or how he was dressed. There could have been some sort of dialogue involving the boy and the Norwegian; direct speech is very common for adult characters in sagas. We could have a reason or motive for the child running past the adults; or how the boy was, or perhaps was not, being supervised by an adult. In this instance the saga's plot does not demand fuller details and so we do not get them, even though self-evidently the saga writer wanted to include this story despite its having no obvious narrative function. In this example the only reasons for the child to be mentioned is the apparent humour in the situation and, perhaps, the opportunity to comment on the anti-social behaviour of Norwegians. Most instances in sagas are similar, in the sense that children enter the narrative momentarily and without much dramatic effect.

---

[4] 'Um daginn eftir tefldi Grímur við Austmann ok rann að borðinu sveinn, er þau Þorkell áttu ok Jórunn, ok rótaði taflinu. Austmaðrinn spyrndi til sveinsins, en hann frat við. Grímur skelldi upp ok hló.' *Droplaugasona saga* ch.13 (Jóhannesson 1950:172).

As we shall see, however, some sagas do include incidents where children are key to saga action, where they have motives, speak and are given other characteristics which are more akin to the way adults are treated. It is only through using such exceptional examples, usually of the children and youth of Iceland's elite, that we can gain any insight at all into how the transition to adulthood was perceived in Iceland in the central Middle Ages.

Age, laws, theory and practice

Before addressing the literary evidence in more depth, a brief look at the legal evidence is necessary because Iceland's earliest compilation of legal material (*Grágás*) provides some apparently easy-to-interpret evidence for age-related status for young people. In this respect it resembles many earlier medieval European legal texts, such as the surviving early Frankish, Visigothic or Anglo-Saxon laws (e.g. James 1988: 216-9; Halsall 1996; Crawford 1999: 40-2, 159, 175-7). There are the usual problems with such prescriptive evidence, however, which any historian faces. Just because the 'rules' say that someone should behave in a particular way does not necessarily mean that they did. We ought also to ask whether in most societies people actually took as much notice of chronological age as the lawmakers who compiled texts such as *Grágás* would like us to believe. Most people might remember their age and those of others in relative rather than absolute terms. It might also be better to suggest that 'practical' age depended on individuals' abilities and social circumstances; at court people might not want a poor negotiator to undertake a lawsuit on their behalf even if they were old enough. On the other hand, if there were no one else to undertake that case then perhaps someone 'too' young might be encouraged to do so with the help of colluding supporters. As we shall see, the narrative sources give a more nuanced view of the social actions of people under 20.

Grágás nevertheless identifies ages or circumstances at/under which younger males and females could do certain things, although not in a systematic way. For younger males *Grágás* suggests that chronological age seems to have been the major determinant of status. For a girl to attain the status of an adult woman, as we shall see, she had to get married. For both, however, it was not considered right that they should be forced to fast until they were 12; up to the same age neither sex could be prosecuted for murder. The implication of both statements would seem to be that children were only mentally and physically strong enough to do certain things once they reached the age of 12. These laws also suggest that until the age of 12 the lawmakers did not think it worthwhile to distinguish between boys and girls.

Grágás also implies that boys began to negotiate some legal rights at 12:

It is lawful for a son to prosecute a killing case if he is between twelve and sixteen winters old if the principal permits it, but he does not need to take over the case formally from anyone. (Dennis, Foote & Perkins 1980:157).

One manuscript also suggests that it was only people younger than 12 who could kill with impunity, suggesting perhaps that while lawmakers could conceive of people under 12 killing, they felt that they were not to be punished for it. Interestingly, the other manuscript of *Grágás* gives 16 as the age for this, suggesting that there was some ambiguity as to how 12 to 15 year olds should be treated (Þórarinsdóttir 2005: 117).

At 16, however, the laws say that males could do a number of more positive things: claim an inheritance; give their (widowed) mother in marriage; prosecute a case for a killing; and decide which household they were to live in. They could even take up cases retrospectively which had not been prosecuted on their behalf before they had reached 16 (Dennis, Foote & Perkins 2000:8, 1980:156, 157). For females the situation was different. At 16 a female could claim an inheritance and an income from properties she owned and, if widowed by the same age, then she could make the same decisions as a 16 year-old male. If as yet unmarried, however, these rights were not acquired by a female until she was 20 (Dennis, Foote & Perkins 2000:8, 1980:158). Thus the perspective we get from *Grágás* is that the transition from legal dependent to legal adult was different for the genders because, as this last stipulation shows, for women, gaining fuller access to the law directly depended on their having been married (Hansen 2002: 2-3; Þórarinsdóttir 2005:117). We have no clear indication as to what age was considered a minimum for a girl to get married. The implication is that some, if not many women, were expected to have been married before 16.

Age and social action in *Sagas of Icelanders*: an overview

While *Sagas of Icelanders* frequently use general terms for boy and girl which cover a wide age range (*sveinn* or *piltr* for boy and *mær* for girl), it is also true that they are often keen to point out children's chronological age, and the material available provides a much more nuanced view than the bold statements about the limited range of legal actions mentioned in *Grágás*. A search of the standard electronic corpus of *Sagas of Icelanders* makes it clear that every age up to and including 20 is mentioned at least once among the tens of references (Rögnvaldsson et al. 1996).[5] Often it is the ages of individuals who are not heavily involved in sagas that are mentioned, even if it is not particularly relevant to the storyline. Sometimes,

---

[5] Keyword searches were made for appropriate terms for ages and numbers such as *tvævetur* (two or two winters/years), *þrevetur* (three or three winters/years), *fimm* (five), *sex* (six) etc.

for example, it would seem that ages are given simply as chronological markers to explain precisely when certain things took place in absolute time. This would seem to form part of the chronological framework which saga writers used, connecting their relative, genealogical dating framework to known absolute dating markers, such as the arrival of Christianity in the year AD 1000. Yet, despite the blurring effect brought about by this and other, arguably erroneous, reasons for mentioning precise chronological ages, there are patterns among the ages given. Certain ages – always given in terms of the number of 'winters' – occur much more frequently than others and this must imply that at some level certain ages were seen as more significant. It might be argued that, as with many aspects of saga literature, children's ages conform to literary *topoi* or act as convenient or mnemonic devices but, even if they do, they must have some significance as readily-chosen points in an individual's life. The vast majority of references to children are to boys, which would seem to suggest a greater interest in the chronological age of males.

Boys in sagas are seen to do lots of things when they are three. At this age the precocious elite male is supposed to be *doing* something. Hörd, the main character in *Harðar saga*, is said to have been precocious (*bráðger*) in all respects at three except for the fact, for no obvious reason, that he was unable to walk (ch. 7). One of the few examples of a baptism of a child is that of the three year-old Hallr Thórarinsson (*Njáls saga*, ch. 102). Egill Skallagrímsson also makes his first significant (anti-) social action at the age of three (see below).

While it might look clichéd, 12 is also a commonly identified age and, again, this is when many elite males are identified as precociously doing adult, masculine things for the first time: Óláfr peacock in *Laxdæla saga* (ch. 16) gets noticed at the Alþing because of his fine dress and weapons; others are seen to reach phenomenal strength at precisely this age (Egill, Hörd); take part in local pitched battles (Thórodd Snorrason in *Eyrbyggja saga* ch. 44); take an active part in court (Brodd-Helgi in *Vopnfirðinga saga* ch. 2); and travel (Gellir Thorkelsson went to Norway with his father in *Laxdæla saga* ch. 74). In contrast, no boys of 10 or 11 are seen to be doing these things. The corpus of sagas identifies some boys as doing these same kinds of things at 13 or 14 but in far fewer numbers. Twelve, then, is not a typical age for boys to be acting as adult men, but it is the earliest age at which saga writers can even conceive of attributing fully adult behaviour to elite males.

There are just a handful of references to 13 and 14 year-olds, but more than ten references to boys of 15, and then few references to 16 year-olds and above. It is the case, for instance, that one 14 year old is identified as a killer (the exceptional Grettir, see below) while another takes joint control of the management of a household (*Laxdæla saga*, ch. 76), but such actions are far more common for 15 year olds. As with the age of 12, no specific action

seems to be identified as defining for 15 year olds, either as a normal or precocious action. 15 year-old males are identified as killing people (Thorgeirr in *Fóstbrœðra saga* ch. 3; Össur in *Flóamanna saga*, ch. 6) and one establishes his own farmstead (*Hrafnkels saga* chs 1-2). At the same time, however, some texts give the impression that at 15 and 16 years of age, boys were still just that – the term *sveinn* (boy, lad) is used of someone of this age just as it is used of much younger boys, and the word almost seems to imply some kind of inferiority to adult males (*Bjarnar saga Hítdælakappa*, ch. 32; *Grettis saga* ch. 48) – and another 15 year old was considered to be too young to take revenge (*Flóamanna saga* ch. 9). Ages beyond 15, however, rarely warrant a mention, which would suggest that action within the more public sphere was unremarkable by the time a male reached 16, 17 or 18. Indeed sagas lose complete interest in people's ages once they reach their upper teens: there are virtually no references to characters' ages again until they reach remarkable old age, such as 70 or 80.

The significance of the age of 12 and, to a lesser extent of 15, is emphasised just as much by the way some saga writers are deliberately *imprecise* about some other ages. On a handful of occasions writers specify that someone was 'one age or another'. In *Finnboga saga ramma,* the hero's son was 'six or seven' when he moved to his foster mother's home (ch. 35); three examples from *Egils saga* exist where someone of 'ten or eleven is identified: a king's son (Rögnvaldr, ch.57), a girl sitting on the floor in one scene in a longhouse (*Egils saga*, ch. 72) and a boy about whom more will be said later (Grím, son of Hegg, ch.40; see below); in *Eyrbyggja saga* a boy was 'a big lad and very manly' by the age of '13 or 14' (ch. 50). It might be significant that the fact that this kind of phrase, the 'age X or X+1' formula, refers to the ages six and seven, ten and eleven, and 13 and 14. They are not about the ages 12 and 15. Given that the ages 12 and 15 occur relatively frequently, and that neither are mentioned in this kind of way, this would seem to reinforce their significance and lessen the significance of ages about which writers were not precise. Perhaps these ambiguously worded statements of age represent ages of no specific significance. While six *or* seven is about the age that a few children are said to have been fostered out, and some historians see this as the age at which children were first fostered, the fact that age is so rarely associated with narratives about fostering makes it is difficult to read very much into this age bracket (Karlsson 2005:54-55). For references to ten or eleven, however, bearing in mind the apparent legal significance of 12, it could be that these indicate a writer thinking generally about someone who is still considered to be a child on the verge of the 12 to 16 years old bracket (cf Þórarinsdóttir 2005: 124). Males of 13 or 14 years might equally qualify as comfortably within that particular phase of social and legal status. In one sense, then, these apparently incidental statements about age seem to confirm the pattern of *Grágás*.

There is still a problem about the frequent references in sagas to precisely 15 as a young male's age. Unlike 12, it is not the age which *Grágás* specifies as one which brings with it changes in status, but it is the last year of an intermediate status. Here, it could be that we are seeing saga writers trying to show that their male heroes were doing 'adult' things before they might have been expected to. On the other hand, it seems strange that there are not more references to these heroes being precocious at 13 or 14. We could read these stories as showing that writers conceived of 15 as an age when boys became men, rather than 16.

Case Studies

Three well-known *Sagas of Icelanders* will now be used to examine the general picture of the phasing of childhood and how that relates to other issues of social status more widely. A famous incident in the lengthy *Njáls saga* also allows us a rare insight into one saga author's views on children of lower status and on marriage. *Egils saga Skallagrímssonar* traces the life of Egill Skallagrímsson through his childhood to his career as a successful warrior outside Iceland before his melancholic old age in Iceland. *Grettis saga Ásmundarsonar* follows the anti-social outlaw Grettir Ásmundarson, who seems to lurch from disaster to disaster as he misreads social situations and is simply unlucky. He eventually dies on an island off the north coast of Iceland, but is notorious for supposedly having survived longer than anyone else as an outlaw.

One of the most famous examples of some children's meaningful contribution to a saga narrative comes in *Njáls saga* (ch. 8). A lot has already been said about this particular episode because it is unique, memorable and relatively lengthy for an episode involving children (e.g. Hansen 2002: 7-10, Jakobsson 2003). Here it will be used to highlight how it demonstrates that usually it is only elite children who are talked about in most saga narratives. The story involves Hrút Herjólfsson, a man cursed because his penis was so large that he could no longer have sexual intercourse. The result of this curse was that Hrút was divorced by his wife. On their way back from court, Hrút and his brother stay at a farm. In the evening while they and other men are talking in what must be the main living space of the longhouse, some children who lived at the farm played a game which saw them re-enact Hrútr's recent past. While one boy pretends to be Hrútr, the other plays his rival and former father-in-law, Mörd gígja, and presumably the girl was supposed to play Hrútr's former wife. The episode is humiliating for Hrút because it shows just how public his business is; Hrútr's brother is instantly so angered by the children's behaviour that he hits one of them. Hrút, however, rather than chastise the children, gives one of the boys a gold ring, which is seen as a sign of his magnanimity.

This episode illustrates a little more than simply that children played in Icelandic farmhouses and that, in this case, Hrútr's sex life (or lack of it) was public knowledge. The boys at least – we do not know about the girl because we are not told – are not simply children, but are called *veizlusveinar*, boys who are from poor families, and who must be being cared for at the large farm of Lundur where the scene takes place. These unidentified children of unspecified age are not the well-behaved children of Iceland's elite, of the class of the saga writers, but the ill-behaved children of people on the lowest social rung who cannot run their own farms. The saga is clearly making two points here which have a literary function, but also relate to a reality. That the poor children at a farm in western Iceland know about Hrútr's humiliating circumstances so soon after the events, is to emphasise the completeness of that humiliation. For these children to know about Hrút's misfortune, everyone in Iceland, of all social statuses, must be talking about it and talking about it in front of children (Jakobsson 2003: 8-9). Yet there is also something unacceptable about the children's behaviour here which, perhaps, the saga's writer would only want to see as the act of the children of lower social status. Arguably, only children who were unaware of Hrút's presence or who were not sufficiently aware of how to behave in front of guests would have played the game they played where they did. At the same time, the whole episode serves as a comment on the adults involved: the people of Lundur have been rather incautious in gossiping about their guests; this brings out a violent, but perhaps defensible, reaction in Höskuld while Hrút demonstrates his equanimity. A story about children therefore only occurs here because it serves to say something about the adults involved.

The much-discussed Egill Skallagrímsson represents one of a number of unreasonable saga characters, the story of whom we can use as some kind of guide for medieval conceptions of appropriate behaviour according to a child's age. Egill is a bad example and does exactly what is *not* to be expected of normal children and of children of high social status. Further to Ármann Jakobsson's arguments about troublesome children in sagas being seen as the product of paternal indifference, other points emerge about saga writers' perceptions of appropriate behaviour for children and on the care of children (Jakobsson 2003). Rather like the incident from *Droplaugarsona saga*, it is tempting to condemn the stories about Egill's childhood as simply comedic, but arguably they still say something about the process of growing up. In this case they also represent the part of a biography of an ancestor of some important later medieval Icelanders: Egill is associated with the wealthy farm of Borg, the home of Snorri Sturluson (d.1241), a major political figure, and a known writer who has often been suggested as the saga's author (e.g. Tulinius 2004).

At three years old Egill is already unusual. He is depicted as precocious, taking part in conversations on an equal level with adults, some of whom already view him as a social liability. When Egill's family is invited to feast at his maternal grandfather's farm, Egill's father decides that, while Egill's two older sisters can go, Egill should stay at home. His father claims:

> You don't know how to behave among men when there's heavy drinking. You're not all that easy to deal with, even though you haven't drunk.[6]

Egill is angry about being left behind and so he immediately finds himself a draught-horse (*eykhest*) – rather than a horse more suited for riding – and tries to get to the social event of his own accord. Egill gets there eventually, after the best part of a day's riding, because he does not follow the right route. When he gets there his grandfather is pleased to welcome him despite his father's misgivings about his social skills. Egill joins in the beer-fuelled poetry competition which is going on, reciting a complex poem for which his grandfather gives him a snack as a reward (sea-snails and a duck's egg). The episode ends with the saga saying explicitly that there is nothing more to say about this particular day's events.

What are we to make of this account of an eloquent, poetry-reciting, horse-riding three year-old? First, it seems safe to conclude that no one who read or told such a story probably ever thought that any three year-old was ever likely to do any of these things. The story is really more likely to be demonstrating that Egill was remarkable precisely because he did things which no one could imagine a three year-old doing (cf. Jakobsson 2003: 15). At the same time Egill's father (and mother?) are made to look uncaring by leaving their youngest child at home. As we learn later on (ch. 40), Egill had had a foster-mother, but in this episode it almost looks as if Egill is being left on his own at Borg. Despite his being competent at some things, Egill is seen to be incompetent in his choice of riding horse – again, there is no adult to guide him here (or prevent him from leaving home) which makes it look like Egill is completely unsupervised. While the text wants to demonstrate that Egill's father knew that his son was trouble, the story seems to indicate that it would have been better to look after Egill than not to.

Egill commits his first truly public misdemeanour at the age of seven at a local 'games' (*leikir*), the sort of regular social event where local men challenged each other to wrestling and other sports. On that fateful day, almost everything about Egill's involvement and the behaviour of other children is a model of impropriety. Egill was taken to the games by being given a lift there on horseback by a friend Thórd, aged 15, who was the son of Grani from the farm Granastadir; Thórd is said to have been fond of Egill. Once at the games Egill joined lots of other small boys (*smásveinar*) who decided to organise

their own separate version of the adults' games. The boys are making the decisions rather than any adults. All the boys pair up to take part in the game. Egill gets paired with the son of Hegg from Heggsstadir, who is said to be ten or 11 and strong for his age. Egill gets beaten at the game by the much older boy and he retaliates by hitting him with the stick used in the game, only for the older boy to throw him down. Egill then turns to Thórd Granason, who gives Egill an axe so that he can avenge the slight against him. Egill kills the son of Hegg, which in turn leads to a fight between the adult male relatives on each side and the deaths of seven of them, including Hegg from Heggsstadir.

Clearly Egill's behaviour marks him out as wholly unusual, yet there is an interesting ambiguity about Thórd Granason. At 15 Thórd's age makes his status ambiguous – he is on the cusp of adulthood – but giving Egill a weapon is the wrong thing to do. Thórd's behaviour could, as in some other examples above, be seen as the kind of 'incorrect' behaviour of a youth of low-to-middling social status. To appreciate fully the significance of the relationship between Egill and both Grani and Thórd, however, we have to investigate saga conventions and what a local, medieval audience of the saga might have seen in the connections between the boys. Grani from Granastadir, for example, ranks as one of the many fringe characters who come from farms we know to be of inferior status in the Middle Ages according to later sources. The text only ascribes Grani with the status of Egill's household servants, rather than running his own farm which might make him someone of moderate status (ch. 28). Despite this connection, Grani is not really seen as tightly bound to Egill's family – unlike many other people in the district, he had not been given land by Egill's father when the area was first colonised. We have a rather mixed picture of Grani's and Thórd's status, although they were clearly inferior to Egill's family. In this respect Egill can be seen to be hanging out with the wrong crowd, with his social inferiors. Similar things might be said about the inappropriateness of Egill having anything to do with the people from Heggsstadir. Heggsstadir and its occupants were as equally insignificant as Granastadir and, being 50km away and in an entirely different district from Skallagrím's farm, the Heggsstadir household would have had no social or economic connections with the men from Borg. Thus, while Egill is inherently difficult to cope with as a precocious and aggressive boy, it takes the disinterest of adults and the involvement of Egill's social inferiors for things to go wrong.

Turning to Grettir, the infamous outlaw and subject of *Grettis saga Ásmundarsonar*, we see that Grettir's childhood is almost equally notorious as showing early evidence of his social dysfunction. As a child, Grettir is put to work around the farm by his father, but he conforms to a pattern identified elsewhere whereby sagas see a son's bad relations with his father and over-

---

[6] "'Ekki skaltu fara," segir Skalla-Grímr, "því að þú kannt ekki fyrir þér að vera í fjölmenni, þar er drykkjur eru miklar, er þú þykir ekki góður viðskiptis, að þú sért ódrukkinn.'" *Egils saga Skallagrímssonar*, ch. 31. (Nordal 1933).

protection from a mother as a problem (Jakobsson 2003: 18). The saga says that:

> Grettir grew up at Bjarg until he was ten years old; then he began to come on rather. Ásmund suggested he did some kind of work (*Grettis saga* ch. 14).[7]

First, Grettir is given the task of looking after the farm's geese and chickens, but he fails in doing this. He loses his temper with the birds, killing goslings and maiming the adult geese. Next, Grettir's father asks him to massage his back when his father is sitting indoors by the fire. Grettir cannot do this either, and in another fit of temper scratches his father with a wool-comb. Last, Grettir is to work outside again, looking after his father's favourite mare. Watching over the horse in poor weather irritates Grettir and in the end he cuts her down her sides with a knife.

Although there is nothing particularly typical about Grettir's reaction to being asked to do chores, his reactions perhaps suggest that he feels his father is treating him too much like a child. Nevertheless, we do get some sense of what work might have been deemed appropriate for some boys of ten: looking after geese was also a task given to children in later medieval England, for example (Orme 2001: 308).[8] The writer also seems to think that all of these tasks would have been undertaken before Grettir was 14, by which stage he was causing trouble at local social gatherings by starting fights during ball games (*knattleikr*). Partly this chronology is there to make the story of Grettir's life easy to follow, but it also makes sense in the context of other sagas where generally it is older boys who take part in such local games (and not the likes of Egill).

While chronological age clearly matters for younger males, it was suggested above that it was less important for females. A couple of examples will serve to investigate the way age and social status are used for dramatic effect in some saga episodes relating to marriage. The first story comes from *Njáls saga* chapter 34 where Thráinn Sigfússon marries the 14 year-old Thorgerd, the daughter of Hallgerd 'Long legs' at the latter's marriage to Gunnar Hámundarson, her third husband. Once at the wedding feast, Thráinn is immediately infatuated with the very beautiful young woman (*fríðus kvenna*), 14 year-old Thorgerd. He is neither unperturbed by the reputation of Hallgerd as a trouble-maker, nor by the youth of his potential bride. He divorces his wife on the spot before proposing to

Thorgerd, or rather putting forward a proposal of a marriage to her grandfather who ultimately defers to others who in turn agree to the match.

There are lots of things one might read into this episode. Clearly there is a tragic element to it in that the men who decide that this is an appropriate match drag the hapless Thráinn into the dispute which is to follow. Thráinn is now tied to the ill-fated Gunnarr by marriage: Gunnarr and Thráinn are both later killed as part of the main dispute in the saga. Other commentators might also point to this case as one of those marriages where a girl's choice of husband is made for her with tragic consequences; Hallgerd had her betrothed and no one dissented. Yet at the same time it might be argued that part of the problem is the youth of the girl because this is one of the few examples where the age of a girl being married is mentioned. Certainly *Grágás* does envisage girls being married before 16, but this might still be a moral tale about the girl's youth. The text says that neither Hallgerd nor Thorgerd objected to the marriage but the rest of the saga makes clear that Hallgerd is disruptive and brings about men's deaths by means of her influence over men. Thorgerd not having objections might not be quite the same as her actively desiring to be married to an older man whom she has not even met.

Equally, the same point might be made about Thráinn as has been made above about Grani and Hegg and their low social status. Although Thráinn is apparently wealthy because he is said to be rich, this might be short term wealth, perhaps only in terms of the number of livestock he owns; the term used to describe him (*auðigr at fé*) might imply that. He comes from the farm Grjótá which, to judge from later sources, was not actually a very impressive farm and certainly not the kind of place with which one might expect the more obviously wealthy Gunnarr and Hallgerd to associate (*Jarðabók* I:155). Thráinn might be seen as 'new money' rather than someone of real substance. Thráinn's incautious approach towards his choice of wives equates with his likely perceived social station and rash behaviour: he would have been better not to have made a snap judgement about marrying a young and seemingly not very independent wife.

A less complicated, but still disastrous marriage, is the first marriage of the 15 year-old Gudrún Ósvífsdóttir in *Laxdæla saga* (ch. 34). Like Thorgerd's mother Hallgerd, Gudrún has several marriages, most of which do not have happy conclusions. Her first is to Thorvald Garpsdalur-chieftain. *Laxdæla saga* is more explicit in saying that Gudrún is not consulted about the marriage and that there is a difference in wealth between Gudrún's family and Thorvald's (despite his name). What should happen in material terms in the event of a divorce is set out clearly in the process of arranging the marriage and, not unexpectedly, that divorce takes place. After only two years Gudrún declared herself divorced and received half of the couple's property. Here, as with the previous

---

[7] 'Grettir óx upp at Bjargi, þar til hann var tíu vetra gamall; hann tók heldr við at gangask. Ásmundr bað hann starfa nökkurt.' *Grettis saga Ásmundarsonar*, ch. 14 (Jónsson 1936: 37).

[8] It seems possible that this episode also shows Grettir as undertaking tasks more appropriate for a child on a large, wealthy farm. Geese and chickens are very rarely mentioned in sagas or other medieval Icelandic sources as searches in Rögnvaldsson et al. 1996 suggest. Compare for references to geese in *Diplomatarium Islandicum* II: 259; III 678, 738, 776.

example, there is a sense that the marriage is ill-advised, partly because of the way it was arranged and partly because of the difference in status of the couple. But again the text is explicit about the female spouse at the time of the marriage which suggests that the writer and their peers saw it as inappropriate for women (*kvenna* – the word used in both texts) under 16 to be married off.

In western Europe in the later Middle Ages it seems to have been the case that for most people puberty began at 12 to 14 (Orme 2001:329; Bullough & Campbell 1980:323-4). For Iceland we might suspect that the chances of people suffering from malnutrition were higher than elsewhere, which might delay physical development, but there is not much evidence to guide us on this. Thus saga writers may or may not have been thinking of Gudrún and Thorgerd as having been of child-bearing age when they got married.

Conclusions

There is a surprising amount – at least to this author – of general agreement between the legal and the narrative sources for 13th century Iceland in the way they see the transition to adulthood. This study is not a complete one in the sense that it does not cover all genres of saga, but the corpus of sagas covered is substantial, and looking at other genres would not add many more examples.

Chronological age was actually of great concern to 13th century Iceland's literary elite when it came to teenagers' (to use an anachronistic term) move into adult society. Even if we cannot believe every claim made in sagas about a particular hero's accomplishments at particular ages, we can perceive a general concern that boys should have been remembered as doing things at the ages of 12 to 16. The higher instances of boys identified as being 12 and 15 would suggest that these were more memorable ages, in terms of storytelling, and in the way people wished to represent social action. For 12 it is likely that this was considered the earliest age at which boys could begin to enter the adult social arena; 15 probably signifies an age at which boys were on the cusp of full adulthood. Girls' chronological ages are far less often stated, but we should not underestimate their importance: in key saga episodes their chronological age was deliberately stated. Influencing all portrayals of people under 20 were saga writers' perceptions of class. Here, the representation of childhood provides a very sharp reminder of social divisions in a society where those divisions are sometimes less obvious than elsewhere.

Looking at Iceland and its medieval literature in a broader perspective, while Iceland will always look slightly odd to other medievalists, let alone any other scholars, it has to be hoped that the study of childhood in this society can feed back into wider debates. Few other medieval societies have such a substantial body of medieval narratives with which to explore many of the topics which have been looked at so far by scholars interested in childhood. It would be nice to think too that Icelandic scholars will soon be in a position to study childhood outside Iceland rather than being on the receiving end of the perceived wisdom of foreign scholars. The development of a stronger interface between Old Norse and/or Viking Studies and the rest of pre-modern historical, archaeological and literary studies can only be beneficial for all concerned.

Acknowledgements

I am extremely grateful to the editors of this volume, Gillian Shepherd and Sally Crawford, for suggesting valuable improvements to this article, as well as to Mary Harlow and Christina Lee; to the audience and participants in a Leeds International Medieval Congress session in 2005 where an earlier version of this paper was presented; to the IAA research seminar participants, and to other colleagues in the Institute of Archaeology and Antiquity and the Department of Medieval History at Birmingham University whose questions and observations have also helped shape my views. Errors of fact and interpretation remain the author's responsibility.

Bibliography

Arnórsdóttir, A.S. (2005): 'Nokkrar hugleiðingar um kynbundið uppeldi á miðöldum' in Á. Jakobsson, Á. and T. Tulinius (eds), *Miðaldabörn*, 101-111. Reykjavík.

Bragason, Ú. (2005): 'Sagas of Contemporary History (Sturlunga saga): Texts and Research' in R. McTurk (ed.), *A Companion to Old Norse-Icelandic Literature and Culture*, 427-46. Oxford.

Bullough, V. and C. Campbell (1980): 'Female Longevity and Diet in the Middle Ages', *Speculum* 55: 317-25.

Callow, C. (2006): 'First steps towards an archaeology of children in Iceland', *Archaeologia Islandica* 5: 55-74.

Classen, A. (ed.) (2005): *Childhood in the Middle Ages and the Renaissance*. Berlin and New York.

Clover, C.J. (1988): 'The politics of scarcity: notes on the sex ratio in early Scandinavia', *Scandinavian Studies* 60: 147–188.

Crawford, S. (1999): *Childhood in Anglo-Saxon England*. Stroud.

Dennis, A., Foote P. and Perkins R. (1980-2000): *Laws of Early Iceland. Grágás I-II*. Winnipeg.

Diplomatarium Islandicum. Íslenzkt fornbréfasafn 834-1600, I-XVI. Copenhagen and Rekjavík.

Egilsdóttir, Á. (2005): 'Kolbítur verður karlmaður' in Á. Jakobsson and T. Tulinius (eds), *Miðaldabörn*, 87-99. Reykjavík.

Finsen, V. (1852-70): *Grágás. Islærndernes Lovbog I Fristatens Tid*. Copenhagen.

Gelsinger, B. (1981): *Icelandic enterprise: commerce and economy in the Middle Ages*. Columbia.

Halsall, G. (1996): 'Female status and power in early Merovingian central Austrasia: the burial evidence', *Early Medieval Europe* 5(1): 1-24.

Hansen, A. (2002): 'Representations of children in the Icelandic sagas'. Paper given at the Sagas and Society conference, Borgarnes, 5th-9th September 2002. http://w210.ub.uni-tuebingen.de/portal/sagas/

Hansen, A. (2005): 'Börn og auður á Íslandi á 13. öld' in Á. Jakobsson and T. Tulinius (eds), *Miðaldabörn*, 27-35. Reykjavík.

Helgason, A., Hickey, E., Goodacre, S., Bosnes, V., Stefansson, K., Ward, R. and Sykes, B. (2001): 'mtDNA and the Islands of the North Atlantic: Estimating the Proportions of Norse and Gaelic Ancestry', *American Journal of Human Genetics* 68: 723–737.

Hreinsson, V. et al. (1997): *The Complete Sagas of Icelanders*. Reykjavík.

Jakobsson, Á. (2003): 'Troublesome children in the Sagas of Icelanders', *Saga-Book of the Viking Society* 27: 5-24.

Jakobsson, Á. (2005): 'Ástin á tímum þjóðveldisins' in Á. Jakobsson and T. Tulinius (eds), *Miðaldabörn*, 63-85. Reykjavík.

Jakobsson, Á. and Tulinius T. (eds) (2005): *Miðaldabörn*. Reykjavík.

James, E. (1988): *The Franks*. Oxford.

Jarðabók Árna Magnússonar og Páls Vídalins I-XII (1913-90). Reykjavík.

Jóhannesson, J. (ed.) (1950): *Austfirðinga sögur*. Reykjavík.

Jónsson, G. (ed.) (1936): *Grettis saga Ásmundarsonar. Bandamanna saga*. Reykjavík.

Karlsson, G. (2004): *Goðamenning. Staða og áhrif goðorðsmanna í þjóðveldi Íslendinga*. Reykjavík.

Karlsson, G. (2005): 'Barnfóstur á Íslandi að fornu' in Á. Jakobsson and T. Tulinius (eds), *Miðaldabörn*, 37-61. Reykjavík.

Kristjánsdóttir, S. (2004): *The Awakening of Christianity in Iceland. Discovery of Timber Church and Graveyard at Þórarinsstaðir in Seyðisfjörður. Part I and II.* GOTARC serie no 31. Gothenburg.

Kristjánsson, L. (1980-6): *Íslenzkir sjávarhættir* I-V. Reykjavík.

Mundal, E. (2005): 'Barn skal eigi lata deyja handa millim', in Á. Jakobsson and T. Tulinius (eds), *Miðaldabörn*, 17-25. Reykjavík.

Miller, W.I. (1990): *Bloodtaking and Peacemaking. Feud, Law and Society in Saga Iceland*. Chicago.

Nordal, S. (ed.) (1933): *Egils saga Skalla-Grímssonar*. Reykjavík.

Orme, N. (2001): *Medieval Children*. New Haven and London.

Rögnvaldsson, E., Kristjánsdóttir, B., Ingólfsdóttir G. and Thorsson Ö. (1996): *Íslendinga Sögur. Ordstöðulykill og texti*. CD-ROM. Reykjavík.

Shahar, S. (1990): *Childhood in the Middle Ages*. London.

Sigurðsson, G. (2000): *Gaelic Influence in Iceland. Historical and Literary Contacts: A Survey of Research*. 2nd edition. Reykjavík.

Sigurðsson, J.V. (1991): 'Börn og gamalmenni á þjóðveldisöld' in G. Karlsson and H. Þorláksson (eds), *Yfir Íslansála. Afmælisrit til heiðurs Magnúsi Stefánssyni sextugum 25. desember 1991*, 111-30. Reykjavík.

Sigurðsson, J.V. (1999): *Chieftains and Power in the Icelandic Commonwealth*. Odense.

Sveinsson, E. Ól. (ed.) (1934): *Laxdæla saga*. Reykjavík.

Thoroddsen, Þ. (1911): *Lýsing Íslands II*. Copenhagen.

Tulinius, T. (2004): *Skáldið í skriftinni – Snorri Sturluson og Egils saga*. Reykjavík.

Vésteinsson, O. (2000): *The Christianization of Iceland. Priests, Power and Social Change 1000-1300*. Oxford.

Vésteinsson, O. (2007): 'Communities of Dispersed Settlements: Social Organization at the Ground Level in Tenth- to Thirteenth-Century Iceland' in W. Davies, G. Halsall and A. Reynolds (eds), *People and Space in Middle Ages, 300-1300*, 87-113. Turnhout.

Whaley, D. (2000): 'A useful past: historical writing in medieval Iceland', in M. Clunies Ross (ed.), *Old Icelandic Literature and Society*, 161-202. Cambridge.

Wicker, N. (1998): 'Selective Female Infanticide as Partial Explanation for the Dearth of Women in Viking Age Scandinavia' in G. Halsall (ed), *Violence and Society in the Early Medieval West*, 205-21. Woodbridge.

Þórarinsdóttir, B. (2005): 'Hirðin og hallærisplanið' in Á. Jakobsson and T. Tulinius (eds), *Miðaldabörn*, 113-135. Reykjavík.

CHAPTER 6

HAD THEY NO SHAME?
MARTIAL, STATIUS AND ROMAN SEXUAL ATTITUDES TOWARDS SLAVE CHILDREN

Niall McKeown

It is at the intersection of the concepts of slavery and childhood that some of the clearest and most radical differences between Roman culture and our own become apparent. We are told that the first emperor Augustus kept a troop of little boys and girls to play with (see Suetonius *Life of Augustus* 83, cf. Aurelius Victor *Epitome* 1.22). It is possible to read Suetonius' comments non-sexually. Aurelius Victor's are less innocent (*serviebat ... libidini*), but one could dismiss them as titillating gossip, suggesting that such behaviour, rather than being general, was counter to the social norms of the writer's time. Aurelius Victor, however, wrote centuries after Augustus' death. Further, if he believes that ordinary Romans disapproved of Augustus' preferences we shall see that this may be as much if not more because of the extravagance associated with the buying of expensive pretty slaves as with any concern over the well-being of the children themselves. We need to take the story, and its implications, seriously.

On one level, *anything* that tells us about Roman slave children is significant. Walter Scheidel has suggested that perhaps 75-80% of Roman slaves were themselves the children of slaves (Scheidel 1997). Slave children were, therefore, a ubiquitous presence. The subject of the sexual use by Roman slaveowners of their slave children is not one to be approached lightly, however. Much of the material is painful to read from a modern viewpoint. In addition, the whole field can be exceedingly complex, lying at the intersection of three often largely separate intellectual universes: Roman childhood studies, Roman slave studies and the study of Roman sexuality. Interestingly the evidence we shall examine has perhaps been given least stress by students of slavery. This might be partly due to the nature of the subject, hardly suitable for text-book treatments of Roman social life. We shall see also that it can sometimes be highly difficult to interpret. I write, however, precisely as a student of ancient slavery, and the importance of this topic to my field will quickly become apparent.

I will concentrate on a small number of writers working at approximately the same time: the end of the first century AD. My main source, Martial, began publishing at roughly the same time as the inauguration of the Colosseum. About 1500 of his epigrams have survived. These are short poems, often (though not always) with a comic or satiric intent, sometimes with a very explicit sexual content (see, e.g. Sullivan 1991). Martial was

renowned during his lifetime and wrote for an educated audience, looking to patronage from Roman aristocrats.

In *Epigrams* 5.34 Martial commends a child's soul, now departed for the underworld, to his parents, who had died some time before. The girl, Erotion, is described as his '*delicias*'. Shackleton-Bailey translates the term as 'pet' (Shackleton Bailey 1993: 385, cf. Slater 1974, Pomeroy 1992: 46-48, Rawson 2003: 261-3, Bernstein 2005: 267). Van Dam suggests the term implies something between a lap-dog and a fool (Van Dam 1984: 72-73, though that seems somewhat perverse given the emotions expressed in this and many of the other poems which use the term). Even Van Dam recognised that it could be used as a term of endearment, as it is, notably, on inscriptions (Van Dam 1984: 73, cf. Nielsen 1990, with Laes 2003: 305-14). Martial goes on to tell us that Erotion was not yet six years old. Martial finishes his short poem thus (I use Shackleton Bailey's translations here and below):

> Let her now play and frolic with her old patrons and lispingly chatter my name. Not hard be the turf that covers her soft bones, be not heavy upon her, earth; she is not heavy upon you.

Epigrams 10.61, published something like a decade later, refers to Erotion's grave. The poet asks anyone who might one day own the land to 'make annual offering to her tiny ghost'.

Perhaps directing such sentiments towards a slave might surprise a modern reader, perhaps not. One doubts whether they would have surprised a Roman as the poems form a sequence of such poems in Martial's work (cf. *Epigrams* 1.88, 1.101), suggesting that there was nothing ironic in the sentiment itself.

Epigrams 5.37 is more of a problem. It was published at the same time as 5.34 but it adopts a rather different approach. It is a longer poem, and the first half is a hymn to an initially unnamed girl (*puella*), praising her voice 'softer than aged swans', whose hair 'surpassed the fleece of a Baetic flock', whose breath was 'fragrant as a Paestan rose bed' etc. Only after the description are we informed that this is Erotion, less than six years old. The poem then apparently changes direction. A 'friend', Paetus, has (allegedly) criticised the poet for grieving so much over the death of a 'little slave girl' (*vernulae*: a home bred slave). Paetus has lost his wife, something evidently much more serious. Martial finishes acidly by remarking how brave Paetus is to go on with such pain: he keeps on living, having come into a fortune. The implication is that Paetus only married his wife for her money and isn't too worried at her loss.

This ending gives an obvious satiric intent to the poem. Does that satiric intent undercut the feelings for Erotion? Given that Martial also wrote poems praising animals (e.g. a puppy, *Epigrams* 1.109), one might suspect that the depth of feeling for the girl might not be quite as it initially seems (see, e.g. Watson 1992: 266). While I would agree with scholars such as Thévanaz (2002), that determining the 'reality' of a Roman poet's emotions is somewhat difficult, we should not, nevertheless, dismiss the possibility of a real bond between master and slave child simply because of the existence of 'pet epitaphs' (see Pomeroy 2003, cf. Statius *Silvae* 2.4 on the death of a parrot). Poems such as Martial *Epigrams* 1.109 actually mirror the epitaph of a person: they 'humanise' the pet. Emotions towards people seem to be affecting the attitude towards animals rather than vice versa. In any case, we shouldn't dismiss the possibilities of deep feelings towards pets. Finally, if 'pet' epitaphs are to undermine the reality of the emotion of epitaphs towards slaves, they should do the same to the epitaphs for free people we find in Roman poetry, something seldom if ever argued.

There is, however, what might be described as a 'rhetoric of embarrassment' involved in grieving over the death of the slave child. In Martial *Epigrams* 5.37 the poet implies that Paetus will despise him for such feelings. This idea actually appears in a range of Roman writings (e.g. Cicero *Letters to Atticus* 1.12.4, Pliny the Younger *Letters* 8.1). Grieving for a slave favourite fits well, however, with some of the more 'humanitarian' elements expressed in contemporary Roman philosophy (see Manning 1989, though cf. Bradley 1994: ch.7 and Garnsey 1996: 153ff on the issue of the impact of such expressions). Apologising for the grief may be nothing more than a mechanism to draw attention to it (and, by extension, to one's decency). We need not take the alleged embarrassment seriously: after all these writers chose to advertise their feelings, and we have to ask why.

Most commentators therefore think that the feelings for Erotion are genuine (or at least represent acceptable feelings to a Roman audience), even if they do find it odd that Martial would use the Erotion character to make his satiric point about Paetus (e.g. Kenney 1964, cf. Watson 1992). Some have argued that Erotion must have been Martial's daughter (by a slave woman) because of the emotions he describes having for her, though the argument seems somewhat circular (Bell 1984). We cannot say if there was any parental relationship. The language of the poem might argue against this. It echoes that found in Roman erotic literature (indeed, the name Erotion may be a hint in itself: as with the other poems of Martial we cannot assume that any individual character is

real). The term *puella* can mean either girl or girlfriend and for much of the poem the reader might well have assumed it meant the latter. Is 5.37 therefore an erotic poem? Some have argued against this. Patricia Watson, for example, has suggested that Romans would not have been able to imagine a physical relationship between an adult male and a five year old girl. Indeed she argues that Martial withholds Erotion's name and age for so long because he is playing with his audience's expectations, hoping to shock them with their own assumptions of what has been going on (Watson 1992: 62-63). A modern audience would certainly feel queasy at the implication of physical love between an adult and a small slave child. The point at issue, of course, is would a Roman audience?

There is, in fact, a whole sequence of poems by Martial explicitly stating a sexual interest in children, albeit almost exclusively male and of a slightly greater age than Erotion. The poems, on occasion, leave little to the imagination (for example *Epigrams* 4.42, 8.46, 9.22, 9.56, 10.98, 11.22 and 11.43). Martial expresses jealousy of those Romans who can buy (and use) very pretty boys. As he put it in 1.58 when he hears of someone who can pay an exorbitant price for a pretty male slave 'my cock is hurt and grumbles about me to myself'.

The Romans had laws detailing how a father might take action against those who misused his free children (e.g. *Digest of Roman Law* 47.11.1.2, 48.6.3.4). Laws protecting slaves, however, are prominent only in their absence. The lack of Roman legislation, particularly with respect to slaves, probably shouldn't surprise, however. Roman legislation operated in a more restricted field than modern law, with a rather stronger distinction between what was public and what was private. In addition, the amount of legislation concerning any form of mistreatment of slaves was comparatively minor (see Watson 1987).

What of non-legal sources? Approximately a century after Martial, Artemidorus produced a work detailing the interpretation of dreams. In it (*Oneirocriticon* 1.78) he suggests that dreaming of having sex with one's own son below the age of six was a very bad omen. How much that tells us about general sexual preferences is, however, somewhat moot.

Depictions of sex in Roman art (see Pollini 1999) and from other literature (for example Strato, *Palatine Anthology* 12.4) suggests, however, that Roman tastes may have been largely directed towards boys between the age 12 and 20, pubescent but without much facial or bodily hair. In this context it should be noted that the acceptable Roman age for marriage (perhaps 12 and above) was also much lower than that generally accepted today in Western Europe. It has further been suggested that physical development may also have been more important in assessing sexual 'maturity' than calendar age (Laes 2006: 247-8). Curiously from a modern perspective, the chief concern was with the *upper* age limit with regards to boys (note the evidence on the 'abandonment' of slave favourites, e.g. Martial 10.66, or Statius *Silvae* 3.4.56-57). The lower limit may ultimately have been a question of aesthetics. Why the greater concern with the upper limit? This may give us a powerful insight into Roman attitudes towards sex. The current orthodoxy is that Roman sexuality was highly phallocentric and hierarchical (see, e.g. Williams 1999, cf. Richlin 1983). Sex was a question of whom men could insert their penises into. All other forms of sexuality were viewed as deviant to a greater or lesser extent. In this context, consorting with a fully grown (and hairy) man behind closed doors might create speculation of who was really doing what to whom, as Martial hints at himself (e.g. Martial *Epigrams* 7.62).

The social importance of penetration (and a corresponding contempt/fear of being penetrated) leads on to a further vital point about slavery, sexuality and children. The Romans adopted or adapted much of the culture of Greek society. That society, however, had been willing to accept pederastic relationships between citizens and the male children of citizens. Adults took the role of the *erastes*, chasing the young boy, the *eromenos*. The *erastes* was (apparently) allowed to penetrate the *eromenos* (for a range of opinions, see, e.g. Dover 1989, Halperin 1990, Winkler 1989). When a Greek boy became an adult, he could no longer decently take on the role of the *eromenos*, but he could take his turn as an *erastes*. It has been argued, however, that Romans were unwilling for even juvenile future citizens to be penetrated. Male and female Romans were protected from penetration outside of marriage (even if, as Christian Laes and others have rightly pointed out, there may have been a gap between ideology and reality).

If Roman citizens were denied access to the bodies of young citizens, it has been argued, the only socially acceptable conduits for pederastic or paedophiliac feelings were slaves. Indeed some modern commentators have gone so far to argue:

> Indeed, in the eyes of the law slaves were property pure and simple, and in general neither the law nor popular morality had anything to say about how a man used his own property (Williams 1999: 30).

Under this scenario, there would be nothing wrong in whatever Martial chose to do with Erotion or any other male or female slave child. There would be nothing for a Roman audience to be shocked about. This interests me as, if true, it runs counter to what one finds in Roman discussions of the physical treatment of slaves. There we find, if not legal regulation (probably of secondary importance to social attitudes), then at least *implied* social norms: limits of the acceptable and unacceptable. While Romans regarded slaves as chattels and could be vicious in their treatment and punishment of them, a number of

ancient sources hint at the norms of physical treatment. For example, in Plautus' comic play *Pseudolus* a character called Ballio is portrayed negatively, partly because he beats his slaves for no good reason (133ff). A wealthy slave owner called Vedius Pollio was pilloried for ordering a particularly hideous death for a slave who had accidentally dropped and broken an expensive goblet (Seneca *On Anger* 3.40.2-5, cf. Dio Cassius 54.23.1-2). The aristocrat Pliny the Younger seems to have gone to some lengths to portray himself as a kind master (Pliny the Younger *Letters* 4.10, 5.6, 5.19, 6.3, 8.16, 8.1, 8.19, see McKeown 2007). Whether or not such sentiments reflect reality, they remain important as sentiments and ideals. When the biographer Plutarch found that the grand old Roman Cato the Elder wanted to sell off sick and old slaves rather than feed them, he felt this was the action of an overstrict personality (Plutarch *Cato the Elder* 5).

With regard to the exercise of physical force upon slaves we can, therefore, find the point at which Romans might become uncomfortable: where they felt treatment strayed into (unjustifiable) mistreatment. It doesn't mean that the life of a Roman slave was anything less than unpleasant, but there were at least informal limits. From a modern perspective, one might have expected some comments about the sexual use and abuse of children too. Why can't we see them?

If Patricia Watson is correct one could, of course, argue that we *have* seen it, precisely in Martial *Epigrams* 5.37. For her the shock value of the poem comes, as we have noted, from Erotion's age. In the absence of any real supporting evidence, however, it is difficult to see how one might go about proving such a position.

Even if Watson were correct, however, it is still clear that Martial assumes that sex with adolescent male slaves is entirely acceptable. But if Martial celebrates the sexual (ab)use of '*pueri delicati*', how far can we assume his poems reflect more general social attitudes? Martial occasionally warned his readers that they should not assume that the morals of his poems were his own (e.g. *Epigrams* 11.15). He is not, however, implying that all his poems are meant to shock, and we cannot be sure which he means. Even if we could make the extra step and conclude that his references to sex with child slaves were designed to shock, we would, even then, have to ask whether this was because sex with young slaves was wrong, or because it was supposed be kept behind closed doors and not discussed publicly.

It seems clear, however, that Martial's penchant for young slave boys is not part of some counter-cultural persona. Firstly, there is an argument from within Martial's own work. The name Zoilus appears a number of times within Martial's poems (*Epigrams* 2.16, 2.19, 2.42, 2.58, 2.81, 3.29, 3.82, 4.77, 5.79, 6.91, 11.12, 11.30, 11.37, 11.54, 11.85, 11.92, 12.54). He represents the kind of ex-slave who had the temerity not only to achieve freedom but also to compete with men such as

Martial for wealth and prestige. He needs to be shown his place. Martial does so by stressing Zoilus' boorish, objectionable, depraved lifestyle again and again. The charge of abusing little children, however, doesn't appear at all. Zoilus (in a metaphor Martial might have approved of) is, therefore, the dog that doesn't bark in the night.

Second, there are a host of other references to sex with young slaves from other Roman authors, e.g. Horace in his *Satires* 2.114-20 or *Epodes* 11.4). Of course, one might argue that Horace and these other authors are 'counter-cultural' too, but their importance within the Latin poetic canon and the number of the references made would suggest that the phenomenon cannot just be dismissed as 'deviant'.

Third, we can compare some of the work of a poet roughly contemporary with Martial, Statius. In several poems (*Silvae* 2.1, 2.6, 3.4, 5.5), Statius celebrates slave or freed 'favourites'. For example, in 2.6 he writes about Philetos who was (he tells us) not chosen by his master for his looks. Those looks, we are told, are manly. The boy was also 'chaste'. Statius stresses that it doesn't matter that the boy was a slave. From all this we may infer that Statius doesn't want his audience to come to the obvious conclusion that Philetos was a good-looking and effeminate slave who was used sexually by this master. Statius' audience would therefore appear to have had clear expectations of the relationship between a master and his favourite, and those expectations were sexual. Some have suggested that Statius' 'praise' of slave favourites is actually designed to draw attention to their sexual use (by pretending to divert attention from it!) and actually forms part of a critique of his aristocratic patrons and even of the emperor (for a discussion, see Laes 2006: 209-10, cf. Newlands 2002: ch.1). While it is technically possible that Statius is representing unease at the sexual relationships between masters and young male slaves, it is unlikely. It would have represented an astonishingly dangerous game (both physically and socially) for Statius to play. More likely he realised he couldn't avoid responding to the traditional reading of relationships with favourites.

So, was the sexual use of child slaves a further expression of their status as chattels and objects that could be bought and sold? Yes, but with a number of caveats. Firstly, we need to bear in mind the extent to which these ties might cut across traditional master/slave relations (see, e.g. Bernstein 2005, cf. Garrido-Hory 1981: 162-72). Sometimes poets seem to envisage a favourite refusing to service their master and engaging in a game of tease (e.g. Martial *Epigrams* 11.58). We need, however, to be careful. Roman masters might have enjoyed the idea that their favourites could say no, but the relationship of slavery gave slaves little or no protection from their master's anger if they took the game of tease too far. In *Epigrams* 11.58 Martial complains of such teasing when his 'pet' demands presents. Well, a master might make promises, he tells us, but, just as one might offer a slave

barber freedom if his razor was at your throat, once free of the threat one would have his arms and legs broken. The slave favourite had better take note. One might compare the similarly nasty sentiments of *Epigrams* 5.46.

It is nonetheless interesting that, as we have seen, *delicium* could be used as term of affection in epigraphy with no apparent suggestion of any sexual relationship. It could even be used on one's own children. It should also be noted that many of the literary references to slave favourites give no clear evidence whether the relationships were sexual or not. Romans also apparently often wanted to read some kind of affective tie into the relationship. The fact that the bulk of our evidence is poetic creates a problem, however. 'Reciprocity' between master and slave may in part be a fantasised reflection of a more 'consensual' form of pederasty between free people found within the culture of ancient Greece which many Romans may have been attempting to copy. Slaves might, of course, have been able to use the expectations created by such fantasies as weapons against their masters. Generally, however, Romans express very little fear that the social hierarchy would be upset by the phenomenon of slave favourites. Martial and other writers could complain bitterly about the cost of slave favourites and their role in bankrupting owners (e.g. *Epigrams* 11.70), but there is little to suggest that such favourites were in any way feared (apart from one cryptic reference in Martial *Epigrams* 12.91 to poisoning). For Roman slaveowners, slave child sex favourites were a source of pleasure, not fear or pain or unease (however much we might like to believe the latter). Where Martial discusses a reprobate being controlled by his sexual need for an (ex) slave he is referring not to a child, but to a woman (*Epigrams* 6.71).

So, were there no restrictions on the sexual proclivities of masters? One could imagine one particular form of social control: the attitude of wives. This is most memorably depicted in Fortunata's violent reaction to Trimalchio's overly public focus on a boy in Petronius' *Satyricon* (74). One might compare Juno's anger with Jupiter's pursuit of Ganymede, mentioned, e.g. at the beginning of Virgil's *Aeneid*, perhaps the most famous single work in all of Roman literature. Catullus 61.119ff also suggests that favourites are something to be put aside at the time of marriage. Martial raises this issue in *Epigrams* 12.96, reproving a wife for needlessly worrying about her husband's attitude towards his page boys (*ministris*). Such affairs are short, he claims, and the boys can give a man something a woman cannot, even if she wants to. It has been argued that Martial 12.96 shows that wives had to accept such relationships if they existed (Williams 1999: 48ff). Could it be, however, that the poem may be designed to shock and so illustrates the opposite? Once again the difficulty of reading Martial's poems in isolation becomes apparent. The bulk of our evidence suggests that keeping a slave favourite could introduce difficulties within a marriage.

So, an accepted social institution, with few limits. There are, however, some unanswered questions in this debate. They may not overturn the position I have sketched above, but they provide food for thought, and potential avenues for future research.

If the sexual use of slave children was accepted, why do the Romans intervene (Martial *Epigrams* 9.5 and 9.7, Statius *Silvae* 3.4.73-77) to make castration and the sale of children for prostitution illegal? If the practice of using slaves sexually, including slave children, is so normal, what is it about it that an author such as Plautus seems to find so funny in his comedies (see Williams 1999: 34-37 for references)? Why is Statius so coy in his poems for his aristocratic friends about even implying sexual relations between master and servant? If it was just one of those things that happened, why try to deny it? Did he suppose he could hope to somehow save the blushes of slave favourites such as Glaucias or Earinus when he was writing for an audience who would have known exactly what was going on behind closed doors? Finally, is it *really* true, as claimed, that all Roman critics of *pueri delicati* were simply criticising the luxury of buying such slaves, not the sex itself? If so, why exactly does Suetonius supply such details of what Tiberius is doing in his decadent exile in Capri (*Life of Tiberius* 44)? Little boys (whom we must assume were slave: Suetonius would surely have been explicit if these had been free children) fellate him as he swims. Exactly what, in Suetonius' eyes, is Tiberius doing wrong? Is it just that he isn't penetrating them as a good, phallic, Roman should? Or is the age of the children part of the obscenity too?

Even granting all these doubts, where does all this uncomfortable material leave us? Martial appears erotically drawn to pretty slave boys between the age (probably) of 12 to 20. His poetry may even include a love poem for a five year old girl, though it is just possible this is designed to shock his audience. Nothing in our evidence, however, allows us to assume that Martial's general tastes belong to some kind of deviant social sub-group within Rome. He may talk more openly about his tastes than prose authors, but this may be more because of different ideas about what one should talk about in different types of texts. There were, apparently, no *legal* restrictions on Martial or his audience moving from poetic fantasy to reality, so long as the object of their desires was a slave. The absence of legal restrictions is probably less significant for Rome than it might be for the modern world, given the relatively restricted remit of Roman legal codes and the different distinctions between public and private. It is fascinating, however, that it is so difficult (certainly when compared to the issue of physical violence towards slaves) to find any *informal* social restrictions on the sexual use of slaves either, though there are, just possibly, one or two hints of this. Perhaps the only effective control on a master's use of slave children was likely to be the attitude of his wife, which our evidence suggests was unlikely to be positive.

The evidence would certainly suggest a degree of expected reciprocity of feeling between master and slave favourite, though such reciprocity was precarious, temporary, and may well have been as much an element of poetic fantasy as reality. Suggestions that the institution of slavery or the lack of privacy within Roman homes was the primary cause of the prevalence of pederastic or paedophiliac relations (e.g. Watson 1992: 259-60; Laes 2003: 314-20; Laes 2006: 232-35) require further comparative research to convince. Overall, however, what we have seen would suggest that, for a Roman, the most important element in the phrase 'slave child' was the term *slave*.

Bibliography

Bell, A.A. (1984): 'Martial's daughter?', *Classical World* 78: 21-24.

Bernstein, N.M. (2005): 'Mourning the *puer delicatus*: status inconsistency and the ethical value of fostering in Statius, *Silvae* 2.1', *American Journal of Philology* 126: 257-80.

Bradley, K.R. (1994): *Slavery and Society at Rome.* Cambridge.

Dover, K. (1989): *Greek Homosexuality.* Cambridge, Mass.

Garnsey, P.D.A. (1996): *Ideas of Slavery from Aristotle to Augustine.* Cambridge.

Garrido-Hory. M. (1981): *Martial et l'esclavage.* Paris.

Halperin, D. (1990): *One Hundred years of Homosexuality.* London.

Kenney, E.J. (1964): 'Erotion Again', *Greece and Rome* New Series 11(1): 77-81.

Laes, C. (2003): 'Desperately Different? *Delicia* Children in the Roman Household' in D.L.Balch and C.Osiek (eds), *Early Christian Families in Context: An Interdisciplinary Dialogue*, 298-324. Grand Rapids, Michigan

Laes, C. (2006): *Kinderen bij de Romeinen.* Leuven.

Manning, C.E. (1989): 'Stoicism and Slavery in the Roman Empire' in *Aufstieg und Niedergang der Römischen Welt* II 36(3): 1518-43.

McKeown, N. (2007): 'The sound of John Henderson laughing: Pliny 3.14 and Roman slaveowners' fear of their slaves' in A.Serghidou (ed.) *Fear of Slaves – Fear of Enslavement in the Ancient Mediterranean*, 265-79. Besançon.

Newlands, C.E. (2002): *Statius' "Silvae" and the poetics of Empire.* Cambridge.

Nielsen, H.S. (1990): 'Delicia in Roman literature and in the Urban Inscriptions', *Analecta Romana Instituti Danici* 19: 79-88.

Pollini, J. (1999): 'The Warren Cup: Homoerotic Love and Symposial Rhetoric in Silver', *Art Bulletin* LXXXI(1): 21-52.

Pomeroy, A.J. (1992): 'Trimalchio as "Deliciae"', *Phoenix* 46(1): 45-53.

Pomeroy, A.J. (2003): 'Heavy Petting in Catullus', *Arethusa* 36: 49-60.

Rawson, B. (2003): *Children and childhood in Roman Italy.* Oxford.

Richlin, A. (1983): *The garden of Priapus: sexuality and aggression in Roman humor.* New Haven.

Shackleton Bailey, D.R. (trans.) (1993): *Martial: Epigrams Volumes 1-III.* London.

Sullivan, J.P. (1991): *Martial: the unexpected classic: a literary and historical classic.* Cambridge.

Scheidel, W. (1997): 'Quantifying the sources of slaves in the early Roman Empire', *Journal of Roman Studies* 87: 156-69.

Slater, W.J. (1974): 'Pueri, turba minuta', *Bulletin of the Institute of Classical Studies* 21: 133-40.

Thévenaz, O. (2002): 'Flebilis Lapis? Gli epigrammi funerari per Erotion in Marziale', *Materiali e discussioni per l'analisi dei testi classici* 48: 167-91.

Van Dam, H. (1984): *P. Papinius Statius, Silvae Book II : a commentary.* Leiden.

Watson, A. (1987): *Roman Slave Law.* Baltimore.

Watson, P. (1992): 'Erotion: Puella Delicata?', *Classical Quarterly* New Series 42(1): 253-68.

Williams, C.A. (1999): *Roman homosexuality: ideologies of masculinity in classical antiquity.* Oxford.

Winkler, J.J. (1989): *The Constraints of Desire.* London.

CHAPTER 7

VITAL RESOURCES, IDEAL IMAGES AND VIRTUAL LIVES: CHILDREN IN EARLY BRONZE AGE FUNERARY RITUAL

Paul Garwood

There has been no previous attempt to evaluate the evidence from child burials in Early Bronze Age Britain or to interpret them in social or religious terms. Indeed, despite a growing literature in archaeology concerned specifically with children and childhood (e.g. Moore & Scott (eds) 1997; Crawford 1999; Sofaer Derevenski (ed.) 2000), there has been almost no discussion of children in the European Bronze Age, either as a general age category or as individuals with social, economic, religious and emotional significance for the living (rare exceptions include Finlay 2000; McLaren 2004 and Rega 1997). The idea that children were social actors and makers and reproducers of cultural life in their own right (cf. Sofaer Derevenski 2000; Lucy 2005: 62) is absent even from recent studies (though see McLaren 2004: 298).

Early Bronze Age child burials in Britain have usually been interpreted uncritically as neutral expressions of certain kinds of social order: as 'family members' who had a right to burial at family monuments, or as members of lineages who were automatically given a formal burial because of their inherited social status. If this was so, it might be expected that child burials would be relatively common and would receive consistent kinds of mortuary treatment at least within the discrete settings of individual monuments. Yet child burials are in fact relatively rare and very diverse in terms of their grave forms and artefact associations. Their rarity, and their presence within the most prominent architectural edifices of the period (circular burial mounds), in fact suggest that child burials were special and unusual events within traditions of funerary practice that were themselves marked by infrequent depositional acts. It will become apparent that to make sense of this evidence we need to understand children as media for expressing adult values, beliefs, ideals or feelings through particular kinds of ritual action at funerary monuments.

Children and childhood in the British Late Neolithic and Early Bronze Age

Our understanding of Late Neolithic and Early Bronze Age society, c. 2500-1500 BC, is based largely on interpretations of monuments and burials and the cultural landscapes of which they were a part (Barrett 1990; Garwood 1991). There is no documentary evidence, virtually no figurative art of any kind, and little evidence for settlements or economic practices that we can put alongside the funerary evidence for a broader appreciation of cultural life in this period. The burial mounds, too, are difficult to interpret in a simple way: some were single-event constructions directly associated with central single graves; others were multi-phase edifices elaborated over long periods, often with multiple burials, some with platforms and wooden structures to guide ceremonial performances. Mounds can occur as single isolated edifices; others were built in impressive linear groups perhaps indicative of lines of dynastic succession (Garwood 1991; Woodward 2000: 78-9).

Child burials, in this context, have been an especially neglected area of study despite a considerable mass of available data. Early assessments of the round barrow evidence (e.g. Fox 1959; Ashbee 1960) made virtually no reference to children except as incidental and marginal adjuncts to 'significant' adult burials. Although the demographic, health and social implications of infant and child burials attracted some discussion in the 1970s (reviewed by Burgess 1980: 161-5, 297-300), most studies of Early Bronze Age monuments and funerary practices published in the 1980s and early 1990s barely mention children except in passing (focusing instead on the significance of ancestral rites, genealogical reckoning, descent and the construction of social identities: e.g. Barrett 1988b, 1990, 1994: 123-29; Garwood 1991; Thomas 1991). In this wider context, only Gibbs (1990) and Mizoguchi (1993, 1995) sought to evaluate child burials and their cultural significance.

Gibbs' study is mainly concerned with gender representations but also takes account of burials of non-sexed 'immature' individuals, contrasting 'earlier' Beaker-associated burials (mainly late 3rd millennium BC) with 'later' Ridge and Groove/Miniature Vessel-associated burials (mainly early 2nd millennium BC). She observes that earlier burials of young people had a far more restricted range of grave goods than adults, suggesting a separation of adult and pre-adult roles and statuses. At the same time, the bodies of children were arranged like those of adults, with gender-related positions and orientations, suggesting strong pre-adult gender distinctions. In the later period, in contrast, most of the artefact types found with adult burials are also found with child burials, suggesting that children in this period were seen as 'integrated mini-adults' (Gibbs 1990: 183), while gender differences were less prominent.

Koji Mizoguchi also identifies age- and sex-related status distinctions in the sequences, spatial ordering and contents of Beaker burials. Adult males usually occupied primary central graves while women and immature individuals were placed in 'satellite' graves around them, or were secondary insertions into central grave pits (1993). In addition, young people were usually buried with smaller and less finely-finished Beakers than those found with adults (1995: 181). These distinctions are interpreted as part of the representation of a 'diachronic linear narrative' of the human life course, that was used by adults, especially males, to "legitimate their domination over non-adults" (Mizoguchi 1995: 184).

Recent discussions of child burials are mostly still incidental to interpretations of other aspects of the evidence. It is especially surprising that studies of the construction of social identities (e.g. Brück 2004; Jones 2005; Matthews 2004; Sørensen 2004), make virtually no mention of children, either as agents who participated in the making of their own identities (cf. Lucy 2005:58-9) or as people given identities in death during funerary rituals. Nor do they consider 'childhood' as a social construct or subject of memorisation (e.g. as a stage in life recalled by those who had acquired adult identities). Although the composition of artefact assemblages found with children is sometimes noted (e.g. Mizoguchi 1995: 181; Sofaer Derevenski 2002: 204), the material culture of child burials has not been examined in detail and there are very few contextual studies of child graves. One exception is Dawn McLaren's study of the burial of a 5-9 year old child with a miniature battleaxe and a miniature ceramic vessel at Doune, Scotland (c. 1870-1530 BC). She concludes that the burial reflected the adult world in miniature (literally), and that 'childhood' as a separate category was given no place in Early Bronze Age funerary ritual, and indeed was perhaps not a part of cultural experience at all (2004: 301). Nyree Finlay's analysis of infant burials in Irish cist graves is also of interest: she suggests that combined women-and-infant burials may reflect a concern with reproduction, related to the importance of descent for assuring status and political success (2000: 418; cf. Christopher Burgess' interpretation (1980: 162) of such burials as a reflection of the hazards of childbirth).

It has been claimed more widely that children in the European Neolithic and Bronze Age are not easily distinguishable from adults in terms of mortuary treatment and dress (Lillehammer 2000; Whittle 2003: 27; though see Welinder 1998 for an opposite view). This could reflect the significant roles played by children in societies that had young populations, high mortality rates, and short overlaps in the lives of children and their adult relatives for the effective transfer of knowledge and skills. Children, in this view, were not just dependents but important economic contributors and home keepers (for example, in caring for younger children) whose attainment of adult qualities and accomplishments was highly valued and celebrated. Young people, it is argued, would therefore have been seen as emergent adults from an early age, and would be accorded mortuary treatment commensurate with their 'adult' roles and capabilities (Welinder 1998). This is consistent with interpretations of

child burials with 'adult' grave goods as those of proto- or quasi-adults (Gibbs 1990; McLaren 2004).

Missing children, virtual lives: conceptualizing Early Bronze Age children

Representations of children in these studies share several features in common. They are all partly based on assumptions about the children that are *missing* from the archaeological record, and they all presume to reconstruct 'social life' by studying the dead. Also, they tend to draw upon the same set of three partly overlapping assumptions about the cultural significance of child burials in this period: that the burial of children was 'natural' or 'inevitable' given the social milieu of the time; that such burials represent 'important children'; and the idea that Early Bronze Age childhoods were intrinsically 'different' to those we experience (i.e. that children in this period represent a cultural 'Other' in their own right).

The idea that children should inevitably have been buried at round barrow sites embodies a simplistic 'reflectionist' understanding of the evidence and of Early Bronze Age society. Because children, it is argued, were members of the 'family' groups that built round barrows, it supposedly follows that they should also have been buried at those places as a matter of course (e.g. Ashbee 1960: 175; Burgess 1980: 297). Also, because these children belonged to small communities with a shared religious outlook, there is the sense that mortuary treatment of children and adults should have been similar. Such assessments of the burial evidence ignore the abundant ethnographic evidence for varied treatment of age and gender categories, the lack of any kind of straightforward relationship between social organization and mortuary practices, and the diversity of social and religious beliefs that might be reified in funerary rituals in any one cultural context (e.g. Bloch 1971, 1981; cf. Barley 1995; see Parker Pearson 1999, for a general survey of approaches to mortuary evidence).

The idea that children in graves were important in a social sense is based on more convincing readings of the evidence. These assume that round barrow burials represent only a small part of the population (Burgess 1980: 171-2; Bradley 1984: 86) so that everyone buried at these sites must have been important in some way (e.g. Ashbee 1960: 170-72; Fox 1959: 20; McLaren 2004: 301). In other words, the 'missing' majority is used to define and measure the importance of the visible dead. It is also notable, given likely child mortality rates of around 50% (Lucy 2005: 50; cf. Burgess 1980: 162-3), that child burials are relatively rare in relation to those of adults: they occur, for example, in about 10% of Irish Early Bronze Age graves (Mount 1995: 109-10, table 5), and represent about 25% of Late Neolithic/Early Bronze Age burials in Dorset (see below). Children thus comprise more of the missing than other age categories, implying that those who *were* formally buried were very special indeed. 'Importance', in this context, has been related to social hierarchy (e.g. positions in higher status kin groups) and religious identity (inherited sacred roles or caste membership), but not economic or political success (achieved in the adult world; e.g. through prestige goods exchange). Although definitions of the elite groups responsible for monument building and prominent funerals are vague, this approach may account in a broad way for distinctions between those buried at mound sites and those who were not (Bradley 1984: 73-89; Braithwaite 1984: 105-6; Barrett 1990; Garwood 1991: 15). The particular significance of children, in this context, is explained in terms of inherited social status and their perceived importance to the continuance and reproductive capacities of lineages (Garwood 1991; cf. Finlay 2000: 418).

There is, however, a problem with this approach, especially the assumption that because not all children warranted formal burial at monuments, those that did must in some way have been especially important. This line of reasoning is dubious: to compare the importance of children buried at monuments, with the 'empty' category of children that were not, is unhelpful because there is no basis for comparison with invisible practices that may have been just as 'important' in other respects. As Sally Crawford notes in her discussion of child burials in Anglo-Saxon England, the exclusion of children from cemetery sites was not because they were unimportant, 'but because their place lay within other realms of social expression' (2002: 177). It is better to assume that the mortuary treatment of all children was meaningful, and never 'ordinary', natural or inevitable.

Recent attempts to explore the nature of 'different' childhoods in prehistory have drawn on a range of new approaches in archaeology concerned with the social construction of meaning, personhood and different kinds of subjectivity (e.g. Díaz-Andreu et al. 2005; Fowler 2004; Thomas 2004: 123-48). Studies of this kind reject universal classifications of childhood and child categories (Sofaer Derevenski 2000; Baxter 2005; Lucy 2005), as well as the moral and sentimental valuations we attach to these (e.g. Lillehammer 2000: 22-3; Sofaer Derevenski 2000: 3-6), and focus on children as socially-constructed beings.[1] These themes, especially cultural difference, are evident in Dawn McLaren's paper in which she argues

that because 'toys' are missing from Early Bronze Age child burials, children therefore lacked a distinctive material culture and thus experienced childhood in ways different to children today (2004: 301; cf. Sofaer Derevenski 2000: 6-7). This is considered further below, but it is important to note here that this argument is again based more on assumptions about what is *not* present in the mortuary record rather than what is actually there to see, and that it depends on very narrow conceptions of both toys and miniature objects (i.e. 'not toys'). Ironically, the specific interpretation of the meaning and purpose of miniature objects proposed by McLaren is not unlike Roland Barthes' interpretation of toys in France in the 1950s as media for inculcating orthodox social values by prefiguring, in miniature forms, the material culture and practices of the adult world (Barthes 1972).

Children in the Early Bronze Age are thus 'missing' in more than one sense. They are rarely observed materially, the majority being absent from formal burial contexts, and they appear to have led virtual, collective, and largely unseen lives as far as most representations of social life in this period are concerned. Rather than investigate the identities conferred on young people in death, most recent studies still treat children as a unitary, abstract category representing one part of an imagined social unit (such as a 'family' or 'lineage'), or as exemplars of cultural otherness. The expectation that mortuary analysis will somehow provide a 'picture' of living Early Bronze Age society also seems to be remarkably resilient. These approaches betray profound misunderstandings of the material culture of death and the nature of funerary ritual.

The child's body as a cultural construct

The human body is a cultural construct not only in the way that it is manipulated by others in death, but also more profoundly in the way that bodily dispositions and actions produced in social practices are reifications of cultural schemes (Bourdieu 1977: 72, 87-95). Moreover, the human body can be seen as a locus of symbolic order, involving as it does a fundamental articulation of biology and culture through bodily functions, social practices, experiences and conceptualizations of the world (see Douglas 1966: 114-39; Bourdieu 1977: 114-24, 143-58; cf. Tilley 1999: 37-9; Sofaer Derevenski 2000: 9-10). As such, the body is an ideal symbolic resource that can be used to express ideas about nature and culture, identity, and the wider social body of which it is a part (e.g. Shanks & Tilley 1982; Thomas & Tilley 1993: Treherne 1995; Thomas 2000). As Alasdair Whittle observes, by studying the treatment of bodies, "it may be possible to glimpse, or at least begin to think about, generative schemes behind bodily action" (Whittle 2003: 27). The body in childhood, in particular, can be seen as an especially powerful medium for addressing the nature of change because of its transformational and malleable physical qualities (James et al. 1998: 156; Sofaer 2006: 127).

---

[1] These themes have been common in historical studies for some time (since Ariès' work on children in the Middle Ages; 1962), strongly influenced by sociological perspectives (e.g. see James and Prout (eds.) 1990; James et al. 1998). It is perhaps surprising that the social determinist and constructivist approaches to classificatory schemes and the symbolic significance of the body in anthropology, which appeared long before comparable approaches in history (e.g. Durkheim & Mauss 1902; Mauss 1935 (1973); Douglas 1966, 1973; Blacking 1977; Ellen 1977), as well as many descriptive accounts of 'other' childhoods in ethnographies, have had far less influence on archaeological interpretations of children than the sociological approaches adopted by historians. This is probably because of the focus on childhood *per se* as a distinct subject in social history, and the fact that many of the archaeologists working on child-related subjects are concerned with historical periods.

There are many dangers, however, in pursuing this theme too simplistically. Recent interpretations of Early Bronze Age graves, for example, suggest that the complexities of lived experiences, as well as ideational categories, were embodied in the individual 'biographies' constructed in funerary deposits (e.g. Thomas 1991; Last 1998: 51); yet young children, who lacked such complex life experiences, were subject to the *same* kinds of 'construction' practices in death as adults. Moreover, children in these studies are generally treated as a single category, even though it is evident that not all children are the same. The differentiation of young people according to age groups is common cross-culturally, often involving rites of passage that impose social and moral discontinuities in early life (cf. Lucy 2005: 55). In addition, children may be engendered from an early age (Sofaer Derevenski 1997; Lucy 2005: 59): there is increasing differentiation in perceptions of the bodily qualities and potentialities of boys in comparison with girls during their early lives, especially with respect to political and economic roles, child-birth and child care. How different age groups and genders were conceptualized and valued in the Early Bronze Age must inevitably have affected how children were treated in mortuary practices, both in a corporeal sense, and with reference to the symbolic universe that was addressed in funerary ritual.

Children may perhaps also be seen as 'plural beings', in the way that they embody multiple identities defined with reference to the past, present and future (Mizoguchi 2000). The way children are raised draws upon a range of social practices, skills, positions and dispositions (*sensu* Bourdieu 1977: 72) that are 'of' the past, derived from living adults (and dead ancestors). Children also demand care and attention in the present, and their lives are bound up with predictions and expectations about their future lives, especially on the part of adults. Mizoguchi argues that the death of a child problematizes the self-identities of adults because of the removal of what the child had come to represent about their social world and its future (2000: 141-2). The funeral, in this light, is a means to address the social concerns of parents and other adults, with the child's body being used as a central symbol, resource or device for articulating and negotiating such concerns. It may not, however, be a straightforward task to distinguish the particular temporal facet of the child's 'being' that is emphasized in a funerary context.

This also highlights the way that children and their bodies may be used as symbolic media just like other kinds of objects. The remains of children in mortuary contexts are not only cultural constructions in a general sense, they are also more specifically 'artefacts' – made things (dressed, adorned, arranged) that are produced by people in ways that are infinitely varied in form and meaning. Moreover, the dissolution of categorical boundaries between people and objects, which means that objects can be made symbolically to 'stand for' people, their actions, biographies or qualities (Kopytoff 1986; Miller 1994;

Tilley 1999: 62-76; Fowler 2004: 53-78), can clearly work in both directions, so that the body as a constructed object can stand for things, qualities and powers. A person's body can thus become a symbolic and highly valued resource (in whole or in part) that can be displayed, consumed, exchanged or expended (e.g. see Chapman 2000: 134-46), and take on meanings that may have nothing to do at all with the individual's social personae or life experiences. What may be described as a 'child burial' may, in fact, be the material outcome of giving, storing or expending a ritually transformed corporeal object or substance that was believed to embody powers or qualities appropriate to the depositional act (an act which, of course, might include transformation by deliberate killing and/or 'sacrificial' rituals; cf. Davies 1997: 68-80; Green 2001: 17-36, 137-97; Taylor 2002).

The children that never were: transformations of intention, identity and materiality

It is evident that the cultural significance of children in the Early Bronze Age and the kinds of strategies involved in manipulating their physical remains varied greatly. There is, however, an even more fundamental condition of the evidence that has far-reaching significance for how we understand child burials in this period: the *ritual* context of mortuary deposition. As Stig Welinder has emphasized: 'what we observe is not childhood but burial rites for children' (1998: 188). Yet observations of this kind are rarely accompanied by any attempt to explore the nature of ritual or the wider implications of this interpretative position for archaeological study.

Ritual, and the dichotomization of ritual/practical (or sacred/secular), have attracted considerable recent attention in archaeology (e.g. Hill 1995: 95-101; Brück 1999; Insoll 2004; Bradley 2005: 28-36), with widespread rejection of characterisations of ritual as a separate kind of behaviour concerned with religious beliefs (as defined by Turner 1967: 19), as symbolic communication (Richards & Thomas 1984), and as a kind of action analogous to the reading of a 'text' (because of its 'distanciated' authorship: Barrett 1991).[2] Recent approaches focus instead on the nature of ritual performance, structured practices and ritualisation (Bradley 2005; Hill 1995). Surprisingly, less attention has been paid to reappraisals of ritual in anthropology which have re-examined the distinctive forms and qualities of ritual action and related kinds of signification (e.g. Bell 1992; Humphrey & Laidlaw 1994; Schechner 1994).

---

[2] Joanna Brück even suggests that ritual is a value-laden Western concept that has no place in prehistoric archaeology (1999: 336-37). She argues that our idea of 'ritual' is a modern Western abstraction, and that it is inapplicable to social agency in prehistory because this involved rationalities different to those structured by our sacred/secular classificatory opposition. In this view, ritual escapes our methodological capacities to distinguish it in the material record because it simply had no existence in prehistoric social life separate from everyday action.

These have particular relevance for an understanding of prehistoric funerary practices.

First, actors in ritual have prior conceptions of the 'ritual-action-to-be', which they mark out as separate from other activities (Bell 1992: 140) and to which they consciously commit themselves (Humphrey & Laidlaw 1994: 5, 106). Ritual actions, in this process, are socially prescribed, perceived by individual actors to be "given" and external to themselves' (Humphrey & Laidlaw 1994) and are interpreted with reference to a 'redemptive hegemonic order' linked to ultimate sources of power (Bell 1992: 141). Meaning thus lies not in the intention of the actor but in the intended purpose of the ritual action to which the actor is committed, and the relation that purpose has to cosmological order. This exposes the absurdity of interpreting burials as reflections of 'society' or cultural 'otherness'. The burial of a child is not a reflection of social relations but the realization of concerns embodied in the intention of the ritual act. The supposed absence of toys from Early Bronze Age burials has no bearing at all on whether children played with toys in this period, or whether childhood was experienced in ways different to ours (*contra* McLaren 2000: 301). That 'absence' is only relevant to the way in which toys were judged inappropriate to the matters being addressed in ritual actions at monument sites.

Second, it has been suggested that all rites of passage share a tripartite structure and that their beginnings (rites of separation), middles (rites of liminality) and ends (rites of re-aggregation) have similar attributes from one ritual and cultural context to another (Metcalf & Huntingdon 1991: 30; cf. Bloch 1992 on the symbolic conquest of vitality in rites of re-aggregation). The apparent universal nature of this process can be explained with reference to the relationship between everyday life in the present, and what is sacred and belongs ultimately to a state of being or place that is not of the 'here and now'. Rituals in this light provide a practical means of engaging with the sacred. Rites of separation set aside daily life and guide participants to a place where ordinary social matters are excluded. In the liminal stage, people in sacred conditions or places (e.g. round barrow monuments) find themselves betwixt and between heaven and earth, in the presence of supernatural forces or entities (gods, ancestors, spirits), in a domain where social norms are suspended. Finally, rites of re-aggregation provide a way for people to leave the sacred and return safely to living society (bringing back something of the sacred with them: absolution, purity, power).

In the ritual process, the burial of the dead thus takes place at a time when everyday society is deliberately put aside in favour of sacred, idealised and stereotypical identities. The burial event takes place during the liminal stage or during rites of re-aggregation, when the dead remain behind or depart in a different direction to the living (to join an ideal society of the dead perhaps), and thus they retain the identities or qualities conferred during the ritual. In other words, despite the hope that burial rites in the past will in some way correspond to lived social relationships, however idealised (cf. Lucy 2005: 63), in fact the transformational process intrinsic to ritual means that an altogether different (if not unconnected) vision of existence was deliberately constructed in the funerary setting. Burial evidence therefore can never provide us with a picture of living society, because funerary ritual is concerned precisely with transforming and re-representing social life.

Materials that are used in rituals, including human bodies, must also be understood in relation to the transformative qualities of ritual. As Maurice Bloch emphasises: 'The ritual process is always focused on a special type of substitution, where one thing 'becomes' another, in the same way as wine becomes the blood of Christ during the mass' (2005: 21). This may even be seen as a condition of ritual: because ritualisation involves a transformation in the intentionality of action (Humphrey & Laidlaw 1994: 88-107), the properties and meanings of the material objects and substances that are present will also be redefined in ways appropriate to the intention of the ritual act: a good example is the transformation of rice in Jain *puja* from an everyday foodstuff bound up with ideas of sustenance and life, to a material symbolising perfection, immortality and the end of life (Humphrey & Laidlaw 1994: 205-6). In a funerary setting, this might possibly involve a process whereby the social dead are simply transformed into the sacred dead, with little loss of 'individual identity' however idealised that may have become, but it could alternatively involve a radical transformation in the meaning of the physical remains of the dead to the point that these remains no longer represent 'people' at all (Garwood in preparation).

These observations provide a basis for evaluating interpretations of Early Bronze Age burials. At a fundamental level, recognition of the transformational properties of ritual, the kinds of interpretation that ritual performances evoke in the minds of actors, and the nature and significance of materials in mortuary contexts, raise important questions about the 'meanings' of burial deposits. At the same time, given that the majority of children who died in the Early Bronze Age were not buried in formal mortuary settings, and that funerary practices can take any imaginable form that people care to devise, a critical issue is why there should be child burials at round barrow sites at all.

Children, too, are good to think with

The answer to this question, in one sense, is straightforward: when it came to addressing the cultural concerns evoked in funerary rituals, children and the remains of children were sometimes especially 'good to think with', to paraphrase both Claude Levi-Strauss on totemism ('natural species are chosen not because they are "good to eat" but because they are "good to think"' (1969: 162) and Maurice Bloch on tree symbolism: 'Why trees, too, are good to think with' (2005: 21)). Yet the potential ways in which children and their bodies may be conceptualized and used symbolically are infinite. In principle, there is no limit to the creativity of symbolic expression or the skein of metaphorical associations that may be involved (cf. Tilley 1989, Miller 1994). What prevents semantic chaos is the social context of action that defines the frame of cultural reference, pre-understandings of social practices in the minds of participants, and the particular socially-constituted instances of *'parole'* through which meanings are articulated and perceived (Miller 1994; cf. Miller 1985: 178-83; Pearce 1994; Hodder & Hutson 2003: 156-205).

In this context, round barrow monuments and graves in all their guises (Garwood 2007) provide us with a guide to contexts of interpretation (concerned primarily with the dead, the past and the cosmos) as well as the kinds of pre-understandings brought to the fore in the enactment of funerary rituals (based on knowledge of the lives of individuals and communities, and of corporeal materials that once belonged to living people – materials associated with life and death, human kinds, biographies and organic processes). At the same time, the ontology of childhood experience (e.g. through engenderment, dependency, play, learning, and child tasks) and adult experiences of children (for example, in birth, caring roles, child behaviour, rites of passage and death), would together provide for a rich language of metaphorical association and representation related to children.[3] It is easy, in this context, to see how understandings of specific life events and the nature of things could be symbolised in funerary ritual in complex and diverse ways. Ideas of fertility, birth, life and death, for example, might be associated with cyclical regeneration, repeated order and 'cosmos' (Bloch 1982; Bloch & Parry 1982). Descent and inheritance could be connected with social reproduction, history and memory; and growth with vitality, potentiality and the life course. There are many ways in which relationships among these themes could be structured, but above all we need to distinguish between symbolic statements that focused on the dead child, and those that were mediated by the child's remains and referred rather to *other* people, objects, states of being, domains and conditions, both present and implicated (e.g. 'ancestors', 'spirits', 'heaven').

There are many problems, however, in trying to discern the significance of child burials given the nature of symbolic expression in ritual action, especially where generalisations are made about children as a unitary category. The idea that children are especially appropriate for symbolising regeneration and future life, because they

are always full of potential for what 'may be' (Whittle 2003: 27), suggests general equivalence in terms of their significance to regenerative processes. But this does not take account of how gendered children, for example, might be conceptualised or valued in different ways in relation to cosmological schemes. The perceived potential of boys belonging to a patrilineal descent group, for instance, would relate to their fundamental role in the biological and social reproduction of social order, real and ideal (as suggested for the Early Bronze Age: Garwood 1991: 14-15). In contrast, the loss of a girl in this context would not be directly relevant to this process, because as a potential exogamous exchange partner her fate would be to contribute to the reproduction of another patrilineage. Funerary rituals for boys are thus likely to be intended to 'presence' and reaffirm cosmological order and lines of descent, while the treatment of girls may mark entirely different concerns (e.g. affinity, marriage, exchange).[4] In cognatic systems, in contrast, which may be endogamous (e.g. some clan structures), the cosmological implications of descent rules may be reckoned more in relation to the capacity for reproduction, both male and female. In other words, there may be more emphasis on 'fertility' or the passage to adulthood rather than gender *per se*.

There is another aspect of representation and meaning that it is important to examine: the body as material culture in sacralised exchanges (cf. Fowler 2004: 113-17, 135-37; Barley 1995: 102-4). Children may be thought of in various ways as 'gifts': from gods or ancestors to a family, for example, or from one lineage to another through marriage exchange. Gifts received, however, can also be given away or re-worked to signify new kinds of qualities and relationships: in this light, those things that children were made to symbolise could be transposed (exchanged) from one place to another as corporeal forms and substances (e.g. as gifts to the gods or as gifts accompanying the burial of others). In Aztec cosmology, for example, 'it was believed that the human body was the vulnerable nexus of vital cosmic forces and was filled with divine essences that needed periodic regeneration … Specific parts of the human body, especially the heart, the head, and the liver, contained animistic entities that were gifts and presences of the gods and could be returned to them as gifts through ritual sacrifice' (Carrasco 1999: 73). This included the ritual killing of children as 'debt payments' (offerings) to the god Tlaloc responsible for the regeneration of life through rain (Carrasco 1999: 85, 132). The burial of infants in and around corn-drying ovens in late Roman Britain may reflect similar

---

[3] It is worth emphasizing that small-scale prehistoric societies were composed largely of young people less than 18 years old (perhaps 50% or more), so that children were abundantly present and prominent in a range of social and economic activities. At the same time, childhood mortality rates at around 50% meant that child death and especially infant death (30% or more) was an extremely common experience for the living community (Lucy 2005: 50).

[4] The death of a girl in a patrilineal system in some ways is ambivalent in relation to social reproduction. In the marriage exchange (that never happened) she may have constituted a 'gift' from one lineage that would inflict profound moral debt on the other – the gift of potential future life itself through the promise of bearing children. This debt is only really 'repayable', of course, through reciprocal exchange of the same kind (immediate or delayed). The loss of a girl, therefore, does have implications for social reproduction (as well as alliance formation), but indirectly, and in ways un-related to the fundamental cosmological status of patrilineages.

	Period 1: c. 2500–2150 BC	Period 2: c. 2150–1800 BC	Period 3: c. 1800–1500 BC
Burials	Mostly single inhumation graves in central positions. Cremation rare. Adult males most common, usually in primary contexts. Occasional burial sequences.	Inhumation burials predominant, often occurring in groups (all ages and both sexes) in complex sequences. Increasing frequency of cremation burials.	Inhumation burials very rare by 1750 BC. Cremation burials predominant, in both central and peripheral positions.
Grave goods	Early Beaker ceramics and associated funerary artefact sets.	Diverse Late Beaker, Food Vessel and other artefact assemblages, along with Collared Urns after c. 2000 BC.	Collared, Food Vessel, Cordoned, and other urn types. Series of 'Wessex' graves with 'rich' artefact assemblages.
Round barrows	Small, mostly single-phase funerary mounds. Elaboration of mound structures rare and fe, timber circles. Open arena ceremonial monuments such as ring barrows and cairns spatially separate from funerary mounds and usually without burials.	Wide range of mound sizes, both single- and multi-phase. Some progressively enlarged, resulting in massive mound structures. Timber circles fairly common. New kinds of open arena monuments (e.g. pond barrows). Some mounds with platforms.	Single-phase mounds predominant, some very large, with shaped external forms such as 'bell' and 'disc' barrows. Mound enlargements and timber circles rare. New open arena monuments very rare but burials continuing at some existing sites.
Barrow groups	Most monuments dispersed. Occasional wide-spaced lines or clusters of mounds.	Large multi-phase mounds usually widely separated in the landscape. Some paired barrows.	Development of large linear round barrow groups.

Fig. 7.1: Summary of Late Neolithic and Early Bronze Age burial types and monument forms, c.2500-1500 BC (after Garwood 2007, tbl.1).

concerns if not necessarily ritual killing (Scott 1991). Children in death, in these cases, were not just good to think with but were also good to 'speak with' and 'act through': as vessels that contained powers and qualities and as meaningful media of exchange within a moral or sacred economy.

Times and places for children

To make sense of the presence of children at Early Bronze Age funerary monuments thus requires an understanding of their significance as media for representing certain beliefs, ideals, values or feelings in the course of funerary and other rituals. The nature of this representation can only become clear, however, if we can relate patterns of mortuary treatment to changes in cultural life and cosmological schemes. Above all, it is essential to discern the *fields of discourse* (Barrett 1988a) that were brought into being during monument construction and burial events, and how these changed over time.

At first sight, the evidence presents great difficulties: the remains of children are fragmentary, not always well-recorded, and are extremely varied in terms of treatment and deposition. Indeed, analysis of child burials has perhaps been avoided because of the apparent intractability of the evidence, a lack of agreement about how to categorise 'children', and chronological

uncertainties about the extent to which different practices were contemporary. These problems can be resolved at least in part by situating the evidence within a chronological framework for monument construction and funerary practices (Garwood 2007). This scheme, summarized in Fig. 7.1, characterises monument forms and burial types under three broad period headings, dated to c. 2500-2150 BC, c. 2150-1800 BC and c. 1800-1500 BC (referred to here as Periods 1, 2, and 3 respectively). Analysis of child burials within this framework reveals some striking distinctions in the treatment of children and different age groups over time.[5]

The age-at-death distributions of Late Neolithic and Early Bronze Age sub-adult burials from datable contexts in southern Britain (to the south of a line between the Wash and the Dovey) are shown in Fig. 7.2. Only child burials with specific age-at-death estimates recorded in

---

[5] The age categories referred to in the discussion are not intended *a priori* to embody a particular Early Bronze Age age-set classification. The intention, instead, is simply to chart the age-at-death distribution of child burials with reference to age ranges that are identifiable using physiological indicators (Buikstra & Ubelaker 1994; Sofaer 2006; 120-24) and accessible in excavation reports. Classifications of age groups and the definition of thresholds for transition from one age- or role-related status to another are enormously diverse and inconsistent from one cultural context to another, while biological attributes and growth stages can also vary due to cultural and economic practices, environmental conditions and dietary habits (Lucy 2005: 51-5; Sofaer 2006: 117-29).

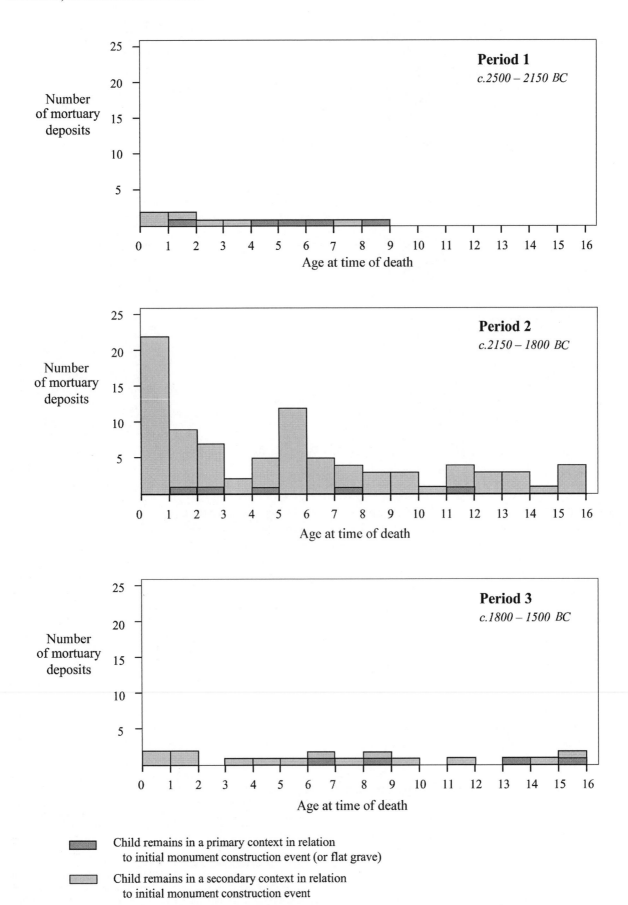

Fig. 7.2: Incidence of well-dated child burials, with known ages-at-death,
at round barrows and other sites in southern Britain, c.2500-1500 BC.

	Barrow sites excavated	Sites with burial evidence	Sites with child remains	Total burials	Child burials/ remains
Period 1	7	6	0 (0%)	7	0 (0%)
Period 2	23	21	14 (66%)	109	42 (38%)
Period 3	16	13	2+ (15%+)	21	2+ (9%+)
Uncertain date (probably EBA)	21	13	2+ (13%+)	35	2+ (6%+)

Period 3 and *Uncertain*: + refers to the presence of un-dated and fragmentary human remains in mound erosion and ditch deposits, some probably Early Bronze Age in date, possibly including children.

Fig. 7.3: Monument use, burials and child remains at Late Neolithic and Early Bronze Age round barrow sites in Dorset.

excavation reports published since 1930 are included (which largely excludes incomplete disarticulated remains, as these often received scant attention or were too fragmentary for ageing).[6] Altogether, 117 burials are included from 59 sites. The data-set is not exhaustive: it is based on the sites listed by Gibbs (1990), Garwood (2003: App.1; 2007: App.1), some additional sites listed in Hopkins 2002, and a review of the author's database of round barrow excavations in southern Britain. Nor are all the age estimates likely to be entirely accurate. Even so, it represents the majority of reliably-recorded, datable, published child burials in southern Britain, and – combined with less detailed but still valuable contextual information from additional sites – provides a broad picture of the changing number, frequency and character of child burials of different age groups over time.[7]

It is immediately apparent that far more child burials date to the period c. 2200-1800, with 88 examples, than the preceding or succeeding periods, with 11 and 18 respectively. This pattern can be evaluated in relation to the wider incidence of mortuary deposition. All of the round barrow excavations in Dorset published since 1920 have been assessed to establish the relative presence/absence and frequency of child burials in relation to the overall occurrence of monument use and funerary activity in each period (see Fig. 7.3).

Dorset was selected because of the large number of excavated sites with good bone preservation. This analysis not only shows that there were more child burials in Period 2, but also that a much higher proportion of all the burial events at monuments in this period involved the remains of children. The overall chronological pattern does not, therefore, simply reflect more, or less, round barrow use: child burials *were* relatively more frequent in Period 2.[8] This point does need to be qualified: child burials in Period 3 may be under-represented as most burials in this period consist of cremated remains which

---

[6] Where child ages are reported in excavation reports as age ranges (e.g. '2 to 4', '5 to 6'), the median age or lower age is used here for analytical purposes (e.g. Figs 7.2, 7.4, 7.5). The selection of the lower age is because of evidence for systematic over-ageing of young people in analyses of anatomical remains undertaken before the 1990s (Lucy 2005: 49). Some of the age groups referred to in this paper correspond in a very broad way to developmental changes in children, although these do not in any way determine how these are culturally differentiated or categorised. Neonates to one-year old children, for example, can be contrasted with those aged between one and three in terms of their locomotion and primary language skills; from three years children develop complex use of language, establish stable gender distinctions and are largely independent in terms of movement and food consumption; between six and 12 years children may master highly complex technologies and are capable of independent strategic action; and from 12 years they may be viable reproductive agents and physically look increasingly like – or are perceived to be – 'adults'. This does not presuppose any particular threshold, or indeed essential dichotomy, in the child/adult transition (Sofaer 2005: 121-24).

[7] References for sites mentioned in the text, in alphabetical order by county and site name: *Berkshire*: Lambourn 17 (Case 1956), *Cambridgeshire*: Barnack (Donaldson 1977; cf. Last 1998), *Dorset*: Down Farm pond barrow (Barrett et al. 1991: 128-38); Fordington Farm (Bellamy 1991); Long Crichel 5 (Green et al. 1982); Crichel Down

Barrows 7 and 12 (Piggott & Piggott 1944), *Lincolnshire*: Deeping St. Nicholas (French 1994), *Northamptonshire*: Raunds Barrow 9 (Healy & Harding forthcoming), *Oxfordshire*: North Stoke (Catling 1951); Radley 919, Radley 4866, and Radley Barrow 12 (Barclay & Halpin 1999), *Somerset*: Tynings Down East (Read 1923), *Suffolk*: Risby (Vatcher & Vatcher 1976), *Wiltshire*: Amesbury 71 (Christie 1967; cf. Barrett 1988b); Amesbury 72b (Ashbee 1984); Durrington Down (Richards 1990); Hemp Knoll (Robertson-Mackay 1980); West Overton G6b (Smith & Simpson 1966).

[8] Round barrows categorised as of *uncertain* date, which have relatively few examples of child burials, probably do not significantly affect this pattern as most appear to be broadly 'later' rather than 'earlier' within the Early Bronze Age (on the basis of indirect dating evidence, stratigraphic sequences and architectural features). If these sites could be assigned to one period or another they would, if anything, strengthen the pattern based on better-dated sites.

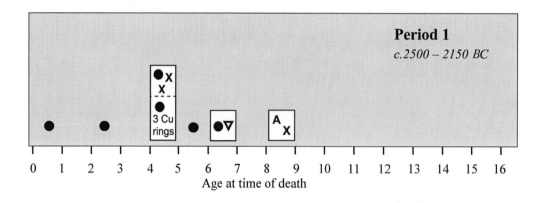

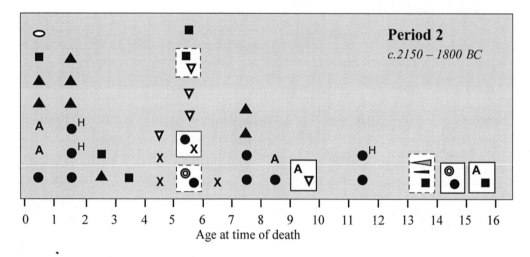

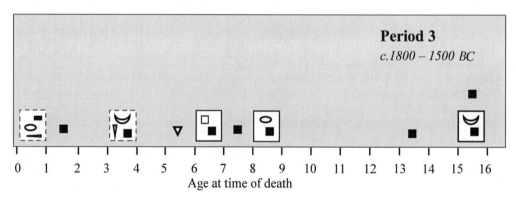

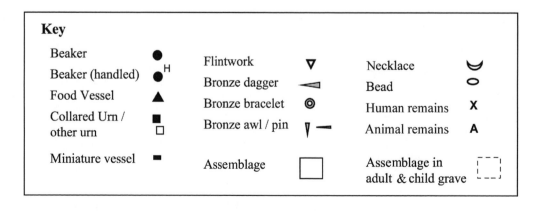

Fig. 7.4: Artefact associations with Late Neolithic and Early Bronze Age child burials (same data-set as in Fig. 7.2).

in some cases cannot be aged or have been subject only to rudimentary analysis. In addition, most such burials, placed in shallow features high in mound structures or around their periphery, have been especially vulnerable to erosion processes.[9] Nonetheless, a survey of the cremated human remains recorded in eroded mound deposits and late secondary (but imprecisely dated) burial contexts in Dorset, suggests that 'children' are not very common: it is likely, therefore, that the level of under-representation is low.

Other contrasts in the frequency and treatment of child burials can be discerned. First, the presence of different age groups varied over time. Most notably, while there are almost no burials of foetuses, neonates and infants less than one year old in Periods 1 and 3, there are 22 examples dated to Period 2 (25% of child burials in this period). In addition, all of the child burials in Period 1 seem to be aged eight years or less, while the ages represented in Periods 2 and 3 span the full range 0-16, with a relatively higher proportion in the 12+ age group in Period 3 (4 burials or 22%, compared with 12% in Period 2). It is also interesting to note that in Period 2, in particular, the 4-8 years age group is more frequently represented than children in the 2-4 and 8-11 ranges (see the discussion of artefact associations below). There are, therefore, different emphases in each period in terms of the ages at which children received formal mortuary treatment at monument sites, with particular focus at various times on three age groups: less than one year, 4-8, and over 12. These must relate to age categories or transitions in the lives of children that were significant to the concerns addressed in mortuary rituals.

Second, there are clear relationships between different age categories and types of grave goods (Fig. 7.4). Above all, objects with children aged less than two years are extremely rare in Periods 1 and 3, but relatively common in Period 2, when this age group accounts for 36% of the burials with grave goods. It is also notable that in Period 2 this age group is especially associated with ceramics, especially Food Vessels (five of eight Food Vessel burials) and handled Beakers (two of three). Other relationships are less distinct but it is evident that in all three periods, children 4-9 were more likely to be associated with objects (including all of the recorded flint artefacts and most of the human and animal remains), than those aged 2-4 or 9-12. More specifically, in Period 2, a contrast can be drawn between the 4-6 age group, associated mainly with lithic artefacts and human (child) remains, and the 7-8 age group associated with ceramics (Beakers and Food Vessels) and animal remains. Finally, some of the artefacts found with individuals over 12 years old in Periods 2 and 3 may have denoted 'adult' identities: these include two of the three metal items

found with young people and one of the two complex bead necklaces. The association between adults and metalwork has been observed before (e.g. Sofaer Derevenski 2002: 204), and necklaces appear mainly to be associated with adult females (Gerloff 1975: 211). It is important to note that the other metal object and necklace were both found in a combined child/adult female burial (at Tynings Down East) and were probably deposited with the woman. The occurrence of grave goods thus parallels the overall pattern of emphasis on certain age groups noted above, but also suggests some distinct associations between these groups and certain kinds of artefacts or materials.

Third, the nature of combined child/adult and child/child burials is surprising. There are no definite examples in any of the three periods of direct associations of foetuses or neonates with adult females, which might be expected in the case of deaths during childbirth or subsequent illness (see Fig.7. 5). Instead, infants less than six months old are associated with adult males (at Barnack, Burials 37 and 67), other children in the 4-6 age group (Radley 919; possibly Radley 12, 601/B/3, and Raunds 9, F741), or with multiple burials (the neonate with disarticulated adult male and female remains at Fordington Farm, Grave 70). Older children in combined burials display no obvious pattern of association or grouping by age, except that in Periods 2 and 3 nearly all of them were found with adult females of various ages from 20 to 50, while those in Period 1 were found with an adult male (Hemp Knoll) or other children (Radley 919, Durrington Down). It is possible that the remains of these children, in some cases, were treated in a similar way to grave goods or as votive deposits. This may be evident where child bodies or body parts were placed around other bodies within graves, or around grave pits, and/or where their mortuary treatment was different to that of other burials, especially after a process of transformation such as burning or disarticulation (e.g. at Durrington Down; Hemp Knoll, Radley 919; West Overton G6b, primary burial; and Long Crichel 7). These kinds of practices seem relatively common in Period 1 and are present in Period 2, but are less easy to identify in Period 3 when nearly all bodies were cremated.

Finally, there are significant contrasts in the monument settings and spatial ordering of child burials. Although primary child burials central to mound structures are very rare, some differences can be seen between Period 1, and Periods 2/3. In Period 1, there is one definite example of a primary child burial at Durrington Down, and several more cases of children (all in the 4-6 age group) in individual 'flat graves' that probably had low mounds (e.g. Radley 919, Lambourn 17). In Periods 2 and 3, in contrast, while there are several young people over 10 years old in primary contexts who may have been treated as 'adults' (e.g. at North Stoke in Period 2; and Crichel Down 12 and Amesbury 72b in Period 3), younger individuals in such contexts are rare (there are primary burials of children aged between four and seven at

---

[9] There are also problems with dating, as many of these burials are unaccompanied by grave goods, radiocarbon dates are rare, and stratigraphic information may simply provide a *terminus post quem* for burial deposits that were late in sequences of funerary activity.

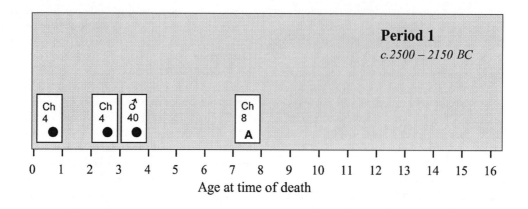

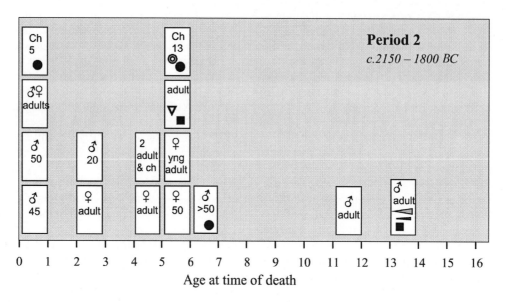

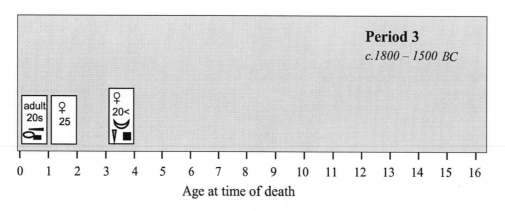

Fig. 7.5: Children interred with older children and adults. Where known, the sex and age of the older individuals and artefact associations are shown (same data-set as in Fig. 7.2; see Fig. 7.4 for key).

Deeping St. Nicholas, Risby and Crichel Down 7) and most children were buried in secondary contexts. There is also a striking difference in monument and funerary contexts. In Periods 1 and 3, most child burials occurred singly at monuments with single construction phases and few other burials (three or less, if any). In Period 2, in contrast, child burials can often be found grouped in relatively large numbers (comprising a large proportion of the burials present) at multi-phase mound sites such as Amesbury 71 (five child burials; 62% of individuals represented), Long Crichel 5 (8; 66%), Barnack (8; 36%), and Radley 12 (4; 44%), and at 'open arena' sites such as the pre-mound phase at West Overton G6b (8; 66%) and the pond barrows at Down Farm (7; 54%) and Radley 4866 (3; 33%).

2500-2150 BC	2150-1800 BC	1800-1500 BC

Age-at-death

0-1
1
2
3
4
5
6
7
8
9
10
11
12
13
14
15

2500-2150 BC

Child burials rare and diverse, though most found with adults or older children (probably as selected material/'artefact' associations), and some with artefacts (Beakers).

Child burials rare but similar in character: most are primary burials associated with artefacts and other materials, especially Beakers and the remains of younger children and animals.

2150-1800 BC

Burials in the 0-2 age group common, especially infants less than 1 year old, neonates and foetuses.

Many associated with ceramics, especially Beakers (notably handled Beakers) and Food Vessels, and animal remains.

Burials of children in the 4-8 age group fairly common. A high proportion associated with artefacts and materials

4-6 age group: lithic artefacts, child remains.

7-8 age group: ceramics (Beakers and Food Vessels), animal remains.

Child burials rare, mostly in secondary contexts, some with artefacts (Beakers).

A few burials, all in secondary contexts. The 14-15 age group possibly being treated as proto-adults/adults, especially those with artefacts and other materials.

1800-1500 BC

A few burials of children in the 0-3 age group.

Often buried with adults: grave goods in these cases probably relate mostly to the adults rather than the children.

Child burials rare, occasionally in primary contexts.

Most child burials associated with artefacts; mainly urns, but also flintwork and other objects.

A few burials, half in primary contexts and most with artefacts (urns and other objects): probably being treated as proto-adults/adults.

Fig. 7.6: Summary of the evidence for child burials in southern Britain by period, showing age groups subject to distinctive mortuary treatment. Bold lines indicate age groups represented by numerous burials and/or especially consistent burial practices. Dark grey areas indicate that child burials of these age groups are either absent or are extremely rare.

It is now evident that there was no single durable tradition of 'child burial' in the Late Neolithic and Early Bronze Age. We are faced instead with several distinct categories of children at any one time, different kinds of mortuary treatment and funerary deposition, and a succession of quite different mortuary and funerary practices from one period to the next (summarized in Fig. 7.6).

Even where practices may at first sight look the same (for example, crouched inhumation burials in pits), it is apparent that the social contexts of burial at different kinds of monuments, and the spatial organization, frequency, sequence and symbolic content of funerary

rituals also changed profoundly over time (see below). As far as different age categories are concerned, very young children less than two years old were especially significant in Period 2 but not in Periods 1 or 3. Young people over 12 years were also marked out in Periods 2 and 3, but perhaps not as 'children': they may already have been seen as adults or adults-to-be (while still lacking the trappings of achieved status, power or personal accomplishment that mark out many 'rich' adult graves). Finally, the emphasis in all three periods on child burials in the 5-8 age group, again in terms of relative frequency and grave goods, perhaps relates to shared perceptions of a phase in the child's life course when personality, independence, sociality, gender and future potential had become manifest, and the loss of the young person palpable in social terms for the first time. This need not imply, however, that the specific conceptualisation or valuation of such a loss was the same in each period.

Social reproduction and cultural representation

Changes in funerary practices and monuments suggest that the cultural contexts, significance and specific meanings of funerary events involving children changed fundamentally during the Late Neolithic and Early Bronze Age. What follows is an attempt to identify some of the concerns evoked in these practices.

Period 1 (2500-2150 BC): at first sight, early deposits of child remains appear to be the most difficult to understand. They are inconsistent, for example, with interpretations of early Beaker graves in terms of the celebration and sacralisation of *adult* role stereotypes perceived to be essential to social reproduction (e.g. Thomas 1991). Nor, as several examples of primary or separate child burials with personal grave goods demonstrate, can they simply represent the subordinate kinsfolk of adults that elsewhere were marked out symbolically as 'satellite' or 'secondary' burials (e.g. Mizoguchi 1993, 1995). Interpretation becomes easier, however, once it is recognized that the diverse range of child burials in this period in fact fall into two quite distinct categories.

First, infants and younger children less than four years old were mostly buried with adults and older children, often in 'satellite' positions or placed within grave pits in positions similar to those of artefacts and other objects. A good example is the burial of a three-year old child at Hemp Knoll, Wiltshire (Robertson-Mackay 1980). The child's body had been placed on the de-turfed old land surface, just to the north-west of the primary grave pit which contained the body of a mature adult male, tightly-crouched in a probable wickerwork coffin, and several distinctive objects including a fine Beaker, an archer's wristguard and the head and hooves of an ox (see Fig. 7.7). There is little question that all the depositional events took place within a short time of one another: both bodies were aligned in approximately the same direction, and both the backfilled grave pit and the child's body were sealed directly beneath the turf mound (Robertson-Mackay 1980: 143). In the absence of formal mortuary treatment of very young children as 'individuals' in this period, it is likely that they were present in burial contexts as votive offerings or gifts to supernatural beings: perhaps as materials that embodied life as a resource (discussed above), deposited in order to placate the ancestors, make entreaties to sources of vitality for the renewal of life, or to pacify malevolent spirits.

Second, the burials of children in the 4-8 age group are very different to those of younger children: they consist mostly of primary burials with artefacts, spatially organised in ways very similar to the lay-out of adult graves. These burials suggest a concern with significant inherited identities and potential adult roles among children who had reached an age where such potentiality had become recognizable and the loss keenly felt. Given the prominence of adult males in early Beaker graves (Robertson-Mackay 1980; Gibbs 1990), and the rarity of female burials in general, it is likely that these were boys rather than girls. The great rarity of these child burials, however, also suggests that there were special circumstances that prompted the decision to proceed with formal burial. The breaking of a descent line, for example, might have evoked great distress and anxiety in relation to concepts of cosmological order. It is interesting that most of these burials occur in isolated settings or (in the case of Radley 919) to one side of a linear arrangement of early Beaker graves (Garwood 1999: Fig.9.7). This may indicate separation of these events from the wider range of funerary activities, which were perhaps more concerned with continuity and reproduction, rather than discontinuity and extinction.

Period 2 (2150-1800 BC): the mortuary treatment of child bodies and the contexts in which they were deposited in Period 2 were altogether different to those of Period 1. This is most clearly appreciated in the funerary practices at large multi-phase mounds (Garwood 2007; cf. Barrett 1988b; Last 1998). These structures represent very strong commitment to specific locations in the landscape, the construction events and ritual performances that took place on and around them, and the dead incorporated within them (with complex referencing of earlier graves in each new burial; Last 1998: 48-51). These activities can be interpreted as ways of reifying stories of origins, belonging and timeless order at significant ancestral locales. The 'growth' of mounds as they were periodically enlarged, and the presence of timber structures and organic deposits, can perhaps be seen as metaphorical expressions of 'organic' qualities and processes, symbolising the continuity and reproductive success of the mound-building groups. At every stage, earlier constructional features, corporeal materials and the memories of past people and events attached to these, were physically absorbed, and assimilated within one composite story of past and present order (Garwood 2007).

In this context, the greater frequency of burials and particular modes of body treatment at multi-phase round barrows suggest that the intention of funerary rituals was to resolve deep concerns about continuity, growth and vitality, and to manage dangerous periods of instability in the order of things (brought about by deaths, but perhaps also other events or periods of perceived social vulnerability). In many cases, burials were added to earlier grave pits or embodied within mound fabrics in such a way that upward vertical sequence was emphasised, perhaps as a metaphorical expression of growth and continuity. It is also evident that many different age and gender categories were buried at these

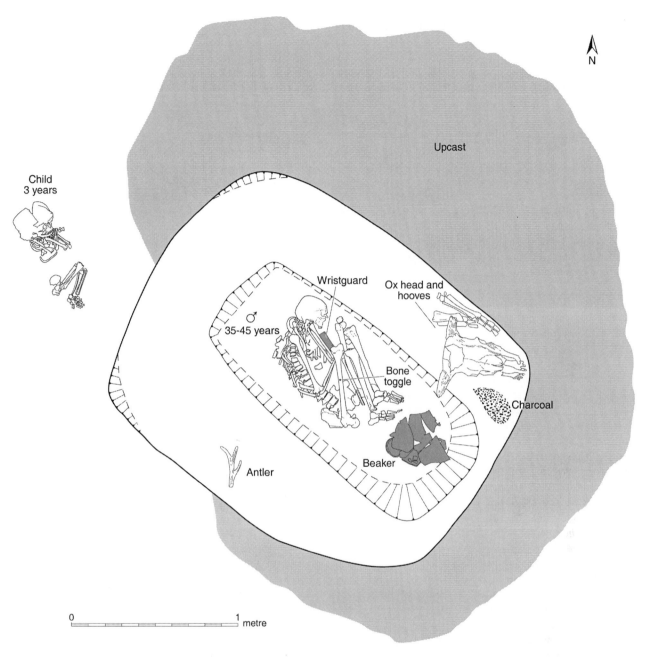

Fig. 7.7: The central burials at Hemp Knoll, Wiltshire (after Robertson-Mackay 1980, figs. 2, 6, 10A).

sites – children, young and old adults, males and females – suggesting a deep concern in funerary rituals with the vital qualities and reproduction of 'corporate' social bodies, rather than individual members of elite groups.

Child remains were treated in much the same ways in both mound and non-mound architectural settings, but their different depositional contexts suggest that funerary rituals may have been interpreted in different ways. Platforms and arenas, for example, while features of mound architecture in this period (i.e. in the form of flat-topped and truncated mounds), were also purpose-built in the form of enclosures such as 'pond barrows', 'ring barrows' and 'ring cairns', which were designed to accommodate repeated ritual actions and depositional

events within open stages (Garwood 2007). Rather than upward growth, the focus of these structures is more inward and downward (inevitably inviting speculation about references to contrasting deities or supernatural domains 'above' and 'below'). Like contemporary mound sites, burials of all age and sex categories can be found at these sites, although child remains, often associated with objects, are especially common (together with the remains of animals; e.g. at Down Farm).

It is important, in other respects, not to assume that all child burials in this period 'meant' the same things or served the same purposes. Although the deaths of children, like those of adults, may well have prompted ritual actions to address losses of vitality and reproductive potential, it is also possible that children served other symbolic purposes. The high proportion of burials of infants less than one year old is especially striking: their presence marks deliberate choices by living adults to incorporate within the central symbols and repositories of group existence a category of children who might be seen to represent life, vitality and its loss, but could not in a straightforward way symbolize growth (being un-grown), group identity (unlearnt), continuity (broken by death) or reproductive potential (unformed and invisible). In this light, the 'burials' of infant bodies may have acted more as offerings of transformed corporeal substances, symbolising or containing sources of vitality, to ancestors or deities on whom future life and regeneration ultimately depended, especially where life itself was perceived to be a 'limited resource' to be recycled or replenished.

Other aspects of the evidence also point to a material culture of death that included wider use of corporeal materials and substances. The young infants found buried with adult males and older children, for example, like those in Period 1 (see above) may have been seen more as 'grave goods' than individual burials in their own right. Moreover, the heavy Food Vessels and handled Beakers found with young infants cannot be seen as functional personal items or as emblems of achieved status, and their rarity and simplicity do not obviously indicate elite display or the marking of inherited status. Instead, the use of these objects for eating and drinking suggest evocations of sustenance, regeneration and sociality: in other words, processes and qualities that were not yet fully recognizable in the bodies or behaviours of dependent infants. The objects may not, therefore, have accompanied the infants as 'grave goods' in any simple sense, but may instead have been set alongside their corporeal remains: both objects and infant bodies being deployed, in parallel, as media in ritual acts intended to engage with sources of life and power (cf. Bell 1992: 141).

Period 3 (1800-1500 BC): there is little evidence for new construction events at old mound sites or the building of new open arenas such as pond barrows after 1800 BC, and burials at these monuments were rare and episodic by 1700 BC (Garwood 2007). Instead, we see very different kinds of mortuary ritual and monumentalism, with the predominance, by c. 1800 BC, of single-phase mound structures and cremation practices, complex treatment of the 'elite' dead (mostly adults, both male and female), and central, sealed burial deposits that appear more like 'final' statements than parts of on-going and inclusive stories of group identity. By raising large mounds soon after funerals, mound builders created prominent monuments indivisible from the individuals embodied within them, projecting unambiguous statements about the 'significant dead' across the landscape. The diversity of burial assemblages and grave lay-outs also suggests that funerary displays and deposits described social and political biographies in individualistic, if idealized and

aesthetically consistent ways (cf. Sørensen 2004). It is clear, however, that each burial was also articulated in relation to others through spatial arrangements of monuments that could be used to assert social and historical relationships (Garwood 2007), especially by adding a new mound to a line of monuments – 'writing' a new chapter in a narrative of dynastic succession and past, present and future glory.

In this context, child burials became rare and more peripheral not because children were now unimportant, but because they were largely incidental to the funerary display and monumentalisation of adult social power, achievement and political success. Above all, the cosmological concerns that had so absorbed people in mortuary rituals in the period c. 2200-1800 BC were no longer as salient, or even relevant, to the issues evoked and strategically manipulated in the course of funerals after 1800 BC. Ritual actions at monument sites now served to transform the significant dead into exemplars or icons of aristocratic moral order and to install them as permanent members of sacralised descent lines. They were embedded within monuments that materially visualised narratives of historical descent and related these to a more distanced timeless cosmological order; it is notable, for example, that many linear barrow groups are aligned on much older ancient monuments or celestial phenomena (Garwood 1999, 2003, 2007). Rather than a concern with recycling fragile and limited sources of life (e.g. as symbolised in young infant burials), or engaging directly with ancestors or deities on whom future life depended, through rituals in which the remains of children had important parts to play, funerary rituals after 1800 BC appear mostly focused on those who could mediate with more distant sources of life and order, by virtue of their ancestry and their consequent position in the order of things. The rarity of very young infant burials in Period 3, and the emphasis on older children who might have taken on 'adult' roles or identities as members of elite lineages, are explicable in these terms. The occasional presence of other child burials, in this context, may relate to specific situations when roles or identities ascribed to certain children, or lines of descent and inheritance, had become matters of special anxiety or contention.

Rare things: time, transformation, and the making of Early Bronze Age 'children'

This paper has presented a preliminary investigation of the nature of child burials and representations of children in the British Early Bronze Age. This subject, hitherto, has been almost entirely neglected: the purpose of this discussion has been to reveal the complexity and significance of the evidence, and possible lines of interpretation.

It is apparent that unitary descriptions of 'child burials' and what they represent are thoroughly misleading. In fact, several different kinds of young people were marked out for special mortuary treatment, and the significance of ritual acts involving child remains at monument sites varied over time. There is a current tendency in British earlier prehistoric studies to focus on traditions of practice in a thematic way (e.g. 'mortuary practices'), and to present gross characterizations of these at a temporal scale of millennia, often with gradualist assumptions about their essential continuity in form and significance over very long periods (e.g. Barrett 1988b; Lucas 1996; Thomas 2000). These interpretations of funerary evidence are unconvincing, especially once the sheer diversity of practices, rapid tempos of change, and radical transformations in the nature of practices and their contextual meanings are recognized (cf. Garwood 2007; cf. Bloch 1986 on the rapidity of change in ritual practices, if not always their meaning). Rather than durable traditions of practice in the treatment of dead children, it is apparent that we are faced with a succession of profoundly different sets of practices, and distinct kinds of social agency and signification. The point of departure for studies of Late Neolithic and Early Bronze Age funerary practices and monuments must be to situate these as precisely as possible in time.

The period framework used here is helpful at a broad level of generalisation for ordering and interpreting some of the activities at monument sites, but inevitably it disguises or conflates short-lived phases of funerary activity within each period. A particular problem, in this context, is accounting for the episodic nature of child burial events within a milieu of funerary practice that largely excluded children. They may perhaps be explained as impulsive sentimental acts by grieving parents (cf. Crawford's interpretation of child burials in early Anglo-Saxon England: 2000: 177), but in the Late Neolithic and Early Bronze Age such burial events appear deliberate and self-conscious: they were rare things that involved strategic choices about location, decisions to proceed, modes of expression and intended significance. The difficulty lies in how to discern the reasons behind such events and their timing. References to social 'stresses', periods of 'anxiety', and situations in which the community felt 'vulnerable' may well be accurate, but they do not explain the particular concerns involved (see above; cf. Bradley 1984, 75, on the timing of Wessex rich graves). This issue deserves more attention, especially through comparative contextual analyses of child burials and their temporal and spatial settings (Garwood in preparation).

We may also begin to understand more about the children that were buried at monument sites by trying to make sense of those buried elsewhere. The evidence is very limited and fragmentary, but one obvious place to start would be cave deposits (e.g. see Barnatt & Edmonds 2002). It is not that this may provide a way of 'reconstructing' a coherent religious system, in which each kind of burial practice occupied an appropriate niche (implying that we might understand the parts by discerning the whole), but rather that in different

practices and in comparisons between them we may recognize the generative schemes and religious concerns that structured the treatment of children in specific contexts of deposition. In all these kinds of mortuary deposits, however, what we encounter are the material outcomes of processes of ritualisation, symbolic transformations and ritual actions, during which children and the remains of children were re-constituted and endowed with new qualities and significance. The study of Early Bronze Age children is thus concerned more with what they became after death, than what they had been in life.

Bibliography

Ariès, P. (1962): *Centuries of Childhood: a social history of family life*. London.

Ashbee, P. (1960): *The Bronze Age Round Barrow in Britain*. London.

Ashbee, P. (1984): 'The excavation of Amesbury barrows 58, 61a, 61, 72', *Wiltshire Archaeological Magazine* 79: 39-91.

Barclay, A. and Halpin, C. (eds) (1999): *Excavations at Barrow Hills, Radley, Oxfordshire. Vol I: The Neolithic and Bronze Age monument complex*. Oxford Archaeological Unit; Thames Valley Landscapes, Monograph 1. Oxford.

Barley, N. (1995): *Dancing on the Grave: encounters with death*. London.

Barnatt, J. and Edmonds, M. (2002): 'Places apart? Caves and monuments in Neolithic and earlier Bronze Age Britain', *Cambridge Archaeological Journal* 12(1): 113-29.

Barrett, J. (1988a): 'Fields of discourse: reconstituting a social archaeology', *Critique of Anthropology* 7(3): 5-16.

Barrett, J. (1988b): 'The living, the dead and the ancestors: Neolithic and early Bronze Age mortuary practices', in J. Barrett and I. Kinnes, (eds), *The archaeology of context in the Neolithic and Bronze Age: recent trends*, 30-41. Department of Archaeology and Prehistory, University of Sheffield. Sheffield.

Barrett, J. (1990): 'The monumentality of death: the character of Early Bronze Age mortuary mounds in southern England', *World Archaeology* 22: 179-89.

Barrett, J. (1994): *Fragments from Antiquity*. Oxford.

Barrett, J., Bradley, R. and Green, M. (1991): *Landscape, Monuments and Society. The prehistory of Cranborne Chase*. Cambridge.

Barthes, R. (1972): *Mythologies*. London (first published in 1957: *Mythologies*. Paris).

Baxter, J.E. (2005): *The archaeology of childhood: children, gender and material culture*. Oxford.

Bell, C. (1992): *Ritual theory, ritual practice*. Oxford.

Bellamy, P. (1991): 'The excavation of Fordington Farm round barrow', *Proceedings of the Dorset Natural History and Archaeological Society* 113: 107-32.

Blacking, J. (1977): 'Towards an anthropology of the body', in J. Blacking (ed.), *The Anthropology of the Body*, 1-28. Association of Social Anthropologists Monograph 15. London.

Bloch, M. (1971): *Placing the dead: tombs, ancestral villages, and kinship organization in Madagascar.* London.

Bloch, M. (1981): 'Tombs and states', in S.C. Humphreys and H. King (eds), *Mortality and Immortality: the anthropology and archaeology of death*, 137-47. London.

Bloch, M. (1982): 'Death, women and power', in M. Bloch and J. Parry (eds), *Death and the regeneration of life*, 211-30. Cambridge.

Bloch, M. (1986): *From blessing to violence: history and ideology in the circumcision ritual of the Merina of Madagascar.* Cambridge.

Bloch, M. (1992): *Prey into hunter: the politics of religious experience.* Cambridge.

Bloch, M. (2005): 'Why trees, too, are good to think with: toward an anthropology of the meaning of life', in M. Bloch, *Essays on cultural transmission*, 21-38. London School of Economics Monographs on Social Anthropology, Volume 75. Oxford. (Re-printed from: L. Rival (ed.), *The Social Life of Trees: anthropological perspectives of tree symbolism.* Oxford).

Bloch, M. and Parry, J. (1982): 'Introduction: death and the regeneration of life', in M. Bloch and J. Parry (eds), *Death and the regeneration of life*, 1-44. Cambridge.

Bradley, R. (1984a): *The social foundations of Prehistoric Britain.* London.

Bradley, R. (2005): *Ritual and domestic life in Prehistoric Europe.* London.

Braithwaite, M. (1984): 'Ritual and prestige in the prehistory of Wessex, c. 2200-1400 BC: a new dimension to the archaeological evidence', in D. Miller and C. Tilley (eds), *Ideology, Power and Prehistory*, 93-110. Cambridge.

Brück, J. (1999): 'Ritual and rationality: some problems of interpretation in European archaeology', *European Journal of Archaeology* 2(3): 313-44.

Brück, J. (2004): 'Material metaphors: the relational construction of identity in early Bronze Age burials in Ireland and Britain', *Journal of Social Archaeology* 4(3): 307-33.

Buikstra, J.E. and Ubelaker, D.H. (eds) (1994): *Standards for Data Collection from Human Skeletal Remains.* Arkansas Archaeological Survey 5. Fayetteville.

Burgess, C. (1980): *The Age of Stonehenge.* London.

Carrasco, D. (1999): *City of Sacrifice: the Aztec empire and the role of violence in civilization.* Boston.

Case, H.J. (1956): 'The Lambourn Seven barrows', *Berkshire Archaeological Journal* 55: 15-31.

Catling, H.W. (1959): 'A Beaker-culture barrow at North Stoke, Oxon.', *Oxoniensia* 24: 1-12.

Chapman, J. (2000): *Fragmentation in Archaeology.* London.

Christie, P. (1967): 'A barrow-cemetery of the second millennium BC in Wiltshire, England', *Proceedings of the Prehistoric Society* 33: 336-66.

Crawford, S. (1999): *Childhood in Anglo-Saxon England.* Stroud.

Crawford, S. (2000): 'Children, grave goods and social status in early Anglo-Saxon England', in J. Sofaer Derevenski, (ed.), *Children and Material Culture*, 169-79. London.

Davies, D. (1997): *Death, Ritual and Belief.* London.

Díaz-Andreu, M., Lucy, S., Babić, S. and Edwards, D. N. (2005): *The archaeology of identity: approaches to gender, age status, ethnicity and religion.* London.

Douglas, M. (1966): *Purity and Danger: an analysis of concepts of pollution and taboo.* London.

Douglas, M. (1973): *Natural Symbols: explorations in cosmology.* Harmondsworth.

Durkheim, E. and Mauss, M. (1967): *Primitive Classification.* Trans. R. Needham (originally published 1902). Chicago.

Ellen, R. (1977): 'Anatomical classification and the semiotics of the body', in J. Blacking, (ed.), *The Anthropology of the Body*, 343-74. Association of Social Anthropologists Monograph 15. London.

Finlay, N. (2000): 'Outside of life: traditions of infant burial in Ireland from *cillín* to cist', *World Archaeology* 31(3): 407-22.

French, C.A.I. (1994): *Excavation of the Deeping St Nicholas Barrow Complex, South Lincolnshire.* Heritage Trust for Lincolnshire. Sleaford.

Fowler, C. (2004): *The Archaeology of Personhood.* London.

Fox, Sir C. (1959): *Life and Death in the Bronze Age: an archaeologist's field-work.* London.

Garwood, P. (1991): 'Ritual tradition and the reconstitution of society', in P. Garwood, D. Jennings, R. Skeates and J. Toms (eds), *Sacred and Profane. Archaeology, ritual and religion*, 10-32. Oxford University Committee for Archaeology Monograph 32. Oxford.

Garwood, P. (1999): 'Radiocarbon dating and the chronology of the monument complex', in A. Barclay and C. Halpin (eds), *Excavations at Barrow Hills, Radley, Oxfordshire. Vol I: The Neolithic and Bronze Age monument complex*, 293-309. Thames Valley Landscapes, Monograph 1. Oxford.

Garwood, P. (2003): 'Round barrows and funerary traditions in Late Neolithic and Bronze Age Sussex', in D. Rudling (ed.), *The Archaeology of Sussex to AD 2000*, 47-68. Great Dunham.

Garwood, P. (2007): 'Before the hills in order stood: chronology, time and history in the interpretation of early Bronze Age round barrows', in J. Last (ed.), *Beyond the Grave: new perspectives on round barrows.* Oxford.

Garwood, P. (in preparation): 'The children that never were: ritual transformations and cultural constructions in Bronze Age Europe'.

Gerloff, S. (1975): *The Early Bronze Age Daggers of Great Britain and a Reconsideration of the Wessex culture*. Munich: Prähistorische Bronzefunde Abt.VI, B.2.

Gibbs, A. V. (1990): *Sex, Gender and Material Culture Patterning in Later Neolithic and Early Bronze Age England*. Unpublished Ph.D. thesis, University of Cambridge.

Green, C, Lynch, F. and White, H. (1982): 'The excavation of two round barrows on Launceston Down, Dorset (Long Crichel 5 and 7)', *Proceedings of the Dorset Natural History and Archaeological Society* 104: 39-58.

Green, M.A. (2001): *Dying for the Gods: human sacrifice in Iron Age and Roman Europe*. Stroud.

Healy, F. and Harding, J. (forthcoming): *Raunds Area Project: the Neolithic and Bronze Age landscapes of West Cotton, Stanwick and Irthlingborough, Northamptonshire*.

Hill, J. D. (1995): *Ritual and Rubbish in the Iron Age of Wessex*. British Archaeological Reports, British Series 242. Oxford.

Hodder, I. and Hutson, S. (2003): *Reading the Past: current approaches to interpretation in archaeology* (3rd edition). Cambridge.

Hopkins, E. (2002): *A Study of Child Burials from the Late Neolithic and Early Bronze Age in Central Southern England*. Unpublished B.A. dissertation, University of Birmingham.

Humphrey, C. and Laidlaw, J. (1994): *The Archetypal Actions of Ritual: a theory of ritual illustrated by the Jain rite of worship*. Oxford.

Insoll, T. (2004): *Archaeology, Ritual, Religion*. London.

James, A. and Prout, A. (eds) (1990): *Constructing and Reconstructing Childhood: contemporary issues in the sociological study of childhood*. New Haven, Conn.

James, A., Jenks, C. and Prout, A. (1998): *Theorizing Childhood*. Cambridge.

Jones, A. (2005): 'Lives in fragments? Personhood and the European Neolithic', *Journal of Social Archaeology* 5(2): 193-224.

Kopytoff, I. (1986): 'The cultural biography of things: commoditization as process', in A. Appadurai (ed.), *The Social Life of Things,* 64-91. Cambridge.

Last, J. (1998): 'Books of life: biography and memory in a Bronze Age barrow', *Oxford Journal of Archaeology* 17: 43-53.

Levi-Strauss, C. (1969): *Totemism*. Trans. R. Needham. Harmondsworth (first published in 1962: *Le Totemisme Aujourd'hui*. Paris).

Lillehammer, G. (2000): 'The world of children', in J. Sofaer Derevenski (ed.), *Children and Material Culture*, 17-26. London.

Lucas, G. M. (1996): 'Of death and debt: a history of the body in Neolithic and Bronze Age Yorkshire', *Journal of European Archaeology* 4: 99-118.

Lucy, S. (2005): 'The archaeology of age', in M. Díaz-Andreu, S. Lucy, S. Babić and D. N Edwards (eds), *The Archaeology of Identity: approaches to gender, age status, ethnicity and religion*, 43-66. London.

Mauss, M. (1973): 'Techniques of the body', *Economy and Society* 2(1): 70-88 (first published in 1936: 'Les techniques du corps', *Journal de Psychologie* 32: 271-93).

Matthews, S. G. (2004): 'Gesture, gender, ethnicity: the instantiated communities of Bronze Age Europe', *Archaeologcal Review from Cambridge* 19(2): 56-72.

McLaren, D. (2004): 'An important child's burial from Doune, Perth and Kinross, Scotland', in A. Gibson and A. Sheridan (eds), *From Sickles to Circles: Britain and Ireland at the time of Stonehenge*, 289-303. Stroud.

Metcalf, P. and Huntingdon, R. (1991) *Celebrations of Death: anthropology of mortuary ritual* (2nd edn.). Cambridge.

Miller, D. (1985): *Artefacts as Categories: a study of ceramic variability in central India*. Cambridge.

Miller, D. (1994): 'Artefacts and the meaning of things', in T. Ingold (ed.), *The Companion Encyclopaedia of Anthropology*, 396-419. London.

Mizoguchi, K. (1993): 'Time in the reproduction of mortuary practices', *World Archaeology* 25: 223-35.

Mizoguchi, K. (1995): 'The 'materiality' of Wessex Beakers', *Scottish Archaeological Review* 9: 175-86.

Mizoguchi, K. (2000): 'The child as a node of past, present and future', in J. Sofaer Derevenski (ed.), *Children and Material Culture*, 141-50. London.

Moore, J. and Scott, E. (eds) (1997): *Invisible People and Processes: writing gender and childhood into Euroepan archaeology*. Leicester.

Mount, C. (1995): 'New research on Irish Early Bronze Age cemeteries', in J. Waddell and E. Shee-Twohig (eds), *Ireland in the Bronze Age*, 97-112. Dublin.

Parker Pearson, M. (1999): *The Archaeology of Death and Burial*. Stroud.

Pearce, S. (1994): 'Objects as meaning; or narrating the past', in S. Pearce (ed.), *Interpreting Objects and Collections*, 19-29. London.

Piggott, S. and Piggott, C.M. (1944): 'Excavations of barrows on Crichel and Launceston Downs, Dorset', *Archaeologia* 90: 47-80.

Read, R.F. (1923): 'Second report on the excavation of the Mendip barrows', *Proceedings of the University of Bristol Speleological Society* 2: 131-46,

Rega, E. (1997): 'Age, gender and biological reality in the Early Bronze Age cemetery at Mokrin', in J. Moore and E. Scott (eds), *Invisible People and Processes: writing gender and childhood into European archaeology*, 229-47. Leicester.

Richards, C. and Thomas, J. (1984): 'Ritual activity and structured deposition in Neolithic Wessex', R. Bradley and J. Gardiner (eds) *Neolithic Studies: a review of some current research*, 189-218. British Archaeological Reports, British Series 133. Oxford.

Richards, J. (1990): *The Stonehenge Environs Project*. English Heritage Archaeological Report 16. London.

Robertson-Mackay, M. E. (1980): 'A "head and hooves" burial beneath a round barrow, with other Neolithic and Bronze Age sites, on Hemp Knoll, near Avebury,

Wiltshire', *Proceedings of the Prehistoric Society* 46: 123-76.

Schechner, R. (1994): 'Ritual and performance', in T. Ingold (ed.), *Companion Encyclopaedia of Anthropology*, 613-47. London.

Scott, E. (1991): 'Animal and infant burials in Romano-British villas: a revitalization movement', in P. Garwood, D. Jennings, R. Skeates and J. Toms (eds), *Sacred and Profane. Archaeology, ritual and religion*, 115-21. Oxford University Committee for Archaeology Monograph 32. Oxford.

Shanks, M. and Tilley, C. (1982): 'Ideology, symbolic power and ritual communication: a reinterpretation of Neolithic mortuary practices', in I. Hodder (ed.), *Symbolic and Structural Archaeology*, 129-54. Cambridge.

Smith, I. F. and Simpson, D. D. A. (1966): 'Excavation of a round barrow on Overton Hill, north Wiltshire', *Proceedings of the Prehistoric Society* 32: 122-55.

Sofaer Derevenski, J. (1997): 'Engendering children, engendering archaeology', in J. Moore and E. Scott (eds), *Invisible People and Processes: writing gender and childhood into European archaeology*, 191-202. Leicester.

Sofaer Derevenski, J. (2000): 'Material culture shock: confronting expectations in the material culture of children', in Sofaer Derevenski, J. (ed.), *Children and Material Culture*, 3-16. London.

Sofaer Derevenski, J. (2002): 'Engendering context: context as gendered practice in the Early Bronze Age of the Upper Thames valley, UK', *European Journal of Archaeology* 5(2): 191-211.

Sofaer, J.R. (2006): *The Body as Material Culture.* Cambridge.

Sørenson, M.L.S. (2004): 'Stating identities: the use of objects in rich Bronze Age graves', in J. Cherry, C. Scarre and S. Shennan (eds), *Explaining Social Change: essays in honour of Colin Renfrew*, 167-76, Macdonald Institute Monographs Cambridge.

Taylor, T. (2002): *The Buried Soul: how humans invented death.* London.

Thomas, J. (1991): 'Reading the body: Beaker funerary practice in Britain', in P. Garwood, D. Jennings, R. Skeates and J. Toms (eds), *Sacred and Profane. Archaeology, ritual and religion*, 33-42. Oxford University Committee for Archaeology Monograph 32. Oxford.

Thomas, J. (1999): *Understanding the Neolithic.* London.

Thomas, J. (2000): 'Death, identity and the body in Neolithic Britain', *Journal of the Royal Anthropological Institute* 6: 653-68.

Thomas, J. (2004): *Archaeology and Modernity.* London.

Thomas, J. and Tilley, C. (1993): 'The axe and the torso: symbolic structures', in C. Tilley (ed.), *Interpretive Archaeology*, 225-325. Oxford.

Tilley, C. (1989): 'Interpreting material culture', in I. Hodder (ed.), *The Meaning of Things*, 185-213. London.

Tilley, C. (1999): *Metaphor and Material Culture.* Oxford.

Treherne, P. (1995): 'The warrior's beauty: the masculine body and self-identity in Bronze Age Europe', *Journal of European Archaeology* 3(1): 105-44.

Turner, V. (1967): *The Forest of Symbols: aspects of Ndembu ritual.* Ithaca.

Vatcher, F. de M. and Vatcher, H.L. (1976): 'The excavation of a round barrow near Poor's Heath, Risby, Suffolk', *Proceedings of the Prehistoric Society* 42: 263-92.

Welinder, S. (1998): 'The cultural construction of childhood in Scandinavia, 3500 BC – AD 1350', *Current Swedish Archaeology* 6: 185-204.

Whittle, A. (2003): *The Archaeology of People: dimensions of Neolithic life.* London.

Woodward, A. (2000): *British Barrows: a matter of life and death.* Stroud.

CHAPTER 8

COMPANIONS, CO-INCIDENCES OR CHATTELS? CHILDREN IN THE EARLY ANGLO-SAXON MULTIPLE BURIAL RITUAL

Sally Crawford

The bodies of children, though generally under-represented in early Anglo-Saxon inhumation cemeteries, are conspicuously present in a minority early Anglo-Saxon burial rite, where one or more bodies were placed simultaneously in the same grave (Crawford 1999: 108). In early Anglo-Saxon England from the 5th century AD to the conversion to Christianity in the 7th century, the predominant method for disposing of an adult body was inhumation or cremation with grave goods in cemeteries. The cremation ritual consisted of burning the body (with or without artefacts); collecting the ashes; and placing the remains in the ground, sometimes in a container, of which the most archaeologically-conspicuous type is a pottery urn.[1] Additional small and miniature artefacts were sometimes added to the cremation pot. Anglo-Saxon inhumation cemeteries, which are the focus of this paper, normally consisted of single supine burials, laid out without much regularity across the cemetery area. Early inhumation cemeteries rarely display any archaeologically discernable boundaries. Men, women and children are usually found distributed relatively evenly over Anglo-Saxon cemeteries, and those buried with and without grave goods do not show any strong clustering, though some possible clusterings on the basis of age, gender or grave wealth have been observed at some cemetery sites (Lucy & Reynolds 2002). Graves were rarely intercutting, suggesting that most graves were marked in some way, and there was not normally any pressure of space, so any re-use of burial spaces was not due to constraints within the cemetery (Chadwick Hawkes & Grainger 2003: 11). The size of the average excavated early Anglo-Saxon inhumation cemetery suggests that most served relatively small communities of three or four households over a period of one or two centuries. Anglo-Saxon graves are notable for their great variety, in terms of grave orientation, grave structure, and grave furniture. Analysis of grave goods has shown that the most significant aspect of grave good deposition was its correlation with gender (Brush 1998; Crawford 1991; Härke 1990; Stoodley 2000). The prevailing theoretical interpretation of burial with grave goods in both inhumation and cremation contexts is that the rite offered

a means for conspicuous display of status, social identity and political affiliations, though the burial ritual may also have had familial and religious dimensions (Pader 1982; Filmer Sankey & Pestell 2001; Geake 1997; Crawford 2004).

Though a number of Anglo-Saxon inhumation cemeteries have been excavated and published (Meaney 1964), some to a very high standard, all studies of the mortuary ritual of this period are hampered by some fundamental problems with the evidence. Because Anglo-Saxon cemeteries of this period tend to sprawl across the landscape, only a handful have been fully excavated, so most of the available data comes from partially-recovered populations. Evidence for the age and sex of the mortuary population is variable according to skeletal preservation, and, in published reports, gender distinctions are based on observable skeletal morphology, so children's skeletons cannot be sexed. Furthermore, the population distribution for Anglo-Saxon skeletons makes it clear that the archaeologically recoverable skeletons represent a selected proportion of the mortuary community: children, especially babies, are famously under-represented in the Anglo-Saxon cemetery evidence (Crawford 1991, 1999: 25; Buckberry 2000). Though there may be archaeological explanations for the 'missing infant phenomenon', the inescapable conclusion is that dead children could not normally have been buried in the adult folk cemetery – any infants and children that are found in these cemeteries, therefore, must be considered to have been a deliberately selected proportion of the total (Crawford 2000). On the basis of the surviving evidence, it is not possible to say what circumstances, either related to the social context of the child, or related to the context of its death, may have lead to the decision to include a child's body within the community cemetery (Crawford 2000).

The use of the term 'children' in this paper is not intended to convey any biological sense of those who are not 'adult'. It is a well-established paradigm that age categories, like gender, are a social construct, albeit one closely linked to physiological development and changes (Sofaer 2002: 119). Failure to recognise the culturally variable character of childhood in studies of Anglo-Saxon mortuary ritual has led to confusions and misreadings of the cemetery evidence, a problem compounded by inconsistencies in age categories used across site reports, and even within the same publication (Crawford 1991). However, studies of the archaeological evidence, in

---

[1] The evidence from cremation cemeteries is particularly hard to assess in the context of social responses, because relatively little bone survives to give information on the age, sex or health of the deceased. In addition, it appears that pyres might have been repeatedly built on one site, because bones from more than one individual, which do not represent a whole skeleton, may appear in a single cremation urn. This suggests some contamination at the point of bone collection from the pyre, though it is possible that the cross-contamination was deliberate (Richards 1987; Williams 2005b).

conjunction with the earliest documentary evidence, indicate that any body assigned an age of ten years or above at the time of death could have been perceived as an adult within Anglo-Saxon society, at least in ritual terms (Crawford 1991). Children's graves are characterised by a comparative lack of grave goods, and by the range of adult artefacts they do not possess, rather than by any child-related objects (Crawford 2000). In this respect, Anglo-Saxon children truly were 'sub-adults', defined by what they were not; children's burials reflected incomplete achievement of 'adult' grave goods. Key amongst the 'missing' artefacts for children were 'gendered' items: weaponry for men, and jewellery, girdle hangers and dress fasteners for women. The most common grave goods for children were gender-neutral artefacts such as pots and knives (Crawford 2000; Stoodley 2000).

Younger age thresholds are not easy to identify in the archaeological record. Cultural distinctions between the very young, completely dependent child and older children are implicit in Old English vocabulary and later documentary sources, but if they exist in the archaeological record for the early Anglo-Saxon period, they are not sensitive to current methods of analysis and observation (Crawford 1999: 54, 2007). On the one hand, then, it is possible to argue for a culturally-constructed transitional date from childhood to adulthood of around 10 to 12 years of age, when some boys received weapon sets, and some girls were buried with brooch sets and chatelaines, while any transition from dependent infancy to young childhood, though anthropologically and comparatively likely, can only be mooted. In these circumstances, and however unsatisfactory the compromise may be, this paper will offer an osteologically-determined age for the burials under discussion where that is possible, and the word 'child' will be used to mean a child in Anglo-Saxon cultural terms (i.e. under the age of 10 to 12). Other age ranges and terms used have to be dependent on the information available within the published excavation reports, and should not be assumed to reflect any culturally-determined age category.

Multiple burials

Although the dominant burial form in earlier Anglo-Saxon furnished inhumation cemeteries was supine, single burial within one grave, some excavated cemeteries include a small number of exceptions to the rule of single burial. Multiple burial was a small but significant variation to the norm, which involved adult males and females of all age ranges, and children, with and without grave goods.

The multiple burial ritual has been reassessed recently by Nick Stoodley, who proposed the following simple categorisation of multiple burials: 'grouped' burials in individual graves; sequential burials in a single grave,

which can be subdivided into deliberate insertions of new bodies into existing graves, or accidental overlap with earlier graves; and contemporary burials in one grave, either side by side or one on top of another (Stoodley 2002). Only in the last type, where there was simultaneous burial of two or more bodies in one grave, does it appear certain that two or more deaths occurred either simultaneously, or within a very short space of each other. Early Anglo-Saxon bodies do not show archaeologically visible signs of having been preserved or stored out of the grave for more than short periods after death.

Where different post-mortem processes occur, as they clearly must in the case of different types of 'multiple' burial, it is not surprising that, as Nick Stoodley argued, multiple burials had multiple meanings (Stoodley 2002). However, there is a consistent conceptual difference between these different categories of mortuary groupings, in terms of how these groups were created, and in terms of the cultural and behavioural significance of these different methods of associating bodies within the mortuary ritual. The most profound variation lies in the processes that took place at or around the moment of death. A cluster of individual burials, deliberately intercutting burials, and secondary burials intentionally inserted into pre-existing graves, all make statements of remembrance or association between bodies over an extended chronological period. The first body or series of bodies in the sequence remain in a 'systemic context' after death, in that the body retains a meaning and a place in social memory after the point of death and burial (Schiffer 1976: 27-28; Hallam et al. 1999; Johnson 1989; Williams 2003: 5). Where two bodies are buried simultaneously (that is, where the archaeological evidence within carefully-excavated sites shows absolutely no signs of re-cutting or re-use of the grave), there can have been no definite expression of the continued social presence of the dead in the life of the living, nor any reinforcement of temporal links between one body and another.

The normal focus of mortuary interpretation is on what happened after death: the process of burial and the burial itself. Contemporary, simultaneous burials allow us a rare opportunity to say something about the 'death event' of an individual within Anglo-Saxon society, rather than about what happened to the body *after* death. The death of one individual happened at the same time as, or immediately before or after, the death of another member of the community. Subsequent to the deaths, a deliberate decision was made (except in the case of women buried with *in utero* babies, where the buriers may not necessarily have been aware of the foetus) to deviate from the predominant ritual and bury the two bodies in the same grave. We cannot say that all simultaneous deaths in the community were given multiple burials, but we can say that, in addition to any other unknowable social factors (age, wealth, familial relationships), the

Grave number	Body 1 (SEX (WHERE KNOWN) AND AGE IN YEARS)	Body 2 (AGE)	Body 3 (AGE)	Body 4 (AGE)
49	1	F - 17-25		
67	1 - 1.5	F - 17-25		
79	2 - 3	F - 17-25		
113	3 - 4	M - 17-25		
11	8	F - 'adult'		
16	9	F - 35-45		
85	F - 13-15	F - 35-45		
104	M - 16-18	M - 25-35		
98	M - 17-25	F - 'adult'		
4	F - 45+	M - 'adult'		
96	5	F - 8	M - 15-17	
26	10 - 12	12 - 14	M - 20-25	
31	M - 18-20	M - 25-30	M - 25-30	
119	2	M - 22-30	M - 30-50	M 'adult'

Fig 8:1 Age and sex combinations in multiple contemporary burials at the early Anglo-Saxon cemetery of Empingham II, Rutland (derived from Timby 1996).

coincident death-event of two or more people played some significant role in determining their subsequent non-standard mortuary disposal in the same grave.

Not all Anglo-Saxon cemetery sites include multiple burials in their rituals: all the graves at Alton, Hampshire, for example, contained single bodies (Evison 1988). However, a striking aspect of the multiple burial ritual where it was practiced is the disproportionately large number of children found in them (Crawford 1993: 84-85). At the furnished inhumation cemetery of Worthy Park, Kingsworthy, Hampshire, for example, every simultaneous double burial included a child (Chadwick Hawkes & Grainger 2003). At Nassington, Northamptonshire, the only two infant burials recovered from the site (which consisted of approximately 40 excavated bodies) were in double burials (Leeds 1944).

To give a more detailed picture of the age groups involved in the multiple burial ritual, Fig 8.1. offers a breakdown of the body combinations at Empingham II, Rutland (derived from Timby 1996). In all, 14 of the 136 graves at this site contained the bodies of more than one person. Children are strongly represented in multiple burials at Empingham II – nine of the 31 children aged less than ten years of age in this mortuary population (29% of the children) were in multiple burials, including a two year old in the site's only four-person grave. All age and gender combinations are represented here, with the notable exception of children with children. Over half of the Empingham II multiples include a child under the age of ten years. This pattern is replicated across the Anglo-Saxon inhumation burial ritual, with some sites, such as Lechlade (10 out of 15 multiples), Nassington, Northamptonshire (all multiples), and Berinsfield, Oxfordshire (all certain contemporary multiples), having

considerable higher ratios (Stoodley 2002; Leeds 1944; Boyle, Jennings et al. 1998).

These figures are potentially skewed by the inclusion of women who died during pregnancy, as noted above. At Westgarth Gardens, Suffolk, two of the three multiple burials are of adult females with infants (Graves 9 and 48: West 1988). At Worthy Park, Kingsworthy, three of the five double burials at the site are of women with infants. The positioning of the few surviving infant bones in Grave 21 led the excavator to suggest that the associated adult female might have died in pregnancy, though heavy post-burial disturbance in the pelvic area, and the woman's age (she was identified as being around 50 at the time of death) make such a diagnosis less convincing. Grave 26 at Worthy Park leaves much less room for doubt: the infant associated with a female aged between 18-30 still had its feet enclosed within the woman's pelvic girdle. The infant's body, resting between the female's legs, had been covered by a layer of chalk rubble. This seems a case of 'obstetric calamity', where complications associated with the birth led to death and burial for a mother and infant who literally could not be separated (Chadwick Hawkes & Wells 1975). However, infants are also found in association with adult males, so infant/adult female pairs cannot automatically be assumed to represent childbirth mortality unless, as in the case of Worthy Park Grave 26, a death in pregnancy seems indisputable.

Child pairs are relatively uncommon in the multiple burial ritual as a whole. As already noted, there were no child pairs at all at Empingham II, Rutland (Timby 1996), and neither were there any at the large cemeteries of Berinsfield, Oxfordshire (Boyle 1995), Lechlade, Gloucestershire (Boyle et al. 1998), Polhill, West Kent

(Philp 1973), Worthy Park, Hampshire (Chadwick Hawkes & Grainger 2003), and Castledyke South, Humberside (Drinkall & Foreman 1998), for example. An exception to this pattern is the site of Great Chesterford, Essex (Evison 1994). The excavated portion of the cemetery at Great Chesterford consisted of 161 inhumation graves, 23 cremations, two horse graves and one dog burial (Evison 1994: xi). Dating evidence from the site was poor, but the earliest burials may be assigned to the mid-5th century, and the latest burials were deposited c. 600 AD. Aside from the animal inhumations, the site is very unusual in having a large number of children's graves. There were at least 82 burials of juveniles under the age 15, of which 65 were infant or foetus graves (children under the age of two), not including two infants found within the pelvic girdle of female adults (Evison 1994: 33-35). Mulitple, simultaneous burials at the site consist of Grave 142, containing a horse and a male adult; Grave 86, containing a juvenile and a dog; Grave 95, containing two infants aged under two months at the time of death; Grave 150, with two infants aged between 2-4 months at the time of death, and Grave 83, which contained the remains of at least six foetuses, all aged between 36 and 40 weeks. As the excavator commented, 'it is possible that graves 95 and 150 might represent burials of twins or even triplets, but it is difficult to imagine how six or more foetuses of the same age can be buried in the same spot, unless the grave was marked and reopened each time for the burial of a full-term stillborn' (Evison 1994: 31). Given the position of this grave pit in the cemetery, the conditions of excavation, and the probable size of the living population serving this cemetery, the pit containing six foetuses has to be considered as a non-contemporary series of burials.

Explanations for multiple simultaneous burials

One benign explanation of simultaneous death and burial might be that two close members of a family, not necessarily mother and child, might have succumbed to the same illness and died more-or-less together, and their shared grave reflects the close bond of affiliation or affection between the two (Crawford 1993: 85). Simultaneous death in small communities may have represented a stress or 'insult' to the community which required special rituals (in this case, multiple burial) to repair it (Crawford 1993: 89; Stoodley 2002: 120). This 'stress' might have been particularly acute where the deaths involved a mother and child; in other medieval contexts, pairings of women and infants in one grave have been interpreted as simple reflections of the hazards of childbirth, or as reflecting social concerns with reproduction (Finlay 2000: 418). The relationship between the adult and child bodies in some Anglo-Saxon graves may be interpreted as expressing emotional bonding between children and adults; at Empingham II, one of the adult females appeared to have been cradling a child within her arms, and at Lechlade, Gloucestershire, there is a clear case of a child aged between 15 and 18

months being embraced by an adult female in the grave (Grave 81) (Timby 1996: Boyle et al 1998). Similar emotional ties may have existed between other members of the family, of course, and anecdotal supporting evidence can be found in the later Old English documentary sources. While the written evidence belongs firmly to the milieu of Christianised Anglo-Saxon England, older, pre-Conversion social mores and structures remained embedded in later Anglo-Saxon society, and the written sources offer our closest anthropological parallels in time and space to elucidate the proto-historic social structures of Anglo-Saxon culture in the period before the Conversion. The earliest hagiographies, for example, refer to a period shortly after, or contemporary with, the last phases of furnished burial, and the lists of carers who brought children to visit saints for a miracle cure include father, kin and neighbours as well as mothers (Crawford 1999: 39). Writers of hagiography were consciously modelling their reports of Anglo-Saxon saintly miracles on older traditions, but it is probable that the details of daily life reflected an Anglo-Saxon reality (Ward 1976). A very late 12th century *Life of St Peter of Cornwall and Launceston*, recording events relating to pre-Conquest Anglo-Saxon society, even offers an exact parallel for some of the old male/young child pairings seen in the earlier Anglo-Saxon mortuary evidence: when a holy man died, as his funeral cortege was making its way to the church for burial, the body of his granddaughter was brought out of her house, she having 'died in a state of innocence, immediately after baptism, and still dressed in white'. The hagiographer records that she was buried in her grandfather's coffin, placed on his knees (Hull & Sharpe 1985: 27).

Within the simultaneous multiple burial ritual where children are present, the children always have fewer grave goods compared to the adult, though both juveniles and adults bodies may have been furnished. At Polhill, Kent, for example, Grave 69 contained the remains of a male adult over 45 years of age buried with a knife, bronze buckle and spearhead, and a child aged about five whose only surviving grave good was a knife (Philp 1973:180). Where both the adult and child have grave goods, it might be argued that it was nothing about their relative social status, but about the coincidence of their deaths, which may have been the primary factor in determining that these bodies were given simultaneous multiple burial (Crawford 1993: 89; Stoodley 2002: 120). Coincidental deaths within an Anglo-Saxon community, perhaps caused by disease, might seem the simplest and most obvious explanation for the presence of children in the simultaneous multiple burial ritual, but this suggestion is weakened by the consideration that, while children are most likely to succumb to infectious disease, child/child pairings are extremely rare in the Anglo-Saxon inhumation cemetery evidence. A more normal pattern of death through outbreaks of disease would be to find more children buried together, given the higher rates of mortality in childhood and infancy (Woods 2007: 378).

One group of early Anglo-Saxon multiple burials where the death of one of the grave's occupants has not been interpreted as coincidental are adult/adult pairings where one of the burials (usually female) was prone. The case of a probable 'live' burial at Sewerby, Yorkshire, has been discussed in some detail. In this example, both the lower (supine) female burial and the prone female buried above her in the same grave had grave goods, and were amongst the 'richest' women in this relatively poor mortuary community, so social inequality or slave status is not necessarily the explanation for the prone burial; explanations based on witchcraft or deviant social behaviour have been sought instead (Hirst 1985: 38-40). In a ritual where the normative burial was supine, prone burials, as in the Sewerby example cited above, suggest at the least deviance, and possibly a lack of respect. The existence of a 'prone' burial ritual has been called into question; the apparent deviance of the burial ritual might be attributable to post-mortem cadaveric spasm (Reynolds 1988; Knüsel et al. 1996). Though dead bodies may move within mortuary spaces, the argument that the majority of Anglo-Saxon prone burials might have been caused by post-mortem decay processes assumes the presence of coffins or burial 'lids' which have not been identified archaeologically, and in part derives from a culturally anachronistic distaste for the concept of soil being thrown onto a body without an intervening coffin or covering (Reynolds 1988: 716). Multiple side-by-side burials where one body is prone, while the others are supine and undisturbed, make cadaveric spasm a much less likely explanation than that there was a deliberate intention to bury one body face down. Later Anglo-Saxon 'execution' cemeteries such as the Sutton Hoo, Suffolk example, illustrate beyond doubt that Anglo-Saxons were capable of mutilating bodies post- or peri-mortem, and used prone burial as a way of marking deviant or criminal social status (Carver 2005: 12). Examples of child/adult pairings where the child's body was prone are not difficult to find: examples include Empingham II, Grave 113, of a young male adult and child, where both the child (under the adult's legs) and the adult were prone; Empingham Grave 119 where one child aged two 'was completely overlain' by an adult; and Norton, Cleveland Grave 116 of an infant who was buried prone by the side of female (Timby 1996; Sherlock & Welch 1992).

While prone (secondary) adults in the multiple burial ritual have been interpreted as 'live' burials, can the presence of children in the multiple burial ritual be predicated on the assumption that the two or more deaths represented by a multiple burial were 'natural' and 'coincidental'? Where animals have been found buried or cremated with humans, they have invariably been interpreted either as food offerings (especially in the case of sheep or pigs), or as grave-goods to 'accompany' the human burial (horses, dogs) (Wilson 1992: 101; Bond 1996: 83). Where cremated animal remains are found in urns adjacent to urns containing human bone, the former are habitually termed 'animal accessory vessels' (McKinley 1994; Bond 1996: 78). In other words, the

archaeological reading of human/animal pairings is consistently different from the reading of human/child pairings, where the former sees the animal's presence as grave good/deliberate and the latter sees the child as equal/coincidental within the grave. Is this reading based on the evidence, or on modern ideas about the status of children?

Bodies or objects?

In her recent review of the way the human body is represented in archaeological practice and theory, Jo Sofaer noted that the separation of people and objects is 'deeply ingrained in the discipline' (Sofaer 2006: 62). This explicit separation of 'body' and 'object' in the grave is embedded in discussions of Anglo-Saxon mortuary ritual; in his recent review of early medieval mortuary archaeology, Howard Williams rightly argued for a more interdisciplinary approach to the mortuary ritual, taking into account anthropological theories on the 'dividual' social person, and on the 'biography' of objects, yet throughout, the central relationship in the grave is presented as being between the human body on one side and the artefacts accompanying it on the other (Williams 2005). Yet there is a case for arguing that bodies and objects cannot be so readily separated, and that there is considerable archaeological evidence for the objectification of bodies (Brück 2001; Green 2002; Fowler 2002; Fowler 2004; Chapman & Gaydarska 2007; Lally 2007; Garwood, this volume). Bodily integrity and sacredness should not be privileged when interpreting the use of bodies in the past (Yates 1993; Meskell 1999; Scheper-Hughes 2001: 3; Sofaer 2006: 64).

Across different cultures, living and dead bodies may be commodified in a number of ways, ranging from a traffic in human organs; the collection of relics of the 'special dead'; the use of bodies as war trophies; slavery; prostitution; apprenticeship; and giving bodies in gift exchange (Thomas 2002; Sofaer 2006). Later Anglo-Saxon culture provides a number of examples of such commodification. Slavery and prostitution were a documented part of Anglo-Saxon society, and slavery at least was a trade which included the bodies of infants and children (Crawford 1999: 174; Pelteret 2001). In the later Anglo-Saxon period, there was a lively trade in saint's relics, and bodies/body parts of criminals and victims of war were put on public display, most famously the literary example of the severed arm of the monster Grendel, which adorned the hall of Heorot in the Old English poem *Beowulf* (Swanton 1978: lines 833-836).

Evidence for use of body parts as objects in the early Anglo-Saxon period are rare by comparison, though the human teeth found in a pouch in an early Anglo-Saxon grave at Marina Drive, Dunstable, Bedfordshire, may qualify, suggesting that parts of bodies could be transformed, kept, displayed and deposited in the grave: that some Anglo-Saxon body parts became objects, retaining a 'biography' beyond the moment of separation from the body (Matthews 1962). At Castledyke South, Barton-on-Humber, at least three graves contain additional teeth. The 'extra' teeth are briefly discussed under the heading 'amulets and related objects; animal and human teeth' (Drinkall and Foreman 1998: 289), where it is recorded that the 'extra' teeth in Graves 25, 42, and (possibly) 26 may have either been 'carried by the individuals concerned, or else deposited in the grave fill as part of the burial ritual' (Drinkall & Foreman 1998: 289). Grave 25 contained a female aged 35-45 years and three teeth from 'a smaller individual'; Grave 42 was of a female aged 45 or more, with two incisors of an individual aged ten or more, and Grave 26 was of yet another female aged 45 or more, with the addition of a canine tooth and two incisors (Drinkall & Foreman 1998: 42, 48). A further body, that of a 10-11 year old in Grave 32, also had the human teeth of a six year old deposited within her grave, in a pouch which also contained a copper alloy ring, a glass bead, a pebble and a scrap of iron. Though the discussion in the site report hints that the extra teeth in these cases ought to be classed as 'objects', the site catalogue reflects the usual archaeological tendency to separate the human body from the grave goods. In each case, the teeth are assigned to 'Individual B' rather than being listed as 'finds', and consequently the surplus teeth are completely absent from the plans of the graves.

Though the collection of items from Castledyke South Grave 32 might evoke the 'child's cache' at Assiros, discussed by Diana and K. A. Wardle (this volume), it should be noted that, in ritual terms, the girl in Grave 32 was an adult, and collections of such miscellaneous items which seem to 'lack utilitarian purpose' (Dickinson 1999: 368) are typically associated with adult women in the Germanic burial ritual (Meaney 1981: 247-62). Such women are usually discussed in terms of their possible status as 'wise women' or healers, and the miscellaneous items collected together in their pouches are regarded as 'amuletic' (see especially Dickinson 1999).

At the furnished inhumation cemetery of Edix Hill, Cambridgeshire, containing over 120 bodies, 13 of the 18 multiple-burial graves contained children under the age of 12. Three of these multiple-burial graves show similarities, both with each other and with the multiple burials from Castledyke discussed above. Grave 13 contained the body of a female aged 25 who was suffering from debilitating and deforming arthritis and congenital/developmental pathologies. In terms of wealth, her grave goods carried the highest score of the Phase I burials (those belonging to the 6th century); she was buried with a cruciform brooch, a small-long brooch, a disc brooch, a necklace made up of 46 beads (including 35 amber, one polychrome glass and one crystal bead), silver rings, wrist clasps, a belt with buckle and strap end, a knife, latchlifters, and a purse with fragmentary contents. Her body was covered by a thin layer of soil, and then an infant aged less than one year was placed over the adult female's left shoulder with a buckle, small knife and pot, before the grave was filled in over the two contemporary burials. The first body to be inserted into Grave 18 at Edix Hill, dating to the second phase of the site's use, was a female aged 17-25, who was suffering from leprosy. Her body had been placed on a bed – a form of grave furniture particularly associated with elite female burials in the Germanic world (Speake 1989). Her rich grave goods (she had the highest wealth score of any of those buried in Phase II) included a necklace of 29 beads, silver rings, a key, two knives, a bucket, a weaving batten, a comb and a box, in which were a spindlewhorl, a copper-alloy sheet, a fossil sea urchin, a sheep astragalus, glass, a metal rod and iron fragments. The body of a child aged about three years was placed over her burial, followed by the body of an adult. It is possible that two further burials catalogued as Grave 17, a double burial which overlay Grave 18, may in fact have been two further insertions into Grave 18. Grave 84 contained the body of a female aged 25-35, whose arthritic and deformed body with multiple congenital and developmental pathologies was buried with a long string of beads (2 glass, 29 amber and one bone), a buckle and a nail. The body of a perinatal infant, definitely contemporary with the female burial, was underneath the adult's head in the position of a pillow.

In all three of these burials, then, the primary focus of the grave appears to have been the body of an adult female. All three women were wealthy, or very wealthy, in terms of grave goods; all three showed skeletal changes representing bodily disfigurement as a result of chronic illness; and all three shared one further characteristic – the inclusion of a small child within the grave (Malim and Hines 1988). In addition to these three, Grave 82 contained the badly disturbed remains of a woman suffering from arthritis and 'other special pathological features' and a child aged 3-4, and Grave 60 might provide a further example of the same pattern: this grave contained the body of an arthritic female aged 25-35, who was buried on a bed with a variety of grave goods, including a pin, buckles and a silver ring: due to disturbance, it is not clear whether a baby's body was associated with this grave or with a female buried in Grave 61. The women might have been the mothers or carers of the children, but there are some peculiarities in the positioning of the children which argue for other explanations, particularly the placing of the infant in Grave 84, which lay under the adult's head.

Not all wealthy, physically impaired women at Edix Hill were buried with infants – Grave 69 contained the single body of a female with arthritis aged about 18 years, whose grave goods included wrist clasps and a bag group, while the rich woman in Grave 93, whose body carried 'changes suggestive of leprosy', was not associated with any other burials. However, the association of impaired adult female/special (wealthy) burial/child burial is a persistent minority ritual thread at Edix Hill across the whole period of the site's use, echoed with slight variation at Castledyke, and also visible in some form at other pre-Conversion sites such as Beckford (Hereford and Worcester) and Lechlade (Gloucestershire), and later Anglo-Saxon burials at Flixborough (Lincolnshire); Whithorn (Dumfriess and Galloway) and Yarnton (Oxfordshire), indicate that an association between women with deforming physical impairments and infant burial may have continued well into the Christian period (Crawford forthcoming).

Discussion

A recent and welcome trend in the discipline of the archaeology of childhood has been an emphasis on the need to interpret children as dynamic and active participants in the past; asserting, controlling and creating their own physical spaces and artefactual environment (for example Sofaer Derevenski 1993; Lillehammer 1989 and 2005). It is increasingly possible to identify the child as a social actor in the past. The emphasis on the child as having agency in the past rightly redresses a narrative which has placed children as passive onlookers, almost invisible in the archaeological record except when used or manipulated by adults to enact adult concerns and adult agenda (Moore and Scott 1997, Proust 2000). The mortuary ritual represents an arena where the modern conflict between identifying children as having agency clashes most dramatically with the theoretical assumption of children as adjuncts to adult narratives. Interpreting the 'place' of children in the past – either as people or possessions – is particularly acute when it comes to their dead bodies. A child that dies represents a challenge to social, familial and community cohesion in a number of ways because it is not 'natural'. Abbot Aelfric of Eynsham, writing in the late Anglo-Saxon period, agreed with his continental exemplars in describing the death of a child as 'the bitter death', in contrast to the death of a young adult ('the unripe death') and the death of an old adult ('the natural death') (Thompson 2004:10). The death of a child was painful because it was not natural. The feeling of loss at the death of a child may be linked directly to the value a child had to those who nurtured it. In this context, a child had greater 'value' than an old adult.

Following trends developed by prehistorians, Anglo-Saxonists have become aware that mortuary objects might be seen as having 'biographies': they were created, used, then 'died', by deposition in hoards or votive places, or through recycling (Parker Pearson 1993, Gosden and Marshall 1999, Williams 2005). Some artefacts may have been created with the specific intention that their 'lives' would end in votive or ritual deposition: such intent is relevant to understanding the relationship between people, the things they create, and the way they use these things as commodities for social, political and theological transactions, before, during, and after deposition (Osborne 2004). The period under study in this paper – early Anglo-Saxon England from the 5th to the 7th century – witnessed a massive haemorrhage of material wealth into the grave ritual, effectively 'killing'

enormous quantities of artefacts as they were permanently removed from the community as grave goods, in both cremation and inhumation contexts. Animals – horses, dogs and sheep in particular – were also apparently included in this act of conspicuous deposition and loss. In his insightful paper reviewing the state of early medieval mortuary archaeology, Howard Williams rightly pointed out that objects within the mortuary ritual are not merely evidence for status or identity, but are 'a means of managing death pollution and interactions between the living, the dead, and the supernatural' (Williams 2005: 207). Objects (including animals), then, communicate, mediate and manage; objects have 'life courses' and 'biographies'. 'Objects' have become more like people. At the same time, however, it needs to be recognised that human bodies might become objects. The *Life of St Peter of Cornwall and Launceston*, already cited, offers a literary example of how a 'companion' body may transgress the bounds between body and artefact, even if only in a metaphorical way: as the body of the holy man was processed through the town, and: 'passed in front of the house of his son-in-law, behold, suddenly from that house instead of a banner there was carried out to meet him the body of the daughter of his son-in-law' (Hull and Sharpe 1986:27). In this miracle story, the body of the child has been explicitly transformed into an object: she comes to the burial not as a focus for parental or familial grieving, but as a triumphant symbol and objectified reinforcement of her grandfather's spiritual and religious status.

The presumption that all human bodies are central and pivotal to the burial rite, in which objects play a secondary, supportive role, is challenged by the simultaneous multiple burial ritual. In the case of multiple burial, the bodies can only be central if an assumption is made that both bodies died, coincidentally and naturally, at the same time, and are read as partners in the ritual, whose coincidental deposition is based on unknowable relationships and accident of death. Any alternative explanation, of course, raises the possibility that one or more of the bodies in the multiple burial ritual perhaps did not die naturally and coincidentally. Though human sacrifice has 'long been out of fashion' for archaeologists, as Miranda Green has commented, there is no good logical reason for assuming that a dog in a burial is a sacrifice or 'accessory', but a second human body in a burial is simply a coincidental death (Green 1998: 8). While there is no unequivocal evidence for the sacrifice of humans in early Anglo-Saxon archaeology, Iron Age examples of pair burial or multiple burial have been cited as probable cases, especially the recurrent presence of children buried with adults at cemeteries such as the Iron Age cemetery at Carrowjames, Co. Mayo (Green 1998: 8). As Miranda Green also noted in this context for the Iron Age, 'the ritual killing of children may have had especial potency associated with their value. After all, killing the young meant quite literally sacrificing the future' (Green 1998: 9). Need an element of sacrifice be sought to explain the presence of children in the Anglo-

Saxon burial ritual? A converse proposal would place the emphasis on the child and the stress of the child's loss to the community: perhaps children whose bodies were selected for inclusion in the inhumation ritual needed 'adults' to accompany them in the grave, which might explain the relative predominance of children in the multiple burial ritual (but would not explain those infants and children buried on their own) (Crawford 1996). It is also possible to interpret the association with disabled adult females and infants discussed above as a negative reflection of the social status of the adults, rather than offering any comment on the child: their disabilities may have rendered them child-like and so their bodies were associated with infants. At Edix Hill and Castledyke, however, these women were very rich (and not at all child-like) in terms of their artefact assemblage. The value of their grave goods, juxtaposed with the presence of the contemporary infant or small child burial, raises the alternative possibility that the infant body added 'value' to the grave assemblage of these socially and physically 'special' women.

Archaeological parallels and documentary evidence together suggest that there is no good reason to suppose that the Anglo-Saxons always privileged all bodies in the burial ritual, nor that one or all of the bodies found within the multiple burial ritual should not have had a role as 'objects', rather than as bodies. Given that the multiple burial ritual was not normative within Anglo-Saxon mortuary ritual, it might be argued that all the bodies within the multiple ritual should be read as having a different form of social identity from other bodies in the cemetery. However, the evidence discussed above implies that adults, rather than children, held the dominant identity in the ritual. Some condition of life or death, found more commonly in children than in adults, predicated their inclusion in the multiple burial ritual. Not all the bodies in the burial ritual were equal, and greater consideration could be given to the liminality of children as social actors, and to the possibility that their presence within the multiple burial ritual is as a result of objectification and association. As archaeologists, it is right that we look for evidence of infants, children, women and other members of the non-'normative' groups as agents engaged in controlling, shaping and manipulating the archaeological environment (Moore and Scott 1997). However, we also need to be aware that children's bodies in general, and infants' bodies in particular, may not have had agency at all. Children, like artefacts, are made and 'belong' to the parents who made them. An unthinking imposition onto the early medieval period of concepts of individuality and the separation of objects and bodies that are unique to Western modernity may be interfering with our ability to identify the most valuable 'objects' within the Anglo-Saxon furnished burial ritual – the bodies of the 'accompanying children' buried in multiple graves.

Acknowledgements

Thanks are due to the University of Birmingham for research leave in 2005, and to the Institute of Archaeology, Oxford University for a Visiting Research Fellowship which provided a supportive environment for research and exchange of ideas. The IAA Research Seminar Series on childhood provided a stimulating and creative environment in which to explore some of the ideas developed in this paper. I very am grateful to Mike Lally for allowing me to read and cite his unpublished paper on bodies in the Iron Age, and for his work in bringing together archaeologists of infancy and childhood at two successful and stimulating Childhood Archaeology Research workshops. Thanks are also due to Gillian Shepherd, for insightful comments and scholarly ideas. Any misconceptions or errors in this paper remain, of course, my own.

Bibliography

Bond, J.M. (1996): 'Burnt offerings: animal bone in Anglo-Saxon cremations', in K.D. Thomas (ed), *Zooarchaeology: new approaches and theory: World Archaeology* 28(1): 76-88. London.

Boyle, A., Dodd, A., Miles, D. and Mudd, A. (1995): *Two Oxfordshire Anglo-Saxon cemeteries: Berinsfield and Didcot,* Thames Valley Landscapes Monograph 8, Oxford, Oxford Archaeological Unit. Oxford.

Boyle, A., Jennings, D. Miles, D. and Palmer, S. (1998): *The Anglo-Saxon Cemetery at Butler's Field, Lechlade, Gloucestershire, Volume 1: Prehistoric and Roman Activity and Anglo-Saxon Grave Catalogue.* Thames Valley Landscapes Monograph 10. Oxford.

Brück, J. (2001): 'Body metaphors and technologies of transformation in the English Middle and Late Bronze Age', in J. Brück, (ed.), *Bronze Age Landscapes: Tradition and Transformation,* 149-160. Oxford.

Brush K.A. (1998): 'Gender and mortuary analysis in pagan Anglo-Saxon archaeology', *Archaeological Review from Cambridge* 7: 76-89.

Buckberry, J. (2000): 'Missing, presumed buried? Bone diagenesis and the under-representation of Anglo-Saxon children', *Assemblage* 5 www.shef.ac.uk/assem/5/buckberr.html

Carver, M. (2005): *Sutton Hoo, a seventh century princely burial ground in its context.* Reports of the Research Committee of the Society of Antiquaries of London 69. London.

Chadwick Hawkes, S. and Grainger, G. (2003): *The Anglo-Saxon cemetery at Worthy Park, Kingsworthy Near Winchester, Hampshire.* Oxford University School of Archaeology Monograph 59. Oxford.

Chapman, J. and Gaydarska, B. (2007): *Parts and Wholes: Fragmentation in Prehistoric Context.* Oxford.

Crawford, S. (1991): 'When do Anglo-Saxon Children Count?' *Journal of Theoretical Archaeology* 2: 17-24.

Crawford, S. (1993): 'Children, death and the afterlife', *Anglo-Saxon Studies in Archaeology and History* 6: 83-92.

Crawford, S. (2000): 'Children, grave goods and social status in Early Anglo-Saxon England' in J. Sofaer Derevenski (ed.), *Children and Material Culture* 169-79. London.

Crawford, S. (2004): 'Votive deposition, religion and the Anglo-Saxon furnished burial ritual', in R. Osborne, (ed.), *The Object of Dedication. World Archaeology*, 36 (1): 87-102.

Crawford, S. (forthcoming): 'Baptism and infant burial in Anglo-Saxon England', in I. Cochelin and K. Smyth, (eds), *Debating the medieval life-cycle*. Turnhout.

Dickinson, T. (1993): 'An Anglo-Saxon "Cunning Woman" from Bidford-on-Avon, Warwickshire', in M. Carver (ed.), *In Search of cult: archaeological investigations in honour of Philip Rahtz*, 45-54. Woodbridge.

Drinkall, G. and Foreman, M. (1998): *The Anglo-Saxon cemetery at Castledyke South, Barton-on-Humber*. Sheffield Excavation Reports 6. Sheffield.

Evison, V.I. (1988): *An Anglo-Saxon cemetery at Alton, Hampshire*. Hampshire Field Club Monograph 4. Winchester.

Evison, V.I. (1994): *An Anglo-Saxon cemetery at Great Chesterford, Essex*. Council for British Archaeology Research Report 91. York.

Filmer-Sankey, W. and Pestell, T. (2001): 'Snape Anglo-Saxon cemetery: excavations and surveys 1824-1992', *East Anglian Archaeology* 95.

Finlay, N. (2000): 'Outside of life: traditions of infant burial in Ireland from *cillin* to cist', *World Archaeology* 31(3): 407-22.

Fowler, C. (2002): 'Body Parts: Personhood and Materiality in the Earlier Manx Neolithic', in Y. Hamilakis, M. Pluciennik and S. Tarlow (eds), *Thinking through the Body: Archaeologies of Corporeality,* 47-70. London.

Fowler, C. (2004): *The Archaeology of Personhood*. London.

Geake,H. (1997): *The Use of Grave Goods in Conversion-Period England, c.600-c.850*. British Archaeological Reports British Series 261. Oxford.

Green, M.A. (1998): 'Human sacrifice in Iron Age Europe', *British Archaeology* 38: 8-9.

Green, M.A. (2002): *Dying for the Gods: Human Sacrifice in Iron Age and Roman Europe*. Gloucestershire.

Gosden, C. and Marshall, Y. (1999): 'The biographical role of objects', in *The cultural biography of objects. World Archaeology* 31(2): 169-78.

Hallam, E., Hockey, J. and Howarth, G. (1999): *Beyond the body; Death and Social Identity*. Routledge, London.

Hamerow, H. (1993): *Excavations at Mucking, Volume 2: The Anglo-Saxon settlement*. London.

Härke, H. (1990): '"Warrior graves"? The background of the Anglo-Saxon weapon burial rite', *Past and Present* 126: 22-43.

Hawkes, S.C. and Wells, C. (1975): 'An Anglo-Saxon obstetric calamity from Kingsworthy, Hampshire', *Medical and Biological Illustration* 25: 1229-1235.

Hirst, S.M. (1985): *An Anglo-Saxon inhumation cemetery at Sewerby, East Yorkshire, York University Archaeological Publications* 4. York.

Hull, P. and Sharpe, R. (1985): 'Peter of Cornwall and Launceston', *Cornish Studies* 13: 5-53.

Johnson, M. (1989): 'Conceptions of agency in archaeological interpretation', *Journal of Anthropological Archaeology* 8: 189-211.

Knüsel, C.J., Janaway, R.C. and King, S.E. (1996): 'Death, decay and ritual reconstruction: archaeological evidence of cadaveric spasm' *Oxford Journal of Archaeology* 15(2): 121-128.

Lally, M. (forthcoming): 'Bodies of difference in Iron Age Southern England', in O.P Davis, N.M. Sharples and K.E. Waddington (eds), *Changing perspectives on the first millennium BC*. Oxford.

Leeds, E.T. and Atkinson, R.J.C. (1944): 'The Anglo-Saxon cemetery at Nassington', *Northamptonshire Antiquaries Journal* 24: 100-128.

Lillehammer, G. (1989): 'A child is born: the child's world in an archaeological perspective' *Norwegian Archaeological Review* 22(2): 89-105.

Lillehammer, G. (2005): 'Archaeology and Children', *Kvinner I Arkeologi I Norge* 24: 18-35.

Lucy, S. and Reynolds, A. (2004): *Burial in Early Medieval England and Wales*. Society for Medieval Archaeology Monograph 17, London.

McKinley, J. (1994): *Spong Hill Part VIII: the cremations*. East Anglian Archaeology 69. Dereham, Norfolk.

Malim, T. and Hines, J. (1998): *The Anglo-Saxon Cemetery at Edix Hill (Barrington A), Cambridgeshire*. CBA Research Report 112. York.

Matthews, C. (1962): 'The Anglo-Saxon cemetery at Marina Drive, Dunstable,' *Bedfordshire Archaeological Journal* 1: 25-47.

Meaney, A. (1964): *A Gazetteer of Early Anglo-Saxon Cemetery Sites*. London.

Meaney, A. (1981): *Anglo-Saxon amulets and curing stones*. British Archaeological Reports British Series 96. Oxford.

Osborne, R. (2004): 'Hoards, votives, offerings: the archaeology of the dedicated object', *The Object of Dedication. World Archaeology*, 36:1, 1-11.

Pader, E.J. (1982): *Symbolism, Social Relations and the Interpretation of Mortuary Remains*. British Archaeological Reports International Series 130. Oxford.

Meskell, L. (1999): 'Writing the body in archaeology', in A.E. Rautman (ed.), *Reading the Body: Representations and Remains in the Archaeological Record,* 13-21. Pennsylvania.

Moore, J. and Scott, E. (1997): *Invisible people and processes: writing gender and childhood into European archaeology*. Leicester.

Parker Pearson, M. (1993): 'The powerful dead: archaeological relationships between the living and the dead', *Cambridge Archaeological Journal* 3(2): 203-229.

Pelteret, D. (2001): *Slavery in Early Medieval England.* London.

Philp, B. (1973): 'The Anglo-Saxon cemetery at Polhill, Kent', in B.J. Philp, (ed.) *Excavations in West Kent 1960-1970*, 164-214. Kent Archeological Rescue Unit. Kent.

Proust, A. (2000): 'Childhood bodies; construction, agency and hybridity', in A. Proust (ed.), *The body, childhood and Society*, 1-18. London.

Reynolds, N. (1988): 'The Rape of the Anglo-Saxon women', *Antiquity* 62: 715-8.

Richards, J.D. (1987): *The significance of form and decoration of Anglo-Saxon cremation urns.* British Archaeological Reports British Series 166. Oxford.

Schiffer, M.B. (1976): *Behavioral Archaeology.* New York.

Scott, E. (1999): *The Archaeology of Infancy and Infant Death.* British Archaeological Reports International Series 819. Oxford.

Sherlock, S.J. and Welch, M.G. (1992): *An Anglo-Saxon cemetery at Norton, Cleveland.* Council for British Archaeology. London.

Sofaer Derevenski, J. (1993): 'Where are the children? Accessing children in the past', *Archaeological Review from Cambridge* 13(2):7-20.

Sofaer, J. (2006): *The body as material culture: a theoretical osteoarchaeology.* Cambridge.

Speake,G. (1989): *A Saxon bed burial on Swallowcliffe Down*, Historic Buildings and Monuments Commission for England Archaeological Report, 10. London.

Stoodley, N, (2000): 'From the cradle to the grave: age organization and the early Anglo-Saxon burial rite', *Human Lifecycles. World Archaeology* 31(3): 45-72.

Stoodley, N. (2002): 'Multiple burials, multiple meanings? Interpreting the early Anglo-Saxon multiple interment' in S. Lucy and A. Reynolds (eds), *Burial in Early Medieval England and Wales,* 103-110. Society for Medieval Archaeology Monograph 17. London.

Scheper-Hughes, N. (2001): 'Bodies for sale – whole or in parts', *Body and Society* 7(2-3): 1-8.

Swanton, M. (1976): *Beowulf* . Manchester.

Timby, J.R. (1996): *The Anglo-Saxon cemetery at Empingham II, Rutland; excavations carried out between 1974 and 1975.* Oxbow Monograph 70. Oxford.

Thomas, J. (2002): 'Archaeology's humanism and the materiality of the body', in Y. Hamilakis, M. Pluciennik, S. Tarlow (eds), *Thinking through the body: archaeologies of corporeality,* 29-45. New York.

Thompson, V. (2004): *Dying and death in later Anglo-Saxon England.* Anglo-Saxon Studies 4. Woodbridge.

Yates, T. (1993). 'Frameworks for an Archaeology of the Body'. In C. Tilley (ed.) *Interpretative Archaeology,* 31-72. Oxford.

Ward, B. (1976): 'Miracles and history; a reconsideration of the miracle stories used by Bede', in G. Bonner, (ed.), *Famulus Chrisit; essays in commemoration of the 13th centenary of the birth of the Venerable Bede,* 70-76. London.

West, S. (1988): *Westgarth Gardens Anglo-Saxon cemetery, Suffolk: Catalogue.* East Anglian Archaeology 38. Suffolk.

Williams, H. (2003): 'Introduction: The Archaeology of Death, Memory and Material Culture', in H. Williams (ed.), *Archaeologies of Remembrance. Death and Memory in Past Societies,* 1-24. New York.

Williams, H. (2005a): 'Review article: rethinking early medieval mortuary archaeology', *Early Medieval Europe* 13(2): 195-217.

Williams, H. (2005b): 'Cremation in early Anglo-Saxon England – past, present and future research', in H-J. Häßler (ed.) *Studien zur Sachsenforchung* 15, 533-49. Oldenburg.

Wilson, D. (1992): *Anglo-Saxon paganism.* London.

Woods, R. (2007): 'Ancient and early modern mortality: experience and understanding', *The Economic History Review* 60 (2): 373-399.

CHAPTER 9

POOR LITTLE RICH KIDS?
STATUS AND SELECTION IN ARCHAIC WESTERN GREECE

Gillian Shepherd

Sometime in the second half of the 8th century BC, a boy of perhaps 12 died in the Greek settlement of Pithekoussai on the island of Ischia in the Bay of Naples. His grave was added to the tightly-knit plot of burials which probably belonged to his extended family, but unlike most Pithekoussians who died young, he was cremated. Instead of being buried in the trench, or fossa, grave that was normal for individuals of his age, his body was burnt on a cremation pyre and the ashes collected and deposited under a stone tumulus, a rite normally reserved for affluent and older individuals at Pithekoussai. This link with the mature members of his social group was made all the more explicit by the physical linking of their graves: the boy's tumulus was attached to that of an earlier cremation; a little later, two more tumuli were added to the plot and their walls made contiguous to those of the two earlier graves. The contrast between the boy's grave and those of his young peers would have been further underlined by the fact that it overlay three fossa graves of young individuals, including the rich grave of a girl of about 15; and a few years later another fossa grave containing a 13 year old and several enchytrismoi (pot burials of children) were added to the plot. The memory of the boy's lavish funeral might also have lingered in the minds of those who witnessed it: in addition to the expense of a cremation, no less than 27 vases were smashed and burnt on the funeral pyre, together with a silver serpentine fibula which may have signified adult male status at Pithekoussai. One of the vases is particularly distinctive: now dubbed the 'Nestor Cup', it is inscribed with lines of verse which are not only one of the earliest examples of Greek writing found to date but also the earliest reference to Homer. The somewhat ribald content of the inscription ('desire for fair-crowned Aphrodite') on the cup, as well as the fact that it was accompanied by other drinking equipment, also suggests the adult male social context of the symposium, or drinking party (Buchner & Ridgway 1993: 212-23; Ridgway 1992: 55-7; Becker 1995).

The case of Late Geometric II Tomb 168 at Pithekoussai raises a number of issues pertinent to the disposal of sub-adults in the Greek world in general and Greek settlements in Italy and Sicily (Western Greece) in particular during the 8th-6th centuries BC. The first is the type of burial method chosen: in addition to its 'adult' nature, it represents a version with no very close parallels in Greece, including Euboea, the likely place of origin of many Pithekoussians. A second feature is the incorporation of the grave in a plot and the clear declaration of an affiliation with a social group that that

entails. The grave is also conspicuously wealthy: at other sites in the Western Greece small numbers of child graves are likewise distinguished by their ostentation, which at times rivals and even surpasses that of their adult counterparts. Some of these graves, like the Pithekoussai one, also breach the age distinctions normally applied in the Greek world at burial and such selection of certain children for particular burial may also be detected in fluctuating rates of archaeologically visible child burials at Greek sites in the West. A major feature of declining child occupancy in cemeteries appears to be the demise of enchytrismos (pot burial: see Fig. 9.1), a method common at Pithekoussai and other Greek settlements in the West in the earlier Archaic period, but less so in the 6th century when those children who did receive formal disposal were more likely to be buried in an 'adult' manner or in close association with adults. Given that these graves are the product of adult action and decision, such evidence of distinction and selection are likely to be as much linked to the aims and priorities of the adult world as they are to any perception of children and childhood which existed in Greek antiquity. It is this factor of adult manipulation in the representation of their children at death which is examined in this paper.

Fig. 9.1: Late Geometric enchytrismos burial at Pithekoussai (T. 660; Buchner & Ridgway 1992).

As for other ancient societies, child mortality in the ancient Greek world may be assumed to have been very high: life tables generated for pre-industrial stationary populations suggest that on average 42.27% of the population will die before the age of fifteen (Weiss 1973). For many Greek cemeteries of the Late Geometric to Archaic periods (c. 750-480 BC), however, such figures do not always emerge from excavation analysis: sometimes they appear too high, as in the case of Pithekoussai where graves of children account for some 66% (Ridgway 1992: 48-52) of the total sample; or too low, as for example in 10th-8th century Athens (Morris 1987; 1992: 78-81) and periodically in the Western Greek cemeteries discussed below. Here several factors need to be borne in mind. The first is the extent of excavation, and the possibility that limited excavation has unwittingly targeted an area of a weakly 'age-zoned' cemetery and encountered a glut (or lack) of child burials: such may be an explanation for the very high rate of child mortality at Pithekoussai, where the 493 published Late Geometric burials were excavated in an area which represents between 2.5-5% of the whole cemetery; another explanation may be a rather higher death rate for the 50 years or so covered by the Pithekoussai graves.[1] Most of the cemeteries discussed here, however, have been the subject of extensive exploration, but discrepancies between predicted and actual levels of child deposition may also be explained by a second possible factor: namely that the cemeteries do not necessarily provide an accurate representation of the living population. This may take the form of more explicit zoning on the basis of age, as in the cases of the Archaic 'child' cemeteries found in Athens, Anavyssos, Eleusis and Phaleron in Greece (Kurtz & Boardman 1971: 71-2; Houby-Nielsen 2000:155-61); equally certain groups may simply be absent from the mortuary record and are most likely to have been disposed of in manner which is not archaeologically visible, be it in within the main cemetery or elsewhere.[2] This is most likely to be the case for the Western Greek sites discussed below, where cemeteries at certain periods display implausibly low numbers of child burials, yet where, despite well over a century of extensive exploration, corresponding 'child' cemeteries have never been identified.

A third factor is the difficulty in identifying child burials in the first place. A number of the cemeteries discussed here were substantially excavated in the late 19th and early 20th centuries, when the significance of age distinction was not fully recognised and skeletal analysis non-existent. As a result, although child burials are at times noted, this tends to be limited to the observation of enchytrismos as the method employed for young children and the occasional description of a grave as 'small' or a skeleton as 'young'. The rapid rate of decay of the bones

of the very young was recognised by early excavators: Paolo Orsi, reporting on his excavations at Megara Hyblaea in Sicily in 1889, assures the reader that he personally examined in detail the 'sepolcri ad anfora' and in almost all cases detected small bones and cranial fragments (Orsi & Cavallari 1889-92: 771-2). Equally, some child burials may be assumed from storage and other receptacles where bone material is absent but there are other indicators, such as grave goods, that the vessel held a burial. It is also possible that early excavators simply missed small bone fragments or misidentified them as animal bones (or indeed vice-versa): this may well be true for some burials also containing adults, given the evidence at many of the sites discussed below for multiple burials of children and adults.[3]

Given these caveats, some working rules need to be established. Most of the sites under study here have produced impressively large samples – often over 1000 graves – for the ancient Greek world and may accordingly be taken as fairly representative of the main trends in burial for their time and place. Enchytrismos burials may be assumed from receptacles and grave goods, even where skeletal remains are not reported; finds of child burials in other receptacles such as fossa graves or sarcophagi are also often explicitly noted. In other cases, where reports may be less specific, child burials may be assumed from grave length in the absence of skeletal evidence. The description of a grave as 'small' without specific dimensions is not necessarily a reliable indicator given the enormous size of many adult graves. More recent excavations (e.g. Meola 1996-98) have followed the general rule that a grave with an internal length of 1.5m or less may be classified as 'sub-adult', assuming the supine inhumation position which is usual for Western Greece: this may be applied to older excavation reports where dimensions are provided. The possibility that cremation may conceal a number of child burials is probably not a major consideration here: although cremation was practiced, most Greek states in Italy and Sicily preferred inhumation and while there is certainly some evidence for the cremation of children in the Greek world – for example in Crete (Levi 1927-9) and exceptional cases like the Pithekoussai boy – in general it appears to be a rite reserved for older individuals.[4] Clearly, however, adolescents may be

---

[1] Cf. Ridgway (1992) 102; Morris (1996) 57 nt. 1; Cf. also the West Necropolis at Megara Hyblaea, where the 19th century excavator Orsi thought he could detect an area for child burials within the greater cemetery (Orsi & Cavallari 1889-92: 770; cf. however Iacovella 1996).

[2] Apart from children, other groups such as slaves are not readily identifiable; recent analyses of skeletal material from Pantanello (Carter 1998: 45, 145, 154), and Osteria dell' Osa (Bietti Sestieri 1992: 100) in Italy as well as Pithekoussai (Becker 1995) also claim significant under-representation of adult males in cemetery populations.

[3] In particular this may apply at Megara Hyblaea: Prof. M. Gras has kindly informed me that a number of the burials he excavated in the South Necropolis contained probable child remains as well as adult skeletons and that he suspects similar burials may have been overlooked by Orsi in the 19th century excavations in the West Necropolis (M. Gras, *pers. comm.*).

[4] See further Garland (2001: 78-9) and Oakley (2003: 176), who both also note Pliny's observation (*Natural History* 7.72) that it was a universal custom not to cremate an individual who had not reached the teething stage. Whatever the ritual significance of cremation in the ancient Greek world, it is possible that practical reasons also lay behind the tendency to reserve the method for adult disposal: children have low levels of body fat which makes combustion more difficult, a problem encountered even in modern crematoria which as a result tend to discourage cremation for children, despite its widespread use (in Britain at least) for adult disposal (Dr M. Brickley, *pers.comm.*).

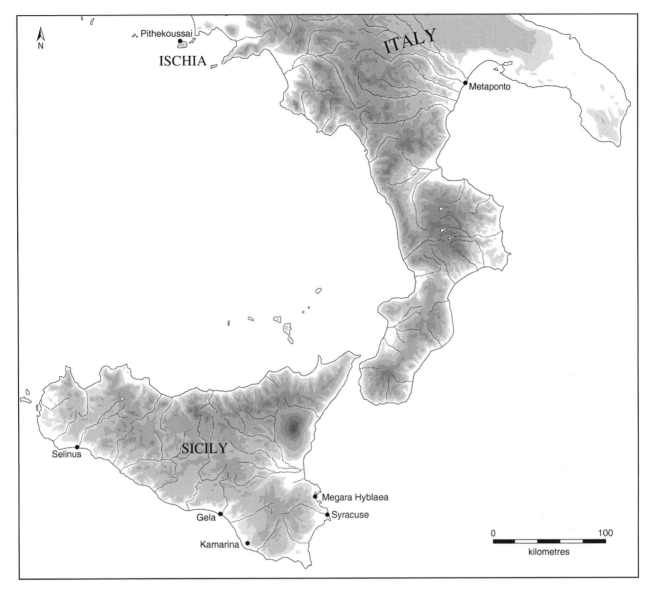

Fig. 9.2: Map of Sicily and Southern Italy, showing sites mentioned in the text.

difficult to detect, both in terms of grave length and the possibility that they may been cremated, and present a grey area in terms of how they should be classified: social constructs of 'child' and 'adult' do not necessarily rely on physical maturity and the transition point between the two is not readily identifiable for Archaic Greece.[5] Furthermore, as indicated by the Pithekoussai boy and further argued below, some children could be represented as adults at death, whatever their designation in life. Given the necessary reliance here on indicators such as grave size and hence biological age, the figures suggested by Morris (1987: 58) of 45.2-51.8% for the proportion of burials of individuals under ten years old in an ideal cemetery where the full dying population is represented are more useful here in avoiding the ambiguity of

adolescence, and may provide a benchmark with which to compare rates of retrievable child burials from cemeteries in Sicily and Southern Italy.

Continuity and Change

The Greek settlements in question were established in Italy and Sicily in the later 8th and 7th centuries BC (Fig. 9.2) and include Pithekoussai, Syracuse, Megara Hyblaea, Gela and Selinus, all of which have produced very substantial grave samples. The establishment of Pithekoussai was probably rather earlier: there is still much of the site to be excavated and the number of graves together with their elaboration suggests that the community was well settled by the middle of the 8th century. For Sicily, the 5th century BC historian Thucydides (VI.3-5) provides quite specific foundation dates (together with the names of founding states) for some of the settlements: thus Syracuse was founded by

---

[5] The evidence is better for the Classical period, especially Classical Athens: see for example Golden 1990:12-22; Beaumont 2000; Beaumont 2003: 62, 76.

95

Corinth in 733 BC, Megara Hyblaea by Megara in 728, Gela by Rhodes and Crete in 688 and Selinus, a sub-colony, by Megara Hyblaea in 628. The accuracy of this information is debatable, not least because Thucydides was writing some 300 years later, other authors offer different dates and settlement may have been a process rather than an event, but they are broadly acceptable and their sequence corresponds to that of the pottery found in them (Morris 1996). Older studies of Greek activity in the West tend to assume that parties of settlers were composed solely of individuals from the cities or areas named by Thucydides (e.g. Dunbabin 1948); more recent work has suggested that the founder state was the place of origin of the oikist (leader) and perhaps the core of the settlers, and numbers were supplemented by individuals from other parts of Greece and, in time, through intermarriage and co-habitation with indigenous populations (Shepherd 2005 with references). The assumption of many modern authors that these were state-supported enterprises may also be unfounded and at least some settlements abroad may have been the result of private enterprise (Osborne 1998).

Whatever the ultimate origin of the settlers, however, their burial customs were on the whole very coherent and do not imply a medley of customs maintained by culturally independent sub-groups. While there are certainly some graves which do stand out as very different and could conceivably represent people of differing origin – notably some of the more elaborate cremations made in a context of more customary inhumation – most variations in burial are best explained in terms of wealth and social status and, of course, age. Enchytrismos was frequently employed in the 8th and 7th centuries and to a lesser extent in the 6th for the disposal of very young children (see further below). At Pithekoussai, where enchytrismos accounts for 27% of burials, the method was certainly employed for very young children, while older children were generally inhumed in fossa graves (Ridgway 1992: 48). A similar situation is likely to be true for the other sites as well: although precise skeletal data is lacking, many children would presumably have simply outgrown containment in a storage vessel by the time of their deaths and there are sufficient examples of other receptacles of small size (fossa graves, sarcophagi) to indicate that these were used for older children.

It is clear that the enchytrismos graves, together with some other forms of child grave, account for a very significant proportion of all the burials made at these sites in the Greek West. They can also represent methods less evident in the graveyards of their historical mother-cities. Syracuse provides a good example: enchytrismos accounts for around a quarter of the burial receptacles in the areas of the Fusco Necropolis which date predominantly to the late 8th and 7th centuries. The method was also used at Corinth, but to a much lesser extent: in the North Cemetery, which provides the best evidence for Corinthian burial in this period, only two

child burials identified for the Protocorinthian period (c. 720-630 BC) were in urns; the rest were all in sarcophagi (Blegen et al. 1964: 50). It is possible that some other fragmentary urns found in this and other cemeteries originally contained enchytrismos burials, but equally they may represent grave offerings of urns placed outside the sarcophagi used regularly for adults as well as children.[6] In the 6th century, Corinthian burials likewise show a preference for sarcophagi rather than storage vessels for the disposal of children (Blegen et al. 1964: 73; Dickey 1992: 39). In contrast, sarcophagus graves exclusively for children at Syracuse are less frequent and instead the fossa grave, which was also most often used for adults, was the most common burial receptacle after storage vessels (Shepherd 1993: 113-4). In addition, sarcophagus burials in general at Syracuse have a distinctly different character from those at Corinth: a number of them were multiple burials and could include children amongst their occupants (see further below), whereas at Corinth multiple burial was almost entirely unknown. For Syracusan inhumation burials in general, whether in fossa or sarcophagus, the corpse was laid in an extended position rather than the contracted one traditional in Corinthian burials (Shepherd 1995 with references).

Similar observations may be made for the other sites under study here: namely, that burial customs in general do not correspond closely with those in use in the historical mother-city preceding and during the foundation period or indeed subsequently (Shepherd 1995) and, further, that funerary methods for children are often amongst the more conspicuous differences between the inheritable practices of the mother-city and those actually adopted by the foundation abroad. The burials of Megara in Greece are not well known, but indications are that, as at nearby Corinth, the monolithic sarcophagus was extensively used, while in Megara Hyblaea vessel burials for both adults (cremations) and children were more common in earlier periods, with monolithic sarcophagi and built chamber tombs (hypogeic cellae) more frequently used from the mid-7th century. The published burials of Selinus, founded in the later 7th century, display little in common with those of her putative mother-city Megara Hyblaea: secondary cremation was predominantly employed for adults until the late 6th century, when inhumation in fossa graves started to become more prevalent; fossa graves were routinely used for children throughout the Archaic period and enchytrismos burials are highly unusual, as are monolithic sarcophagi (Spanò and Spatafora 1982; Leibundgut Wieland 1995; Meola 1996-8; Kustermann Graf 2002; Shepherd 2006: 313-14). At Gela, the enchytrismos burials are sometimes used to stress the Rhodian character of the settlement and there may be some connection here. On the other hand, the method was not employed on Crete and given the popularity of

---

[6] Cf. Dickey (1992: 37) who proposes criteria by which pot burials may be distinguished from grave offerings.

enchytrismos in other contemporary Sicilian Greek states and the tendency for certain burial types to reappear at different sites (notably the monolithic sarcophagus) perhaps as a result of competitive emulation, a more local influencing factor seems just as likely. At any rate, the Geloans did not choose to reproduce the secondary cremations for adults common on both Rhodes and Crete: such cremations as there are tend to be primary and their numbers are exceeded by the inhumations. The latter are usually in monolithic sarcophagi in the 7th and 6th centuries and, increasingly, in terracotta sarcophagi (bauli) in the 5th (Shepherd 1995: 61 with fig. 4).

In sum, despite numerous assertions in the past that the burial customs of the Western Greek settlements, in common with other cultural features, duplicated those of the mother-city, the differences are conspicuous and those relating to the disposal of children are among the most obvious. The cultural dependency and nostalgia for the 'Old Country' often postulated by scholars of the late 19th and earlier 20th centuries for Archaic Greek 'colonies' (despite their political independence; e.g. Dunbabin 1948) does not seem to have been carried through to this particular area of social expression, nor, arguably, to others, despite the fact that such practices were readily transferable to new environments. Rather, there seems to have been a concerted effort to establish new systems of burial which, while falling into the broad categories of burial method employed by the Greeks, were nevertheless sufficiently distinctive in their particular combinations and details to distinguish one particular state from another, including the putative mother-city – much as those of any other Greek state did. In addition to signalling the particular cultural profile within a larger, overarching identity (be it Hellenic, or sub-Hellenic – Dorian, Ionian etc.) typical for ancient Greek states, the new burial systems also seem to have provided a cohering point of reference for a population which may well also have been considerably more mixed in its origins than older studies of the Greek West have been prepared to admit, incorporating Greeks from areas other than the historical mother-city and members of the local Sicilian or Italian population. Disposal methods for deceased children – who must have accounted for up to 50% of all deaths in a settlement – constituted a very significant proportion of these revised burial customs. As such, they were critical to the new funerary profile.

The manipulation of child burial does not, however, seem to have been confined merely to tinkering with the method of formal disposal. As noted for the Pithekoussai boy above, other distinguishing features of child burials at Western Greek sites indicate that they were carefully constructed with a view to demonstrating a range of other social agendas also. These include the incorporation of children into multiple burials or tight grave plots; the deposition of wealthy grave goods with children; and, by the late Archaic period, the exclusion of many children from the realm of formal burial altogether.

Inclusion and Exclusion

In contrast to the 50 years or so spanned by the excavated Geometric graves at Pithekoussai, the other sites under study here rarely achieve the level of visible child burial to be expected from an ancient cemetery. Numbers of identifiable child burials are higher for the earlier Archaic period (8th-7th centuries) but appear to drop dramatically in the 6th century, mainly through the widespread discontinuation of enchytrismos as a burial method.[7]

At Syracuse, for example, the earliest burials are found in the areas of the Fusco Necropolis which are closest to the ancient city (Orsi 1895). Here child burials appear with some frequency: of 362 burials some 38% are those of children and a quarter of all burials are enchytrismos graves. In the 6th century, when the cemetery was expanding (Orsi 1893) and new burial grounds were being opened around the city (notably the Giardino Spagna Necropolis: Orsi 1925; see further Shepherd 2006), this picture changes significantly: proportions of child graves drop to between 11-20% of cemetery populations and enchytrismoi become rare. Those children who were given visible burial were treated much in the same manner as adults, mainly through burial in fossa graves and often noticeably less in the way of grave goods than was previously the case (see further below).

Similar situations occur at Megara Hyblaea and Gela. The earliest graves at the former are in the South Necropolis and are not yet fully published. However, a preliminary report on a section of the necropolis suggests that it dates primarily to the late 8th and 7th centuries; child graves account for more than 50% of the total and were frequently enchytrismos depositions (Cébeillac-Gervasoni 1976-7: 597). In the West Necropolis, which was in use from at least the mid-7th century and throughout the 6th (Orsi & Cavallari 1889-92; Orsi & Caruso 1892), levels of child burial remain high for the area closer to the city (48%) where earlier burials are found and enchytrismos remains common, accounting for a least half of all child graves; a number of child graves also have conspicuously wealthy grave goods.[8] Further away from the city, however, the proportion of identifiable child graves drops to 28% of all burials and enchytrismoi all but disappear: those children who were formally buried were placed in monolithic sarcophagi, much like their adult counterparts; some still have rich grave assemblages, in line with the general increase in expenditure on grave goods (especially metal) in 6th century Megara Hyblaea. At Gela, the composition of the Borgo Necropolis (7th-6th centuries) displays an enormous number of enchytrismoi, which together with

---

[7] For further discussion of fluctuating levels of child burials in Western Greek cemeteries, see Shepherd 2006.

[8] See also Orsi (1913) who treats the metal work in some unpublished graves in the West Necropolis: the contents indicate that at least some of these graves date to the 7th century and may reflect groups of early graves bordering the Cantera Valley to the west of Megara Hyblaea (cf. Orsi & Cavallari 1889-92: 769; Cébeillac-Gervasoni 1975: 13-14).

the relatively few child burials of more 'adult' type account for around 50% of all interments. In the Capo Soprano Necropolis – which represents the westward expansion of the Borgo in the later 6th and 5th centuries – the level of detectable child burial drops dramatically to 13% and once again it is the enchytrismoi which were dispensed with.

Briefly, similarly low rates both of child burial and the employment of enchytrismos as a disposal technique may be seen elsewhere in Western Greece for cemeteries where age-related data is available. At Kamarina, founded by Syracuse in 598 BC (Thucydides VI.5), the 6th century Rifriscolaro Necropolis shows a substantial drop in the use of enchytrismos in the second half of the 6th century (Pelagatti 1976-77: 523-4). At Selinus, child burials do not ever account for more than 20-22% of all burials in the Buffa Necropolis over the period of its use (late 7th-5th centuries) and a mere three graves were enchytrismoi; although three further children were protected by terracotta basins, most children were deposited in simple fossa graves which were used for adults also in the 5th century (Meola 1996-8). The same is true for the Timpone Nero and Gaggera sectors of the Manicalunga Necropolis (6th-5th centuries; Spanò and Spatafora 1982; Leibundgut Wieland 1995; Kustermann Graf 2002; Shepherd 2006: 313-14). At the Pantanello Necropolis at Metapontum, child graves account for up to only 29% – and frequently much less – of burials for any period between the 6th and early 3rd centuries (Carter 1998: 144 with fig. 15.1) and enchytrismos is rare, with most children deposited in the simple fossa or tile graves which were likewise commonly used for adults.

The overall trend seems clear: although children are reasonably (if not fully) well-represented in earlier Archaic cemeteries, by the 6th century changes are afoot in terms of the manner in which children were treated at death. The most conspicuous feature is the apparent decline of enchytrismos as a method of burial and with it, one must assume, either a shift to informal burial of many children in the cemeteries or their exclusion from formal city cemeteries altogether. There is little very specific age information available for these child graves, but the cessation of enchytrismos as a major burial method and the lack of any obvious replacement technique suggests that the very young may have been the first to be excluded, while formal disposal was reserved for a much smaller cohort composed of older children with more distinct social personae or those who had otherwise secured a place in adult-oriented cemeteries, perhaps through lines of descent or inheritance.

There is evidence from elsewhere in the Greek world that different age groups within the general category of 'children' received differential treatment and other studies have emphasised the need for closer examination of age-subdivisions within childhood: Sanne Houby-Nielsen's work on child graves in Athenian cemeteries between the 6th-4th centuries detects three age subdivisions based on grave layout and goods up to the age of 10, while the graves of older children and adolescents are not distinguished in form from those of adults; she argues that particular significance was placed upon the burial of infants and children in Archaic and Classical Athens due to the importance of producing legitimate children who would hold citizenship in this period (Houby-Nielsen 2000: 152-3). In contrast, for the Hellenistic period, when the formal disposal of very young children was low, a well in the Athenian Agora which was closed c. 150 BC has produced the remains of an estimated 450 very young children (predominantly neonates, but also foetuses and infants) as well as faunal remains including over 130 dogs; although factors such as epidemic may account for this, normal practice is arguably the explanation (Houby-Nielsen 2000: 155; Little 1999; Snyder 1999; Rotroff 1999; Liston & Papadopoulos 2004: 23-25). Some analogous set of age-related scales may have become more sharply defined in the 6th century Greek West. In the absence of specific information regarding the skeletal evidence, however, the question must remain open, and it possible that some of the retrieved child burials were those of a few very young children who were given formal burial.

Whatever the specific ages of the children involved, however, it remains the case that their graves become harder to distinguish from those of adults in the later Archaic period, or indeed to distinguish at all. At all times, conspicuous breaching of age boundaries and the use of a more elaborate 'adult' form of burial could occur, such as in the case of the boy at Pithekoussai (see also further below on bronze cauldrons), but as numbers of retrievable child burials at Sicilian sites decline for the later Archaic period and enchytrismos recedes as a burial method, there is an observable assimilation of child burial types to adult for those children who did receive formal burial, especially in the use of monolithic sarcophagi (see further below); particular age-specific burial forms become harder to identify. This shift occurs in the context of other contemporary alterations in burial patterns which manifest themselves about a century or so after the foundation of the settlement.

Essentially, this involves the emergence of more distinct social stratification in the cemeteries, demonstrated most clearly through ostentatious, elite burial receptacles: finer quality, ornate monolithic sarcophagi at Syracuse; enormous built hypogeic cellae at Megara Hyblaea; or huge moulded and painted bauli at Gela. However egalitarian the original foundation may have been, it is not likely to have remained so, as land and wealth was redistributed through factors such as marriage and inheritance. Fifth century literary sources refer to aristocrats at Megara Hyblaea and an elite group known as the Gamoroi (landowners) at Syracuse (Herodotus VII.155-6). By the 6th century, sufficient time may have elapsed for social distinctions to form and crystallise, and for new elites with their own notions of inherited status to emerge and coalesce. Clearly, funerary practice was one arena where claims to status could be articulated and maintained through a more restricted and stratified burial system. The exclusion of most children was another method by which social distinctions could be made manifest in the burial system, particularly if their relatively rare inclusion could serve to emphasise issues of descent and inheritance.[9] In the 5th century, when burial forms and goods in general become plainer and cheaper in Western Greece (Flaim 2001) and disposable wealth was presumably directed towards other ends, the denial of formal burial to a large proportion of children was already well-established and continued to operate as a defining social factor in Western Greek cemeteries. Yet although the practice of large-scale exclusion appears relatively late in the Archaic period in tandem with other shifts in the burial record, the practice of distinguishing certain children at death in fact seems to have begun rather earlier in the history of these settlements.

Multiple burials and grave plots

While most burials, whether of adults or children, seem to be more or less discrete in the cemeteries under study here, there is nevertheless a distinct tendency towards multiple burial or tight grave plots which indicate that certain groups within each society wished to assert and maintain an identity through funerary affiliations. Such clusters frequently include children, whose membership of the group is thus plainly declared. The obvious explanation for these groups is that they represent the members of a particular family or perhaps extended household. While this cannot be confirmed and other reasons might lie behind the formation of particular groups at burial (such as simultaneous death), it is nevertheless worth noting that the recent biological analysis of burials in the 6th-3rd century BC Pantanello Necropolis at Metaponto in Southern Italy has revealed evidence of blood relationships between members of particular grave plots (Carter 1998: 149-65). At Pithekoussai grave plots are particularly conspicuous and most graves form distinct clusters which have been interpreted as family groups (Ridgway 1992: 52-4). In contrast, multiple burial was unusual in Archaic Greece: some of the best evidence comes from Crete and Rhodes, where successive cremations could be added to chamber tombs or pyres respectively (Brock 1957; Kinch 1914: 53 ff.), but elsewhere single inhumation was the normal practice. At Corinth, for example, multiple burial was exceptional - significantly, one of the very rare cases has been interpreted as that of a mother and child or possibly two children (North Cemetery T. 149) - and even evidence for grave grouping is limited (Blegen et al. 1964: 15-16, 66-8, 179; Dickey 1992: 132-4). In this respect also Western Greek practice forms a significant contrast with that of Greece itself.

In Sicily, grave plots can be true multiple burials, in which two or more corpses are contained in a single receptacle, or very conspicuous plots where the burials are in some way contiguous, or a combination of both.[10] The Fusco Necropolis at Syracuse provides some good examples, where in the 7th century around 14% of graves may be described as multiple: T. 436 is a 7th century group incorporating a monolithic sarcophagus containing an adult and child and two further skeletons laid out on its cover slab; Ts 450-52, a group formed between later 7th and early 6th centuries, was also a monolithic sarcophagus containing an adult and child, but with two vessels containing enchytrismos burials placed at the eastern corners of the sarcophagus lid (Orsi 1895). Similar plots may be seen at Megara Hyblaea, especially in the 6th century when approximately 40% of graves are multiple - such as Ts 39-40 in the West Necropolis, a sarcophagus containing four children with at least one (and possibly two) enchytrismos burials on its cover (Orsi & Cavallari 1889-92) - although here most multiple burials are simply contained in a monolithic sarcophagus. They usually comprise two skeletons neatly laid in opposite directions, but cases of three or four interments are not uncommon. Again, such burials frequently include children: T. 72, for example, was a sarcophagus containing an adult and child. Some sarcophagi contained only children, such as T. 39-40 (above) and T. 8V which held five small corpses (Orsi and Cavallari 1889-92). At Gela multiple burial is less common (about 10% of Archaic graves), but again plots are visible (e.g. Orsi 1906: fig. 38) and a limited number of children were selected for burial in association with adults in monolithic sarcophagi or indeed other children (e.g. Ts 91-3; 101; 262; 307-11, 315; 462) while most of their peers were in storage vessels or tile graves (Orsi 1906).

In these necropoleis, then, a certain number of children - along with an equally limited number of adults - seem to have been affiliated with particular groups and as such are distinguishable from the more 'free-floating' discrete burials in the cemeteries. One possible explanation for the appearance of such groups is influence from the native Sicilian population, which regularly practiced multiple burial in rock-cut chamber tombs. Although it is difficult to obtain detailed skeletal information from these tombs, it seems likely that they included at least some children and it is also highly likely that that there was intermarriage between Greeks and Sicilians as well as other forms of co-residence.[11] There are, however,

---

[9] For further discussion, see Shepherd 2006; see also Morris (1987; 1992: 78-81) for similarly stratified cemeteries in 10th-8th century Attica.

[10] There are also examples of less overt, but nevertheless likely groupings as well: see for example, those noted by Orsi for the Fusco Necropolis at Syracuse such as Ts 141-2; Ts 144 and 144bis (Orsi 1895). It is difficult to know whether or not multiple burials were simultaneous or successive; the reality was probably a combination of both, and grave goods do sometimes indicate successive depositions.

[11] The quality of skeletal evidence from Sicilian chamber tombs suffers as a result of a number of environmental factors and also from recording methods of the 19th and early 20th centuries, when many of the major Sikel necropoleis were excavated. For further discussion see Shepherd 2006; on the evidence for intermarriage, see Shepherd 1999 with references.

additional factors which may indicate that other social priorities were in operation also. One very conspicuous feature of these groups – whether they are tight plots or true multiple burials – is their regular association with a monolithic sarcophagus, although there is no reason why other burial receptacles should not have served the purpose equally well. This link is also directly reflected in the chronological range of multiple burial at different sites: with the demise (or, in the case of Megara Hyblaea, increase) in the use of the monolithic sarcophagus, so too does the incidence of multiple burial fall and rise and with it the inclusion of children in these plots.

As noted above, at Syracuse this takes the form of other burial types (unprotected, enchytrismoi) clustered around a sarcophagus which itself contained one or more burials; the rock-cut fossa graves, some of which were of enormous dimensions, were rarely used; a similar situation exists at Gela: the earlier monolithic sarcophagus burials attracted groups but when the sarcophagus was replaced by the terracotta baule from the mid-6th century, the option of multiple burial was not transferred to the new container despite, again, the very considerable size of some of the bauli. At both sites, the monolithic sarcophagus was a high status receptacle: at Syracuse, it became increasingly less common and also of finer construction as the Archaic period wore on and by the 6th century most Syracusans were buried in fossa graves and multiple burial was likewise much more infrequent; at Gela, where stone supply was particularly problematic, it must have always represented a high-expenditure option. If the formation of plots within the cemetery indicates the desire of some groups (themselves possibly subsections of a single social category) to maintain and/or assert a collective identity at death, then the association of these groups with monolithic sarcophagi further indicates that these groups wished to claim some level of social status as well. The inclusion of some – but not necessarily all – children who could claim affiliation with the group as well as adults implies that lineages and possibly inheritance required signalling and that generational links and progression could be demonstrated through child burial just as effectively as through adult.

The multiple burials of Megara Hyblaea display a somewhat different pattern, which may well be due as much to the increasing prevalence of the monolithic sarcophagus as to a desire to create exclusive groupings: in contrast to the other sites, multiple burials in general actually increase throughout the 6th century at Megara Hyblaea when the monolithic sarcophagus is the standard receptacle for the formally buried population. Given the prevalence of the sarcophagus, it is not inconceivable that economic motives played a role in the use of multiple burial: the simple use of a sarcophagus for two corpses (whether child or adult) is noticeable. Nevertheless, there is clear evidence of grave plotting (as opposed to multiple occupancy) in which children make a restricted

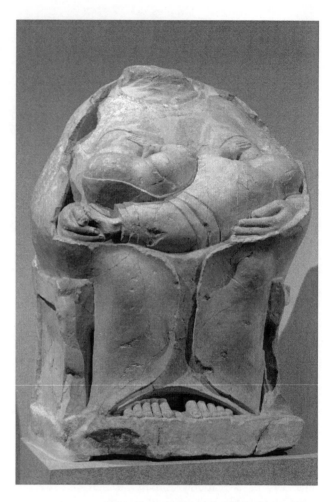

Fig. 9.3: Kourotrophos statue from Megara Hyblaea (North Necropolis), mid-6th century BC. Museo Archeologico Regionale Paolo Orsi, Siracusa. © Assessorato Beni Culturali e Ambientali e P.I. della Regione Siciliana.

appearance, as for example the West Necropolis plot of Ts 16, 17, 21 and 22 (Orsi & Cavallari 1889-92). In the North Necropolis, a small, wealthy and geographically isolated necropolis opened in the mid-6th century, groups of hypogeic cellae line the road into the city (Gentili 1954). Here enchytrismos burials are conspicuous by their absence, and while skeletal evidence is lacking, most hypogeic cellae do not seem to have contained multiple burials, despite their size and vault-like appearance. Yet the evidence suggests that at least one child managed to qualify for burial here: in the plot of Tombs H-O, Tomb L was a small, stone-lined fossa grave which, with an internal length of 1.05m, must have been that of a child. The significance of children within the broader burial ritual may also be revealed by a grave marker from the same plot, one of the very few Archaic Sicilian Greek markers to survive from antiquity. Associated with Tomb I is the famous 'kourotrophos' statue, an extraordinary piece sculpted from local limestone which depicts a seated, curvaceous female nursing two infants which are enclosed in the protective curve of her arms (Fig. 9.3). As a large-scale sculpture, presumably originally placed on the tomb, the group highlights the significance of children within a funerary context; indeed the sculpture, which dates to the mid-6th century BC, is one of the very few pieces of monumental Greek sculpture of the Archaic period to show children (cf. Beaumont (2003: 61), also on small scale terracotta kourotrophos figurines).

In contrast to Megara Hyblaea, both monolithic sarcophagi and multiple burial are very uncommon at Selinus. In the enormous Buffa Necropolis (late 7th-5th centuries BC), for which 1268 burials have recently been published, a mere 15 burials were in monolithic sarcophagi and only eight multiple burials are reported (Meola 1996-8). With one possible exception (T. 642) all the monolithic sarcophagi were of a size that indicated child occupancy and of these two were reported as multiple; a related case may be the fictile sarcophagus T. 226 which contained a child and had six inhumations above its covers. There is however some evidence for grave plotting at Selinus: for Buffa Meola proposes groupings on the basis of circular or exedral arrangements of graves which were enlarged over time. The plots are not clearly demarcated, although may have been more obvious in antiquity through markers; earlier graves also appear to be more scattered and as such may indicate the establishment of discrete plots which merged with each other as space became less available throughout the 5th century. Again, some children were selected for burial within these plots in the context of the general under-representation of children in the necropolis (see further below). A similar situation occurs in the contemporary Gaggera and Timpone Nero sectors of the Manicalunga necropolis where both monolithic sarcophagi and true multiple burials are similarly rare and children are also significantly under-represented. The Gaggera group, which includes a few highly unusual mass graves as well as widely spaced small plots, may represent a particularly exclusive or elite cemetery, similar perhaps to the North Necropolis at Megara Hyblaea (Kustermann Graf 2002; Leibundgut Wieland 1995).

The Pantanello Necropolis at Metapontum in Italy may be another such case: as noted above, scientific analysis suggests that the grave plots in the cemetery belonged to family groups. These plots could include child graves (e.g. Nucleus 3), but equally children are again under-represented in the cemetery overall (Carter 1998: 144-5). Here too, some children 'qualified' for formal burial and affiliation with the group. Most, however, did not.[12]

In sum, these sites appear to reveal additional processes of selection in terms of the location of a child burial and its relationship to a larger adult group. This seems to be particularly conspicuous during the earlier Archaic period (8th and 7th centuries) when formal burial of children was more widely practised: multiple burials and grave

plotting was a way of separating not only particular adults but also particular children from the wider populace. In the later Archaic period (6th and early 5th centuries), when children are in general significantly less visible in cemetery populations in Western Greece, multiple burial becomes less critical for the assertion of group identity, but at the same time other methods – burial receptacle (including the use of 'adult' types for children), grave location and selection of children – become more prominent in the assertion of social differentiation through increasingly stratified cemeteries. Grave grouping can still be distinguished, in which some children may be included. Yet for all periods it seems clear that not all children qualified formal burial and inclusion with the adult group. In many respects, those that did are arguably represented more as adults than children in the burial record, which may be an indication that they held particular positions within the family or other social unit – a male inheritor, for example. Such roles could be maintained at death, even if they were never fully achieved in life. Like the Pithekoussai boy, some children were always to be distinguished through material culture – and another way in which this might be demonstrated was through their grave furnishings, which on occasions were as rich or richer than those of the adult population.

Rich Kids?

Particularly in the earlier Archaic period, a number of children's graves are distinguished by the wealth of either the receptacle (or method, in the case of the Pithekoussai boy) or the grave offerings or both. At Syracuse, for example, a minority of children were buried in monolithic sarcophagi (as opposed to a pot or fossa), especially in the 7th century, and although this might be partially explained by greater age (in the absence of surviving skeletal material) it is possible that at least some of these belonged to young children (e.g. Orsi 1895: T. 441) and accordingly represent more elaborate and expensive burials; in a number of cases this is underlined by particularly ostentatious grave goods (for example, T. 428 – see further below). Even more ordinary receptacles might be upgraded: at Syracuse in the early 7th century, some small children were inhumed in elaborate painted pots rather than the coarse storage vessel usual for enchytrismos; similarly elaborate vases were also used in conjunction with adult burials.[13] At Megara Hyblaea, monolithic sarcophagi were also used for some children, especially as child burial declined and the sarcophagus became more common for adults in the course of the 7th

---

[12] Child burials at Pantanello are defined as those of individuals up to 15 years (Carter 1998: 180).

[13] For child interments in such vessels, see for example T. 216 (Orsi 1895, Sir. inv. 13623); T. 394 (Orsi 1895, no inv.); T. 445 (Orsi 1895, Sir. inv. 13844); T. 500 (Orsi 1895, Sir. inv. 13893 and possibly T. 430b (Orsi 1895, no inv.). Others may be associated with adult burials as either containers for secondary cremations (e.g. T. 213A: Orsi 1895, Sir. inv. 13621; T. 375b: Orsi 1895, Sir. inv. 13771) or grave goods (T. 19: Orsi 1893, Sir. inv. 12437; T. 108: Orsi 1893) although in both these cases the possibility that the vessel contained a child cannot be ruled out.

century and the wealth of offerings in certain graves of children is again very conspicuous (see further below) and seems to keep pace with increasing wealth disposal in adult graves. At Gela also a minority of children warranted burial in a monolithic sarcophagus (Orsi 1906). In this respect the more expensive monolithic sarcophagi in the Buffa Necropolis are conspicuous and it is noticeable that with one possible exception they are all of a size that indicates their occupants must have been sub-adults.[14] They are also relatively early graves for Selinus, dating mainly to the first quarter of the 6th century, and as such probably reflect the general tendency in Sicilian cemeteries towards greater wealth disposal in the Archaic period. From the 5th century, plainer, cheaper forms of interment are preferred, with a few vases and little in the way of metal work. More obvious than the grave receptacles, however, is the disposal of numerous and/or expensive goods (notably metal objects) in the graves of children, especially in the earlier Archaic period

The Pithekoussai boy, with his 27 vases and silver fibula, was not so unusual for his time: many of his peers received similarly extravagant goods and indeed often much more metal work. Much of this was in the form of bronze, iron and occasionally silver fibulae as well as other items of jewellery. In the past, these fibulae have been used to argue in favour of widespread intermarriage between Greeks and Italians on the basis that the various fibula types are of Italian origin and as such are part of the traditional dress worn by Italian women.[15] However, it is noticeable that, of the 192 graves at Pithekoussai containing fibulae, approximately half of them belonged to children (Shepherd 1999: 295 with nt. 20). The connection is nicely illustrated by T. 655, a fossa grave containing an adult and a three-year old: the two fibulae were associated with the latter. Sometimes they appear in quantities that are unlikely to have related to any regular form of dress: in T. 652, for example, a baby was accompanied by no less that 22 fibulae; another baby in T. 355 was buried with eleven fibulae of Italian type and two of Anatolian. The latter may also be related to other eastern objects notably the scarabs or scaraboid seals of Egyptian, Syrian, Cilician or East Greek origin: such exotica are regularly associated with children rather than adults at Pithekoussai (Buchner & Ridgway 1992: App. I; Ridgway 1992: 65-7). Fibulae are not so common in Sicily, but where they do occur they are also as likely to be found in conjunction with a child burial as an adult (Shepherd 1999). Again, the quantity can be surprising: T. 428 at Syracuse (7th century; Orsi 1895) was a monolithic sarcophagus containing a child (with another skeleton, probably adult, on the cover) and 26 fibulae; at Megara Hyblaea Orsi viewed T. 501 as possibly the richest grave of the thousand-odd he had unearthed there and described the three children in the grave as 'letteralmente coperti di argenterie' (Orsi 1913: 195).

Size seems to have mattered, since some fibulae were of enormous proportions. The bulky bone-and-amber decorated fibulae measuring 12-13 cm in length in T. 206 at Syracuse and T. 461 at Megara Hyblaea must have been, as Orsi exclaimed, 'straordinariamente grande in rapporto al corpo minuscolo' (Orsi 1895; Orsi 1913: 194).

Nor is wealth in child graves confined to fibulae: the child of T. 428 at Syracuse was given two iron pins, two bronze pins and 39 silver beads in addition to the 26 fibulae; the little monolithic sarcophagus T. 441 contained two silver rings, four fibulae and over 20 Protocorinthian cups; the ivory plaque depicting a winged Artemis figure in sarcophagus T. 139 was found with a young (female?) skeleton (Orsi 1895). Gold is rarely found at Western Greek sites, but at Syracuse the fragment of gold leaf in the "magnificent" sarcophagus T. 436 and the gold button found in sarcophagus T. 465 were both associated with the child in the receptacles and both children also had two bronze fibulae each and the former also a silver button (Orsi 1895).[16] At Megara Hyblaea gold is likewise extremely rare, but T. 499 contained two children adorned with a gold button and star as well as silver rings and two bronze animal fibulae (Orsi 1913: 195). The greater inclination towards multiple burial at Megara Hyblaea makes associating goods with particular skeletons harder, but it is noticeable that burials with very high numbers of goods in their assemblages often contained one or more children and in addition to the fibulae other metal objects, often made of silver, are conspicuous in child graves.[17] Even at Gela, where the Archaic inhabitants were more reluctant to dispose of luxury objects via the grave, child graves are again prominent in terms of their wealth: in the main Borgo Necropolis just under 8% of graves contained metal of any form, yet about of quarter of these were child graves and one of the wealthiest burials in the whole cemetery was T. 60, a monolithic sarcophagus containing four children with a bronze ring and nail, a pair of silver earrings, an iron fibula decorated with bone and amber, and a gold button.

Other cases of the disposal of conspicuous amounts of metal through the disposal of children are the bronze basins used as receptacles for remains. These are usually large, open vessels which resemble shallow cauldrons; some are decorated with a raised beaded edge around the mouth. A scattering of these vessels has been found across Western Greek sites (for a general account, see Albanese Procelli 2004). In general, these vessels seem to have contained cremated remains which are most likely

---

[14] T. 642 has an internal length of 1.58 m and as such is an ambiguous case.

[15] See further Shepherd (1999) with offerings.

---

[16] See further Orsi (1895) *passim*.

[17] For example, Ts 4, 16, 30, 49, 123 and 165 in the West Necropolis (Orsi & Cavallari 1889-92); also in the West Necropolis: Ts 574; 609; 819; possibly also 610 and 613 (all unpublished, but see Orsi 1913); Ts 630, 705, 754, 768, 801, 805, 814, 825, 2V and 6V, all with silver jewellery (Orsi & Caruso 1892). For the South Necropolis, Gras observes that rich tombs frequently belonged to children (Gras 1975: 51).

to be those of adults; while they could relate to a specific ethnic group (perhaps Euboeans), given their wealth, rarity, similarities with equally rare burials elsewhere in the Greek world and possible allusion to the heroic cremation funerals described by Homer, they seem rather to indicate self-consciously 'aristocratic' or 'heroic' burials. Their appearance at Cumae in Italy and Syracuse, Megara Hyblaea, Gela, Akragas, Lentini and Selinus in Sicily in the Archaic period could represent aristocratic competition not only within these particular city states but between them as well.[18] Some of them, however, seem to have belonged to children – for example, Orsi (1895) identified the cremated remains in the basin of T. 219 at Syracuse as those of a child and examples of inhumation burials of children in similar vessels have been observed in recent excavations of 7th-6th century graves at Syracuse (Basile 1993-4: 1321). These must rank amongst the most extravagant child graves anywhere in the Greek West and must have flagrantly displayed familial disposable wealth and (aspired) status; in addition, although cremation was not always employed, the receptacle is again more 'adult' in nature and may also represent some breaching of the normal age boundaries by a very select group of infants or children.

Much grave wealth in children's graves, then, relates to goods which are more readily associated with adult activity in terms of size, function and value. Another example might be T. 261 at Syracuse (Orsi 1895), where a child was interred in the 7th century with an iron axe – a small axe, admittedly, but nevertheless one that would have been perfectly functional, of high value, and – in the 21st century AD at least – not something to be put in the hands of small child. Even offerings of pottery do not always carry clear age distinctions, although small or miniature vase types are found with some regularity in child graves in Sicily and Italy but are not uncommon in adult as well. It is, however, at times possible to identify certain objects which seem to have been considered more appropriate for children and occasionally some which can be described as toys.

At Pithekoussai, the scarabs and related objects which occur so frequently in association with children may have been used as amulets for the very young and as such carried specific age-related significance (Ridgway 1992: 65). One of the most charming objects from anywhere in Western Greece is the painted terracotta model cart from Syracuse, dated to the later 7th century on the basis of parallels with vase decoration and found in association with a monolithic sarcophagus slightly over a metre in length.[19] Jointed figures which appear to be dolls are occasionally found as well as knuckle-bones which may

have been used for games similar to the modern version (e.g. Sir. inv. 11603, from Megara Hyblaea; Orsi 1895: T. 350 bis). At all the sites under discussion here, objects such as shells, eggs and small terracotta model animals are usually found associated with child burials and could be interpreted as playthings: for example, T. 210 at Syracuse is a rock-cut fossa grave containing an adult skeleton and a storage vessel with a small child inside. Amongst the grave goods were terracotta models of a dog, a dove, a crude helmeted figure and two tortoises; there were also two shells and small vases of types also often associated with children, including a jug, cups and a feeder. Since the objects were simply placed within the fossa, there is no definite association between these goods and the child, but it seems highly likely.

Equally, there is sufficient evidence to indicate that the identification of objects as 'toys' or similarly specifically associated with children is ambiguous and can depend more on the context of its use than the intrinsic nature of the object itself. T. 210 also contained a terracotta model of two seated figures. Terracotta figurines (usually of females) are often found in adults' graves; the figurines are also found in children's graves, where they could be viewed as further examples of 'adult' offerings, but equally could be conceived as toys; and the same types are found in a range of sanctuaries (e.g. Orsi 1906: 707-16). In each case, the same object is used but it potentially acquires a different and specific significance depending upon the context of its use and the age of its owner, recipient or donor. One of very earliest graves at Syracuse was that of a child accompanied by a Late Geometric bronze horse figurine (Scavi Cavallari Sir. inv. 6279). Such figurines are well known in mainland Greece, especially in the Peloponnese where they are found in sanctuaries. It is a rare find for a grave in Sicily: was it ever used as a toy, albeit an expensive one? Or was it placed solely in the grave as a votive to the dead? Or was it a means by which parental status, disposable wealth and the particular significance of the child within the household unit could be demonstrated? Or a combination of all three?

Conversely, objects which do appear designed specifically to be used by children can also occur in adult graves: small vessels usually assumed to be feeders for young children due to an integral strainer and nipple/dummy-like mouth have been found in adult graves at Selinus and the hellenised Sikel settlement at Morgantina (Kustermann Graf 2002 T. 81; Leibundgut Wieland 1995; Lyons 1996: 130). While it is possible that these adults were accompanied by a child whose remains have entirely decomposed, the scattering of such cases across various sites suggests that the feeder may have also have been deemed suitable for adults – particularly if they were mothers.

The disposal of wealth via children's graves seems to be particularly noticeable for the earlier Archaic period; with the possible exception of Megara Hyblaea, in the 6th

---

[18] Similar burials are also found in Euboea, notably in the magnificent 'West Gate' group at Eretria (Kurtz & Boardman 1971: 183). The Euboean connections of Cumae might in part at least explain their presence at that site, but other social factors may be responsible for the limited – but distinct – spread of the type to other parts of the Greek West.

[19] T. 20 (Orsi 1895); Sir. inv. 12438.

century and later the use of metal objects at least as grave offerings declined; as noted above, by the 5th century grave goods in general in Western Greece are overall somewhat undistinguished and disposable wealth must have been directed towards other ends. This is certainly true of Selinus, where of the 1268 graves excavated in the Buffa Necropolis a mere 88 contained metal offerings (Meola 1996-98: 263, 345). Yet even in this context some children's graves stand out: the most conspicuous is perhaps T. 313, a small fossa containing no less than three rings, a bracelet, a pendant and 19 buttons or other dress ornaments; to these may be added six imported Corinthian vases and a small bone plaque. Other child graves also containing one or more metal items and pottery (both imported and local) are T. 605 (grater, vessel fragment, hair spiral and four pots); T. 736 (iron knife, vessel fragment and five pots in a monolithic sarcophagus). By the later Archaic period, however, there was perhaps less need to use grave goods as opposed other means to distinguish particular children or particular adults: as noted above, cemeteries appear increasingly stratified in grave types, which for children also meant a greater degree of exclusion from formal burial. Those that were formally buried may have been conspicuous enough.

It is sometimes said, that, while there were exceptions, the Greeks did not expend much care or expense on the disposal of their dead children (eg Garland 2001: 78; Oakley 2003: 174). Given the tendency towards re-using storage vessels or similarly cheap containers for disposal across the Greek world, this is not surprising. But equally the 'exceptional' cases mount up to a point where there are sufficient to indicate that elaborate disposal of children was, if not a common practice, at least a regular practice amongst the ancient Greeks.[20] The evidence presented here indicates that it must have been a well-recognised, if restricted, practice amongst the Western Greeks in the Archaic period, which goes some way towards redressing the observation that the lack of artistic depiction of children in Archaic Greek art reflects their lowly social position (cf. Beaumont 2003: 61).

At the same time, however, these rich child burials occur in the greater context of more numerous plain, cheap child burials and/or the under-representation of children in city cemeteries, which indicates that the motivations for constructing very wealthy child burials may have been more complex than the overwhelming grief of a few rich parents. Such children were selected as the recipients of grave goods which can have more in common with those of adults in terms of wealth and function – as noted above, specifically child-related objects are not always easily detected and grave goods can blur age boundaries. As for the burial techniques discussed above, this may

indicate not only that disposable wealth might be readily demonstrated through burial, but also that these particular children held – or were to have held – special positions within an elite family. Such an interpretation has recently been suggested for the 9th century Geometric grave of the 'Rich Athenian Lady', one of the richest graves from Geometric Athens The re-analysis of the cremated bone material has revealed the presence of the bones of a child carried almost to full term and possibly delivered amongst those of the adult female (Liston & Papadopoulos 2004). The grave has long been thought to be that of a woman whose grave goods represented the wealth and status of her family, but as Liston and Papadopoulos observe, the presence of the child may alter this interpretation and in fact account for the richness of the tomb, especially if the child was her first (male?) offspring. In Archaic Attica, stone sculptures of youthful males (kouroi) were used as grave markers: females and other age groups are only very exceptionally represented. A possible explanation for this emphasis on a single gender and age group is that these sculptures represent adolescent males who died before they could fully assume their place in society or perpetuate an aristocratic bloodline (Beaumont 2003: 65). Although they represent a somewhat older age group, the kouroi may nevertheless be part of a wider practice of identifying through funerary practice not only family status but also an especially significant loss and the disruption of bloodlines or inheritance.

Conclusions

Despite the understandable view that the Greeks of the Archaic period generally did not make much effort with burial of their dead children, as well as the fact that their graves are often difficult to locate, it remains the case that children must have accounted for a huge proportion of the dying population. As such, practices concerning their disposal constituted a fundamental feature of any burial system: the lack of elaboration or the irretrievable nature of their graves should not lead to the implication that child-specific methods or indeed the children themselves were in some way peripheral or tangential to burial customs or the wider social arena simply because the individuals in question had not gained a certain maturity. The evidence reviewed here suggests the opposite: children – in death, at least – were intrinsic to social expression and the sheer number of infant and juvenile deaths provided an enormous arena in which their burials could be actively used by adults to signal certain social preoccupations or conditions. An important aspect of this was not simply the distinction of children from adults, but also of children from other children and the processes which seem to have distinguished one child from another on – judging from the clear patterns which emerge from the evidence – a systematic and also evolving basis (cf. Garwood, this volume).[21] While age-ranges within

---

[20] Other cases might include the Mycenaean child covered in sheet gold (Garland 2001: 78 with fig. 16); three child graves at Lefkandi (Popham & Sackett 1980: 205; and the older child inhumed the enormous 7th century 'Polyphemus Amphora' at Eleusis (Kurtz & Boardman 1971: 72).

---

[21] See also Houby-Nielsen (2000) who argues that particular significance was placed upon the burial of infants and children in

childhood may have played a part here, there is also evidence to suggest that more complicated social processes were at work which went beyond simple categorisation by age.

Burials of children could be used at several levels to express and nuance the social environment of the adult world. At an inter-cemetery level, varying methods of child burial could be part of an overall new package of burial rites constructed to provide a new foundation with its own cultural profile and identity, perhaps especially in relation to the historical mother-city but potentially also as a new cohering system to which groups of differing origins might subscribe; the similarity of the patterns observed between the cities analysed here – in particular the use (or not) of enchytrismos – also suggests a level of interaction and emulation between peer state which is also detectable in adult burial patterns (Shepherd 1995). The ostentatious disposal of wealth in child graves was a useful vehicle for the demonstration of parental status and possibly also the identification of losses which had particular impact in that they disturbed – even jeopardised – the maintenance of a family line which claimed (or aspired to) elite status; yet that line might still be articulated in the funerary arena. The possibility that a future role within a household unit was ascribed to children well before they would in fact adopt it is also indicated by the inclusion of some children as members of 'family' plots, the application of 'adult' methods to formal child disposal and, especially in later periods, by the mere fact of formal burial at all. At all times, processes of selection seem to have operated in which some children were distinguished in the burial record and very often presented as little adults. Those who died as children in the Greek world have been described as the 'special dead' (Garland 2001): all children might have been special, but some children were more special than others.

Abbreviations

T. (Ts) = Tomb(s)
Sir. Inv. = Siracusa inventory number (for an object stored in the Museo Archeologico Regionale 'Paolo Orsi', Siracusa, Sicily)

Acknowledgments

Grateful thanks must go to Sally Crawford for her comments and scholarly insights, which have greatly improved this paper, and to Harry Buglass and Graham Norrie at the Institute of Archaeology and Antiquity for illustrative work. Figure 9.3 (kourotrophos statue from Megara Hyblaea, now in the Museo Archeologico Regionale Paolo Orsi) is reproduced with the kind permission of the Assessorato Beni Culturali e Ambientali e P.I. della Regione Siciliana; thanks must

also go to Giorgio Bretschneider Editore for permission to reproduce the photograph in Figure 9.1. The IAA Research Seminar Series on childhood provided a stimulating environment in which to explore the ideas developed here and I am grateful to all those who commented on this paper. Any errors remain, of course, my own.

Bibliography

Albanese Procelli, R.M. (2004): 'Pratiche funerary a Siracusa in età arcaica: cremazioni secondarie in lebete', *Kokalos* 46: 75-125.

Basile, B. (1993-4): 'Indagini nell' ambito delle necropoli Siracusane', *Kokalos* 39-40: 1315-42.

Beaumont, L. (2000): ' The social status and artistic presentation of 'adolescence' in fifth century Athens', in J. Sofaer Derevenski (ed.), *Children and Material Culture*, 39-50. Cambridge.

Beaumont, L. (2003): 'The Changing Face of Childhood' in J. Neils and J.H. Oakely (eds), *Coming of Age in Ancient Greece. Images of Childhood from the Classical Past*. Yale, 59-83.

Becker, M. (1995): 'Human Skeletal Remains from the Pre-Colonial Greek Emporium of Pithekoussai on Ischia (NA): Culture Contact in Italy from the Early VIII to the II Century BC', in N. Christie, (ed.), *Settlement and Economy in Italy 1500 BC – AD 1500. Papers of the Fifth Conference of Italian Archaeology:* 273-81. Oxbow Monograph 41, Oxford.

Bietti Sestieri, A.M. (1992): *The Iron Age Community of Osteria dell' Osa.* Cambridge.

Blegen, C.W., Palmer, H. and Young, R.S. (1964): *Corinth XIII. The North Cemetery.* Princeton.

Brock, J.K. (1957): *Fortetsa. Early Greek Tombs near Knossos.* Cambridge.

Buchner, G. and Ridgway, D. (1992): *Pithekoussai I.* Rome.

Carter, J.C. (1998): *The Chora of Metapontum: the Necropoleis.* Texas.

Cébeillac-Gervasoni, M. (1975): 'Les nécropoles de Mégara Hyblaea', *Kokalos* 21: 3-36.

Cébeillac-Gervasoni, M. (1976-7): 'Une étude systématique sur les necropolis de Mégara Hyblaea: l'exemple d' une partie de la nécropole méridionale', *Kokalos* 22-23: 587-97.

Dickey, K. (1992): *Corinthian Burial Customs, c. 1100 to 550 BC.* Michigan.

Dunbabin, T.J. (1948): *The Western Greeks.* Oxford.

Flaim, E.K. (2001) : *"Inhument, entombment, inurnment, or immurement" : burial practices in Greek Sicily during the Classical period.* Unpublished PhD thesis, La Trobe University, Australia.

Garland, R. (2001): *The Greek Way of Death.* 2nd ed., London.

Gentili, G.V. (1954): 'Megara Hyblaea – Tombe arcaiche e reperti sporadici nella proprietà della «RASIOM» e tomba arcaica in predio Vinci', *Notizie degli Scavi:* 80-113.

Archaic and Classical Athens and that this was connected to contemporary political conditions.

Golden, M. (1990): *Children and Childhood in Classical Athens*. Baltimore and London.

Gras, M. (1975): 'Nécropole et histoire: quelques réflexions à propos de Mégara Hyblaea', *Kokalos* 21: 37-53.

Houby-Nielsen, S. (2000): 'Child burials in ancient Athens' in J. Sofaer Derevenski (ed.), *Children and Material Culture*, 151-66. Cambridge.

Iacovella, A. (1996): 'Observations sur la distribution des tombes dans une nécropole grecque d' époque archaïque: le cas de la nécropole Ouest de Mégara Hyblaea', *Archeologia e Calcolatori* 7: 373-84.

Kinch, K.F. (1914): *Fouilles de Vroulia*. Berlin.

Kurtz, D.C. & Boardman, J. (1971): *Greek Burial Customs*. London.

Kustermann Graf, A. (2002): *Selinunte: Necropoli di Manicalunga. Le tombe della contrada Gaggera*. Soveria Mannelli.

Leibundgut Wieland, D. (1995): 'DANIMS 25. Necropoli di Manicalunga. Tomba della contrada Timpone Nero (Selinunte)', *Annali della Scuola Normale Superiore di Pisa. Classe di lettere e filosofia*, ser. 3, 25, 1-2: 189-218.

Levi, D. (1927-9): 'Arkades', *Annuario della Scuola Archeologica di Atene e delle Missioni Italiane in Oriente* 10-12.

Liston, M.A. and Papadopoulos, J.K. (2004): 'The "Rich Athenian Lady" was Pregnant: The Anthropology of a Geometric Tomb Reconsidered', *Hesperia* 73: 7-38.

Little, L.M. (1999): 'Babies in Well G5:3: Preliminary Results and Future Analysis', *American Journal of Archaeology* 103: 284.

Lyons, C. (1996): *Morgantina Studies V: The Archaic Cemeteries*. Princeton.

Meola, E. (1996-8): *Necropoli di Selinunte 1 – Buffa*. Palermo.

Morris, I. (1987): *Burial and ancient society. The rise of the Greek city-state*. Cambridge.

Morris, I. (1992): *Death-ritual and social structure in classical antiquity*. Cambridge.

Morris, I. (1996): 'The Absolute Chronology of the Greek Colonies in Sicily', *Acta Archaeologica* 67: 51-59.

Oakley, J.H. (2003): 'Death and the Child' in J. Neils and J.H. Oakely (eds), *Coming of Age in Ancient Greece. Images of Childhood from the Classical Past*, 163-94. Yale.

Orsi, P. (1893): 'Siracusa – Relazione sulli scavi eseguiti nella necropoli del Fusco nel dicembre 1892 e gennaio 1893. *Notizie degli Scavi*: 445-86.

Orsi, P. (1895): 'Siracusa. – Gli scavi nella necropoli del Fusco a Siracusa nel giugno novembre e dicembre del 1893. *Notizie degli Scavi*: 109-92.

Orsi, P. (1906): 'Gela. Scavi del 1900-1905', *Monumenti Antichi* 17.

Orsi, P. (1913): 'Contributi alla storia della fibula greca'. In *Opuscula Archaeologica Oscari Montelio Septuagenario dicata*. Holms.

Orsi, P. (1925): 'Siracusa. Nuova necropoli greca di sec. VII-VI', *Notizie degli Scavi:* 176-208

Orsi, P. and Caruso, E. (1892): 'Megara Hyblaea (commune di Melilli) – Nuove esplorazioni archeologiche nella necropoli megarese', *Notizie degli Scavi*: 124-32; 172-83; 210-14; 243-52; 278-88.

Orsi, P. and Cavallari, F.S. (1889-92): 'Megara Hyblaea, Storia, Topografia, Necropoli e Anathemata', *Mounumenti Antichi* I: 690-950.

Osborne, R. (1998): 'Early Greek colonization? The nature of Greek settlement in the West' in N. Fisher and H. van Wees (eds), *Archaic Greece: New Approaches and New Evidence*, 251-69. London.

Pelagatti, P. (1976-7): 'Camarina – ricerche nelle necropoli', *Kokalos* 22-23: 522-27.

Popham, M.R. and Sackett, L.H. (1980): *Lefkandi I: The Iron Age*, (British School at Athens Supplementary Volume 11). London.

Ridgway, D. (1992): *The First Western Greeks*. Cambridge.

Rotroff, S.I. (1999): 'The Artifacts from Well G5:3 and Some Conclusions concerning the Deposit', *American Journal of Archaeology* 103: 284-5.

Shepherd, G. (1993): *Death and Religion in Archaic Greek Sicily: A Study in Colonial Relationships*. Unpublished PhD thesis, University of Cambridge.

Shepherd, G. (1995): 'The Pride of Most Colonials: Burial and Religion in the Sicilian Colonies', *Acta Hyperborea* 6: 51-2.

Shepherd, G. (1999): 'Fibulae and Females: Intermarriage in the Western Greek Colonies and the Evidence from the Cemeteries' in G.R. Tsetskhladze (ed.), *Ancient Greeks West and East*, 267-300. Leiden.

Shepherd, G. (2005): 'Dead men tell no tales: ethnic diversity in Sicilian colonies and the evidence of the cemeteries', *Oxford Journal of Archaeology* 24: 115-36.

Shepherd, G. (2006): 'Dead but not buried? Child disposal in the Greek West' in E. Herring, I. Lemos, F. Lo Schiavo, L. Vagnetti, R. Whitehouse and J. Wilkins (eds), *Across Frontiers. Etruscans, Greeks, Phoenicians and Cypriots. Studies in honour of David Ridgway and Francesca Romana Serra Ridgway*, 311-25. London.

Snyder, L.M. (1999): 'The Animal Bones from Well G5:3: Domestic Debris, Industrial Debri and Possible Evidence for the Sacrifice of Domestic Dogs in Late Hellenistic Athens', *American Journal of Archaeology* 103: 284.

Spanò, A.G. and Spatafora, F. (1982): 'Necropoli di Selinunte: un'ipotesi di ricerca', *Sicilia Archeologia* 48: 85-92.

Weiss, K.M. (1973): *Demographic models for anthropology*. Memoirs of the Society for American Archaeology 27.

IAA Interdisciplinary Series
Studies in Archaeology, History, Literature and Art

Series Editor: Gillian Shepherd

Dress and Identity

IAA Interdisciplinary Series Volume II

Edited by Mary Harlow

The way an individual chooses to present him/herself sends a series of messages to those around them. This 'language of dress' assumes a set of shared ideas about the social world of the group involved and it is something most individuals in the modern western world are subliminally aware of: is this a black tie/casual/flamboyant affair? For most periods in the ancient, medieval and early modern world the language of dress that we can access is very varied. Evidence comes from literary texts, visual and material culture, and, for some periods, from garments, or parts of garments themselves. From the kaleidoscope of evidence, dress historians have been able to describe the styles of dress worn in particular contexts by individuals in the past, and much of the previous scholarship has concentrated almost exclusively on description. This volume engages with the debates current in the new dress history which seeks to problematise the evidence, to deal with meanings created by specific genres and contexts and to engage with the research that has come from other disciplines, namely anthropology and the social sciences. It is a discipline engaging in theorising itself.

Archaeologists, historians and classicists are now comfortable in this world of interdisciplinary studies. Those who study dress in the past as a way of accessing ideas of status, gender, ethnicity and social class are often forced to work with very disparate source material, thus new methodologies have been honed to further analysis and discussion. The papers in this volume address the historiography of the study of dress in the past, from prehistory to the early modern period. In a series of case studies different methodologies are employed to ask how dress and identity can be unpicked to say something meaningful about past societies.

Contributors: John Carman, Zvezdana Dode, Penelope Dransart, Paul Garwood, Mary Harlow, Ray Laurence, Lloyd Llewellyn-Jones, Gale Owen Crocker, Maria Pirani, Ursula Roth, Ellen Swift, Diana Wardle.